D0881280

The long political career of Henry Herbert Stevens, once a Methodist preacher, was marked by a crusading zeal that made him one of the most controversial political figures of the 1930s. Stevens was first elected to the House of Commons from Vancouver in 1911 and was a minister in the Meighen and Bennett cabinets. He became the most vocal champion of the producers, small retailers, and other Canadians caught by the depression.

In the Price Spreads Inquiry of 1934, his exposure of the pressures which were squeezing small businessmen out of operation and condemning workers to sweatshops brought strenuous protest from big business and eventually opened a rift in the Conservative government. Bennett hesitated. Stevens resigned from both the cabinet and the chairmanship of the Royal Commission on Price Spreads. But he had abandoned only the office, not the campaign. If he would not be heard by the prime minister, he would speak to the people. They listened, enthusiastically.

Although the Tory government responded by endorsing the principle of reform, its proposals were too modest and its actions too tentative to satisfy Stevens and his growing body of supporters. In 1935 he formed and led the Reconstruction party. It proved to be largely an act of political desperation. The party had no ideological base; it was led by a man who, however dissident, was still a Tory; and it had no long-range plans except to force through enough legislation to protect the little man.

Professor Wilbur records a key political episode in Canada's attempt to deal with the Great Depression. This is the first full study of Stevens' vigorous parliamentary career. It reflects the preoccupations and antagonisms of West Coast politics, and the personality and public concerns of a Conservative whose democratic spirit could not be contained by party politics.

Richard Wilbur is a member of the Department of History at Concordia University.

H.H. STEVENS

Photograph courtesy of Associated Screen News Ltd.

RICHARD WILBUR

H. H. Stevens 1878-1973

Canadian Biographical Studies
UNIVERSITY OF TORONTO PRESS
Toronto and Buffalo

CANADIAN BIOGRAPHICAL STUDIES

1. John Strachan 1778–1867
   J.L.H. Henderson

2. Roland-Michel Barrin de La Galissonière 1693–1756
   Lionel Groulx

3. John Sandfield Macdonald 1812–1872
   Bruce W. Hodgins

4. Henry Alline 1748–1784
   J.M. Bumsted

5. The Denison Family of Toronto 1792–1925
   David Gagan

6. H.H. Stevens 1878–1973
   Richard Wilbur

Co-editors Alan Wilson and André Vachon

© University of Toronto Press 1977
Toronto and Buffalo
Printed in Canada
ISBN 0-8020-3339-3

This book has been published during the
Sesquicentennial year of the University of Toronto

Contents

Foreword   vii

Preface   ix

I   The Boy from Bristol   3

II   A New Leader   50

III   The Speech-maker   89

IV   The Stevens Inquiry   108

V   The Waiting Game   144

VI   The Campaign   184

VII   The Return Home   204

Notes   215

Index   233

Foreword

The <u>Canadian Biographical Studies</u> is allied with
the project of the <u>Dictionary of Canadian Biography/</u>
<u>Dictionnaire biographique du Canada.</u>
   These small volumes have been designed primarily
to interest the general reader. They have sought
to fill a gap in our knowledge of men who seemed
often to be merely secondary figures, frequently
non-political contributors to our regional and
national experience in Canada. Our social, educa-
tional, and economic history may perhaps be better
understood in their light.
   In these <u>Studies</u>, the emphasis is upon an interpretation rather than a life. The limitation in
size challenges the author to consider the best use
of anecdote, description of place, reference to
general history, and use of quotation. The general
reader is offered the fruits of recent research.
Not all of the volumes aim at full comprehensive-
ness and completeness: some may be followed later
by larger and fuller studies of the subject. Many
of the studies published, it is hoped, may suggest
new interpretative possibilities not only about the
central figure but about his period.
   The editors have not followed two of Plutarch's
chief standards: the subjects of these <u>Studies</u>

have not been chosen only for their public virtue, or for their acknowledged distinction. Most of them lived out their lives in Canada, but for some their careers were conducted partly in other theatres. Some have been chosen because, though they were once widely known, they have since been undeservedly neglected. Some have been selected not for their obvious leadership or eminence, but because they were sufficiently prominent to represent some of the qualities that guided their age, men of significance if not of first prominence. Some have been grouped in studies that should throw light on interesting families, professional groups, or lobbies in our past.

Thus, the Studies have presented not biography alone, but social, economic and political history approached through the careers and ideas - acknowledged, but often unrecognized - of Canadians of many ranks and diverse times.

Alan Wilson

Preface

Most of the research for this study was based upon
the extensive collection of Stevens Papers now at
the Public Archives of Canada. It is an unusual
holding inasmuch as the former Dominion Archivist,
Dr. W. Kaye Lamb, prevailed upon his long-time
friend and fellow Vancouverite to place his papers
in Ottawa. Stevens not only complied but agreed to
make a lengthy taped interview with Dr. Lamb; in it
Stevens amplified and at times tried to justify some
of his actions during his long parliamentary career.
This interview, which took place 27 July 1955, was
subsequently transcribed and deposited with the main
collection; it is entitled in my notes as the 1955
Interview. This interview deals in a more general
way with the highlights of Stevens' career.

In May 1966, John Munro, then teaching history at
Selkirk College, British Columbia, spent several
days with Stevens, taping his remarks and elaborating
on the interview done by Dr. Lamb. This second
series of tapes, referred to as the 1966 Interview,
was also transcribed, paginated, and deposited with
the main collection.

Another invaluable source for my study was the
Reverend Francis Stevens, eldest of Stevens' five
children. A close supporter and associate of his

father during the 1935 general election, Francis
Stevens not only gave details of the family life
not usually found among the papers of politicians
but also provided additional letters written by his
father to his family, often during periods of great
political controversy. The Reverend Francis Stevens
did even more: he became my other editor, reading
each draft, spotting some glaring errors and making
some excellent suggestions which I hope are reflected
in the final version.

I never met H.H. Stevens personally, although we
exchanged some correspondence in 1959-1960 while I
was preparing a M.A. thesis for Queen's University
on "H.H. Stevens and the Antecedents to the Reconstruction Party, 1930-1935", a topic suggested by
Professor F.W. Gibson, my thesis supervisor and one
of Canada's foremost scholars of this period. At
this time as well, I was able to interview and cor-
respond with several personalities who had played
vital roles, either as participants or observers,
of these years. They included Grant Dexter, long-
time Ottawa correspondent for the Winnipeg Free
Press, R.K. Finlayson, executive assistant to R.B.
Bennett, 1931-1938, Walter Gordon, Lester Pearson,
and Harold Daly. Their comments, especially those
of Rod Finlayson, added much to my knowledge of the
events and indicated to me at least how valuable a
supplement to written historical material such interviews can be.

Mention of such names as Dexter, Finlayson and
Pearson suggest that this work has been a long time
in the making, since they were alive when I began
my research in 1960. Indeed the subject himself
was still with us when I submitted the original
manuscript six years ago. Reasons for this long
gestation period are many. Some, such as publication financing problems, were beyond any one person's control, but whatever the reasons, I personally
feel that the delay has produced a more useful and

more accurate study. For example, I was able to
incorporate some but by no means all of the research
made available in publications appearing after sub-
mission of my first draft. I should like to thank
Alan Wilson for his help with early work on the
manuscript. No one is more aware of the trials and
tribulations of this study than Francess Halpenny,
the indefatigable general editor of the Dictionary
of Canadian Biography, for she has laboured long
and with endless patience, performing far and beyond
the usual duties of an editor. My sincere thanks.

Montreal, August 1976   R.W.

H. H. STEVENS

I The Boy from Bristol

It was a success story straight from the pages
of Horatio Alger. In 1887, a nine-year-old lad,
Henry Herbert Stevens, had arrived in Canada with
his father, a widower, and his two sisters and an
older brother. They had left Bristol for a new
start in the young dominion of Canada. Twenty-four
years later, Harry Stevens was beginning his career
as the Conservative member of the House of Commons
for Vancouver City. How proud his father would have
been had he lived to see this day, 15 November 1911,
when the first session of Canada's twelfth parliament began.

In the past five days Harry Stevens had been
sworn in; he and his wife Gertrude had been introduced to the Governor-General and the Duchess of
Connaught; and now he was preparing to listen to
his desk-mate, R.B. Bennett, the Conservative member for Calgary, moving the address in reply to
the speech from the throne. Harry had not met
Bennett before his election but of course he had
heard the many stories about this successful corporation lawyer. Bennett's masterly role in revealing the Liberals' activities in the Alberta and
Great Waterways Railway scandal was widely known
in western Tory circles. So too was his close

association with Sir Max Aitken, the young Canadian-
born millionaire now establishing himself in the
old country. Bennett had been Aitken's legal adviser
and collaborator in several big mergers, including
those that created the Alberta Pacific Grain Company, the Calgary Light and Power Company, and
the Canada Cement Company. Sir Sandford Fleming
claimed that there was 'much watering of stock'
in the cement merger[1] but his seems to have been
the only voice raised against what most regarded
as commonplace and even necessary activities in
the corporate world. So Sir Sandford must have
been surprised to hear Bennett in his address demand tighter government controls over corporations
and argue that 'the great struggle of the future'
would be 'between human rights and property interests.'[2] The new government of Sir Robert Borden
was also urged to consider some measure that would
'provide a tribunal' limiting the issue of securi-
ties by corporations,' thus protecting the public
so they would know 'the real value of those secu-
rities.'

Harry Stevens probably agreed with this approach
but four days later, when he made his own Commons
début, he stressed another matter. He looked forward 'to some measure which will assist us to keep
British Columbia as a white man's country, and not
as a field to be exploited by Asiatics.'[3] Japanese
in particular were not ordinary fishermen. In
Stevens' view they were 'to a large extent reserv-
ists of the Japanese navy.' He wanted Labrador
fishermen transferred to the west coast 'to relieve
us of the necessity of employing Japanese.' Stevens
was reflecting the opinions of most British Columbians who remembered several racial riots in the
Vancouver area from 1907 to 1910.

Our gift of hindsight enables us to view this
speech in the light of the 1942 expulsion of Japanese Canadians from the west coast. It also enables

us to marvel at the placing of Harry Stevens and
R.B. Bennett in adjoining Commons desks. Their
political lives would be entwined for the next 27
years. Yet their paths never would have crossed
if Richard Harvey Stevens had stayed with his
original plan to take his motherless flock to New
Zealand. That had been his destination in 1887
and he had even purchased the tickets. Three days
before sailing he had abruptly and mysteriously
changed his mind: they would go to Canada instead.[4]
   What did the destination matter after all? Both
dominions were within the Empire and either could
provide more opportunities than tired and depressed
old England. Canada should welcome an experienced
greengrocer with four healthy offspring. William
was almost old enough to work and Harry, with his
love of books, would have no difficulty in school.
The girls, Bessie, 16, and Louise, 14, would make
ideal wives and in the meantime they would continue to see to the family's domestic affairs.
Young Harry had become Bessie's special charge
after their mother (Jane Anne Phillips) had died
when Harry was hardly more than a toddler. Since
his birth on 8 December 1878 he had never been
far from Bristol, so it would have been an excited
nine-year-old who boarded the Vancouver, a sturdy
ship of the Dominion Line, which would transport
the family to Canada. The vessel was sailing under
good auspices during this, her first spring voyage
to Quebec in 1887. The Bishop of Liverpool had
offered words of encouragement and farewell, prais-
ing the passengers for choosing Canada where there
was room for everyone and plenty of work for willing hands. The thousand passengers included '176
persons of good character selected by the Society
for the Promotion of Christian Knowledge ... 22
young gentlemen sent from Manchester and 70 Norwe-
gians who intend to establish a farming and fishing
colony at Comox, British Columbia.'[5]

5

Two weeks later the Stevens family was aboard a
train chugging across the Quebec countryside.
Their destination was Hamilton, but after a short
stay there they journeyed east again to settle in
the bustling town of Peterborough, where they soon
rented a two-storey house on Bonnacourt Street.
Fortunately Richard Stevens had little trouble
finding a position as a greengrocer.

Harry enrolled in Peterborough Central School,
which bore little resemblance to the old St. John's
School he had attended on the edge of Bristol
downs. He was perhaps more at home at the George
Street Methodist church, with the Reverend E.A.
Pearson, the father of a future Canadian prime
minister.[6] Harry and his chum Gilbert Hall used
to ramble all over the building and one afternoon
they hid in the bell tower. When their friends
failed to find them, they were locked in for the
night and their frantic cries were not heard until
the next morning. Harry also got to know the Sunday School superintendent, Joseph Flavelle, who
ran a general store on the main street. On Saturday mornings Harry was often sent to buy the family's weekly supply of butter and vegetables at
the Peterborough market, and, the Flavelle store
being nearby, he would often go there to pick up
other items. Flavelle later moved to Toronto to
become one of that city's wealthiest citizens.
Who could then have predicted that future time
when Harry and his former Sunday School teacher
would be embroiled in a public controversy?

A political career was nowhere in sight during
Harry's Peterborough days, spent close to his
family, school friends, and the Methodist church.
These were difficult years for Richard Stevens as
he struggled to gain an economic foothold during
a world-wide depression. Lacking the capital to
establish himself in his own trade, Stevens decided in 1894 that a better future might be found in

the far west. In retrospect, one of his more significant actions during these Peterborough years
was to take young Harry to hear Sir John A.
Macdonald as the grand old man waged his last campaign in 1891. Although failing fast, Canada's
great politician gave a speech that did much to
convince Harry that when his time came he would
vote Conservative.[7]

Early in 1894, Richard Stevens and William left
for Vernon, British Columbia, where the girls,
now in their twenties, and fifteen-year-old Harry
were to join them. As it turned out, Harry made
his first trip across Canada alone, in sunny July,
and it always remained one of his most memorable.
'There was nothing west of Brandon on the prairies
until you got to Calgary,' he recalled many years
later, 'just open prairies with antelope and all
kinds of jack rabbits.' The buffalo had vanished
nearly twenty years before but he saw Indians
selling polished buffalo horns at many of the
stations. 'At Swift Current the station was a box-
car taken off its wheels'; and the passenger cars
on his Canadian Pacific train were connected by
link and coupling. The spring run-off was excep-
tionally high in 1894; Mara Lake, south of Sicamous
Junction, was in flood and Harry and the other
passengers had to wade along the submerged railway
ties. In fact, they walked to Vernon, and as Harry
wryly noted, 'I never did get a rebate on my
ticket.'[8]

His formal schooling behind him Harry went to
work at McGaw's general store, Vernon's largest.
As Harry recalls, McGaw sold dry goods and groceries and some farm machinery when farming started
up a little later. Harry would often deliver the
groceries, a job he liked because he was fond of
horses. Soon there was another reason. One of
McGaw's customers was the Glover family. They too
were British immigrants who had first chosen

Qu'Appelle, Saskatchewan, but had moved on to Vernon a few months before Harry arrived. Their young daughter Gertrude quickly caught his eye and soon he began dating her and driving her about in his horse and buggy. In many ways they were ideally suited: both were small in stature, but Gertrude, quiet and deliberate, contrasted with the voluble and quick-moving Harry. Both had been reared in the Methodist tradition, and, as with most of their generation, the church would continue to play a vital role in their lives.

Harry was in no position and perhaps in no mood to settle down in 1894. A few months after the family's arrival in Vernon, Richard Stevens died. Harry continued to work for McGaw for nearly two more years; then in 1896 he got a better-paying job firing on the CPR's branch line connecting Sicamous, Vernon, and Okanagan Landing. The engines were kept at the Landing and Harry was his own hostler: he had to get up early and walk the two or three miles to the Landing to fire up the boilers for the day's run. One of the engines had pulled the first transcontinental train into Vancouver a few years before but now was relegated to this branch line. Today, it is on permanent display at Kitsilano, where in 1969 Harry's great-grandsons would 'love to clamber over it and pretend they are driving Bampa's engine.'[9]

Railroading was not for the ambitious young Stevens, however. After a year he concluded that 'a man in the mechanical department never became president,' so he moved on to Penticton where his skill with horses got him a job as stage-coach driver on the two-day run to Grand Forks and Camp McKinney, both booming mining towns a few miles from the American border. By 1899 he had a small savings account and a large desire to make his mark in the grocery business. Probably because it was the largest supply port for the big Yukon gold

rush, Seattle was Harry's next stop. Failing to
find any immediate openings in the grocery business,
Harry apparently permitted his sense of adventure
to override his Empire allegiance and joined the
transport section of the United States army. Early
in 1900 he left for the Philippines and thence
went to China in the American force sent to help
quell the Boxer rebellion. As a civilian volunteer
attached to an auxiliary service, Harry witnessed
no fighting but he marched with the American sol-
diers into Tientsin late in 1900. Here Harry was
placed in charge of a transport unit with instructions to move 80 tons of silver being taken from
the imperial mint as compensation for riot damage
to the international enclave. He also was ordered
to use ambulances to pick up American casualties;
it turned out that 'they were all alcoholics. I
can see them now going up the side of that boat.'
And he concluded: 'If that's what booze does to a
man, no more booze and I left it alone.'[10] A greater
reason for his life-long abstinence undoubtedly
was his Methodist upbringing. This China experience
also profoundly influenced his later views on
Oriental immigration. To Harry Stevens, China was
a foreign and crowded country whose emigrating
citizens could easily undermine the British herit-
age that was the bedrock of British Columbia
society.

Harry returned home to the Vancouver area in
1901 and immediately tried to enlist for service
in the Boer War. The sense of adventure was still
with him, but so too were the effects of a dysen-
tery attack suffered in China; he failed his army
medical. Still footloose and looking for excitement, he and a newly found partner, Tom Foster,
boarded a coastal steamer and headed up to the
mouth of the Skeena River, where they transferred
to a Hudson's Bay Company boat and got off at the
mouth of the Copper River opposite to the site of

the present town of Terrace. They staked claims
for a New York mining syndicate and found 72 per
cent copper in some places, but apparently nothing
was ever done to follow up their discovery. A few
months later, in 1902, Harry and his partner drifted
south again, joining the great mining boom sweeping
the Kootenay area, just a few miles from the American border. Silver and lead had been discovered
here in 1882 and by 1896 new finds of copper, lead,
zinc, and gold had turned the West Kootenay district into an area 'as famous as the Rand. And by
1898, the American capital which had opened most
of the mines and built the first smelters was
being replaced by British and Canadian capital.'[11]
Some of this investment money came from Calgary,
and in particular from the thriving law firm of
Lougheed and Bennett. R.B. Bennett had come to
Calgary from his native New Brunswick in 1897, the
year the Stevens family had moved west to Vernon,
and a few months after his arrival Bennett had
become Senator James Lougheed's junior law partner.
Thus, while Bennett was moving quickly into Calgary's social and corporate élite, his future
parliamentary colleague was staking out copper
claims for a New York syndicate and deciding to
become a miner. In 1902, Harry Stevens went to
work in the Phoenix area near Nelson, where he
joined the Western Federation of Miners and soon
became secretary of his local union.

As Harry recalled, 'the Phoenix Miners' Union
was extremely left-wing' and democratic in that
it used to meet each week to 'decide on the course
of action and the officers were called upon to
explain their actions to the general membership.'
It would often bring in socialist speakers from
Idaho and Washington for its Sunday afternoon
meetings. One such Sunday Harry had the audacity
to challenge a guest but not before he had done
some homework: 'As a matter of fact I had been

10

quite a student of economics. I had read J.S. Mill
and other leading economists of the day and I had
also read Karl Marx and Friedrich Engels' book...
I used to spend all my free time (and we had lots
of it) reading up.'[12] That memorable debate, which
ended in an unofficial draw, was the first of
many that Harry took part in at the camp. It was
also the beginning of a lifetime of debating and
this careful preparation even in a remote British
Columbia mining camp was to set the pattern. A
decade later, when he began his long parliamentary
career, Stevens had mastered a most important
lesson: a successful debater and public speaker
must seek out the facts. It is also worth noting
that, in this first debate, Harry was against the
socialists, against the radicals.

   It was this mental rather than physical digging
that appealed to Stevens. By the spring of 1902
he had had enough of copper mining and headed for
Vancouver with renewed determination to succeed
in the grocery business and probably to renew
closer relations with Gertrude Glover. He went to
work for Thomas Duke and within a year Harry 'was
in full charge of his business' doing all the
buying and bookkeeping for this thriving grocery
firm.[13] He moved to the Mount Pleasant area of
the city and in 1903 'when Dick McBride conceived
the idea of introducing the party system into provincial politics,' Harry joined the Conservative
Association of Mount Pleasant and soon was appointed
its secretary.[14]

   The year 1903 was a critical one for British
Columbia. According to members of a federal royal
commission investigating an industrial dispute
involving the CPR, society in British Columbia was
threatened 'with a breakdown of morality.' The
business community was disillusioned. 'Even the
Canadian Manufacturers' Association had threatened
to withdraw its travellers from the province.'[15]

11

It was this need for moral reform rather than McBride's call to establish the Tory party in provincial politics that probably motivated Harry Stevens toward active participation in public life.

Within a short time Stevens and his Tory friends in the Mount Pleasant district had started a weekly newspaper, the Western Call, 'which had as its objective the cleaning up of some of the mess around the city.' Stevens found evidence of this 'mess' close to home. He caught two of the grocery clerks at Duke's taking the cash instead of ringing it up. Rather than prosecute, he talked things over with them and learned 'they had resorted to stealing to make up for gambling losses in Chinatown.' When Vancouver's police chief failed to investigate the gambling dens, the energetic Harry visited them himself and gave the names and addresses of the proprietors to the Vancouver News Advertiser. 'The result of this was the Chief of Police was dismissed and there was a cleanup of that condition.'[16] Harry Stevens had won his first crusade. As his son Francis later expressed it, 'I am sure that it was a crusading Methodism that first brought him into public life, when he became involved in a movement of Moral Reform in Vancouver.'[17]

Later in 1903, Richard McBride became premier and, as he settled into a reign that would last for twelve years, it seems that he and the powerful Tory political machine looked with less and less favour on the actions and utterances of 'do-gooders' like Harry Stevens. Certainly Harry was never one of McBride's inner circle, a point that would become clear once the reform-minded Stevens decided to enter federal politics and had gathered about him a group of loyal supporters beyond the dictates of the McBride faction. But that was still in the future.

Harry's Methodist faith pervaded all of his

12

actions, both public and private. Shortly after
he moved to the Mount Pleasant area, he became
active in the local church, teaching Sunday School
regularly and often taking services for the elderly
minister, Dr. Ebenezer Robson. Harry never forgot
one service he took, out on the river road at the
foot of Fraser Avenue. 'I had to walk all the way,
5 or 6 miles, and it was snowing when I started.
When I got there, the total congregation present
was an old man who was deaf and a little boy. And
we sat around talking ... Nobody else came.'[18]
During the next few years Harry would often 'carry
the word' to logging camps and school houses in
the more remote regions outside Vancouver. As he
became more engrossed in civic affairs, he had to
give up this activity, but he was carried on the
roll of Mount Pleasant Methodist Church as a
'local preacher' until after it became part of the
United Church of Canada in 1925.

Besides the church, the other most important and
enduring influence in Harry Stevens' life was
Gertrude Glover. A year younger, she was now teaching in a South Vancouver school. They had never
lost touch since the days when both lived in
Vernon; through all Harry's travels and adventures
in China and remote mining camps they had corre-
sponded regularly. Sometime in 1903 or 1904 they
reached an 'understanding' and on 5 July 1905
they began a marriage that was to stretch over
sixty happy years.

Gertie, as Harry fondly called her, was the more
silent partner. Her calm assurance and her complete
devotion to her family made the Stevens home a
happy place, not only for their own five children
but for Gertrude's several sisters who settled
near them in Mount Pleasant. For years Mr. and
Mrs. Glover lived next door, and their presence
must have added greatly to the close-knit but
large family circle. From the first days of their

13

married life, it was apparent that Harry would be
travelling frequently on political business and
the proximity of these relatives must have been a
great help to Gertrude when Harry's Ottawa career
kept him away from home for weeks at a time.
Almost daily correspondence with his wife not only
kept Harry in the family picture; it also provided
him with the benefit of Gertrude's shrewd feminine
intuition and her view of events back in the constituency.

The year 1905 was a major one for Harry Stevens.
Besides getting married, he decided to leave the
grocery business to take charge of the accounting
department of a local trust company. By 1908 that
firm had begun to indulge in certain practices
that Stevens refused to support, so he resigned
and set up his own brokerage, insurance and public
accounting business. What he lacked in financial
assets was offset by great self-confidence and a
growing network of social and business contacts.
His continued interest in the affairs of the Mount
Pleasant Methodist Church, his conventional but
firm views on drinking and racial integration,
his growing participation in the Mount Pleasant
Conservative party, all pointed to a successful
business and political career.

As early as 1903, Harry Stevens and other Tory
Methodists in his community had begun contributing
to the Western Call's anti-liquor campaign. Then,
shortly after the incident with the embezzling
store clerks, Stevens met Dr. Samuel D. Chown,
secretary of Temperance, Prohibition and Moral
Reform in the Methodist Church, and later that
church's general superintendent. Together they
toured the drinking and gambling dens of Chinatown,
forays which strengthened Stevens' conviction that
Oriental culture and traditions - however one
might respect many of them - could not be assimi-
lated into a predominantly Anglo-Saxon and white

14

community.[19] Stevens was not a member of the
Asiatic Exclusion League that caused the 1907
race riots in the Japanese section of Vancouver,
but he 'took a very strong stand against the free
immigration of Orientals.'[20]

By the autumn of 1909 his business had been
greatly extended, reflecting the boom conditions
now prevailing in Vancouver. Historian Margaret
Ormsby paints this picture of the city:

> The new Granville Street high-level bridge was
> almost complete; the Canadian Pacific Railway
> was subdividing Shaughnessy Heights into resi-
> dential property; Kitsilano was filling up and
> handsome new mansions were under construction
> in Point Grey. The British Columbia Electric
> Company was pushing ahead the electric railway
> line which would soon bring the Fraser Valley
> as far north as Chilliwack within Vancouver's
> orbit ... The population of Vancouver was grow-
> ing at the rate of 1,000 persons per month and
> would reach a figure over 110,000 by 1911.
> According to report, the number of real estate
> agencies in the city outnumbered the grocery
> stores by three to one.[21]

From grocery store to real estate: Harry Stevens
was a good example of the spirit of change and
expansion that characterized Vancouver during the
first decade of the twentieth century. He seemed
a logical choice to contest the aldermanic seat
for Mount Pleasant in 1909 and he won with ease.
Re-elected the following year, he became chairman
of the Vancouver Board of Health on the eve of a
typhoid epidemic. 'It must be remembered,' he
later recalled, 'that in those days there were
vast areas where there were no sewers at all and
the water supply was very often in the backyard.'[22]
The efforts of his board persuaded the provincial

15

government to establish the Greater Vancouver Water Board and the Joint Sewage Commission.

Warming to his new role as municipal politician, Harry Stevens was increasingly in demand as a public speaker. In April 1910 he told a local group calling itself 'The Progressive Thought Society' that the chief weakness in the laws was that they could not meet rapidly changing conditions. 'I believe the time has come when the sacredness of private interests must be subservient to that of the public good.' As an example, he cited the local telephone company. 'It practically dictates to the government of British Columbia and to the people of the country what they shall do ... Why? There is only one answer: vested interests.' Public utilities should be controlled in the public interest; land should be held by the government 'in trust for the people and leased to private enterprise.'[23]

Similar ideas were being expressed by many liberal-minded politicians and critics, especially American Progressives. An omnivorous reader, Harry Stevens must have been familiar with the then-current writings of Ida Tarbell, Upton Sinclair, and Lincoln Steffens with their exposures of corruption in the American oil and meat-packing industries and in local politics. As an active Methodist, he must also have been aware of the progressive social creed adopted in 1908 by the General Conference of the Methodist Episcopal Church in the United States. It urged the 'most equitable division of the products in industry that can ultimately be devised,' the reduction of hours of labour, and other economic reforms.[24] At the same time his personal contacts with leading Canadian Methodists such as Dr. Chown must have reaffirmed his basic Protestantism and swept him up in what Richard Hofstadter has called 'the moral indignation of the age.'[25] Of course it did not follow that Harry Stevens disagreed with the economic system, especially as it was being developed in Canada; he was merely at issue with its weaknesses and with those unscrupulous citizens taking advantage of their fellows. The burgeoning city of Vancouver provided many opportunities for men of Stevens' outlook and temperament to become indignant in 1910 and soon this promising local politician would be given a larger stage.

In the summer of 1911 the Mount Pleasant Conservative Association asked Harry Stevens to contest the party nomination in Vancouver for the approaching federal election. His first response was a flat refusal. After all, if elected, he would have to spend weeks away from his family, which now included five-year-old Francis and two daughters, Marjory, three, and Sylvia, just a few months old. Furthermore he could not afford to leave his growing accounting and real estate business. In every respect his interests were rooted on the west coast. A chance to enter the provincial legislature would have been preferable but the only election in the offing was the federal contest. He probably knew also that McBride's inner circle would prefer one of its own to represent the area. In the end it was Gertrude who induced him to reconsider, and go to the bank to borrow the campaign money. He had little trouble with finances, once he presented as collateral a statement of worth amounting to $96,000.[26] A few weeks before nomination day a more formidable obstacle appeared. Premier Richard McBride's right-hand man and attorney-general, William Bowser, asked Harry to step aside in favour of James Findley, a party faithful much closer to McBride. As a consolation, the party hierarchy promised to support Stevens for mayor. He refused even to consider the proposal and at the nomination meeting won on the first ballot by a large majority.

17

The political climate of 1911 seemed ripe for
Harry Stevens. The federal Conservatives had regained Vancouver City from the Liberals in 1908
and this time their candidate was its best-known
alderman. As a native-born Englishman, an active
member of the Sons of England and the Orange Lodge,
Harry Stevens represented the most important
ethnic group in his constituency. In his campaign
he strongly endorsed the federal Tory stand
against Laurier's reciprocity plan, arguing that
it would mean American economic domination of
Canada. The other big national issue was imperial
defence. Robert Borden and the Conservative opposition wanted to make a direct emergency contribution of a warship to the Royal Navy. The Liberal
government of Sir Wilfrid Laurier preferred the
establishment of a Canadian navy. In his own
Vancouver campaign Harry Stevens largely ignored
the naval issue, stressing local matters by promising to get federal aid to expand harbour facilities and to build a rail line from Vancouver to
the Peace River country. On voting day it was
Harry Stevens all the way: he finished 3,200 votes
ahead of his Liberal opponent, J.H. Senkler; a
socialist candidate finished a poor third. Harry
Stevens' parliamentary career was well launched,
supported by the Conservative victory federally,
but neither he nor Gertrude could have predicted
that Ottawa would become a vital part of their
lives for the next thirty years.

Ottawa is a long way from Vancouver, in every
sense of the word. For Harry Stevens, MP, Ottawa
in 1911 was a congenial town inasmuch as it was
for him English-speaking and British in tone.
Gertrude was able to hear his maiden speech in
November for the children could be left in the
capable hands of Mrs. Fraser, a Scottish nurse
who had been a help on other occasions. After
Gertrude returned to them, Harry took a room at

the Laurentian Club, a brisk walk from Parliament Hill. 'I had very little social life,' he recalls, but it was largely a matter of choice. As his son later observed:

Dad was energetic and hard-working. He concentrated on what he was doing - the speech, the project, the investigation, and shut most other things out. He could get along fine in a social gathering; people liked him. But he wasn't convivial. He had a lot of friends, whom he preferred to see in one's and two's rather than crowds. He didn't drink.[27]

At first Harry thought he might use his spare time in studying for a college degree, but the University of Toronto refused his application to take all courses by correspondence. Perhaps it was just as well; he had never had to fit himself into the structured learning process prescribed by universities. He was mostly self-taught, a training that began during his Phoenix mining days and continued when he turned to accounting. Now that his career had branched out into politics, he began to read widely in the loosely related fields of history, biography, economics, and politics. It was not surprising that Harry Stevens was among the most frequent users of the parliamentary library.

The 1911-12 session could not pass quickly enough for Harry; the bachelor's life was not for him. During the summer recess, he and Gertrude decided to bring the three children east with them for the next session. Francis' sixth birthday was 8 October, past the September deadline for entering school, so they could all go to Ottawa for the relatively short period. Patricia joined the family circle in 1912 and was part of the eastern trek the following year. Fortunately for western members

such as Harry, the parliamentary sessions over
the winters of 1913-14 and 1914-15 did not begin
until after Christmas, but as it turned out 1915
would be the last time they all would go east.
The frequent moves had caused Francis to miss the
required drill in mental arithmetic, so reluctantly
it was decided that Gertrude and the children should
from now on remain behind in Vancouver. The arrival
of Douglas in 1915 emphasized the necessity for
this decision. But in one real sense Harry Stevens
was never separated from his family. Each night
without fail he would write home, and just as
faithfully Gertrude would reply. After reading
his daily letter, she would leave it out for the
older children, Francis and Marjory, to read.
'And we did. We always knew what he was doing and
what he was thinking. In spite of the fact that
he was away for weeks, months at a time, he was
never a stranger to us.'[28] Then, during the glori-
ous west-coast summers, they would all troop out
to the 'ranch.' It was near White Rock, about
thirty miles from Vancouver, and consisted of an
old cottage, a run-down orchard, about twenty
acres of cleared land, and a hundred acres of
bush. Harry's delight was 'to work and sweat there,
hacking it out an acre at a time, with blasting
powder and a team of horses, with ax and peevee,
crosscut saw (no chain-saws then) and mattock.'[29]
The children would often sleep in tents, within
easy reach of the famous White Rock beach. This
warm family environment was Harry's mainstay as
the demands of Parliament grew, and the wartime
sessions stretched into months.
    Harry Stevens' first contacts with Prime Minister
Borden came out of plans and promises to develop
Vancouver's harbour facilities. 'Up to that time,
the federal government hadn't spent one dollar on
them. I immediately undertook to promote the
dredging and widening of the First Narrows, and

[eventually] they widened it to sixteen hundred feet.'[30] During his first few years as an MP, Harry made no major speeches, but he was always in attendence at the House, ready to add his comments and criticisms whenever the subject of Vancouver was raised. For instance, on 24 April 1913 he was quickly on his feet to reply to Frank Oliver. The colourful Liberal member from Edmonton had expressed concern over the possible violation of Indian treaty rights in the BC government's attempts to buy the 80 acres of the Kitsilano reserve at the mouth of False Creek, well within the expanding city limits. The provincial attorney-general, William Bowser, had offered the twenty Indian families $11,250 each. Harry Stevens admitted that this offer had been made without the knowledge or consent of the federal government but he supported the move. He argued that the proposed Vancouver Harbours Board would have this False Creek area within its jurisdiction and therefore it should be held 'for public purposes.' For that matter, he did not believe that it was in the best moral or physical interests either of the city or of the Indians that they should be allowed to remain there. In the end the white man continued to get his way. As the Canadian Annual Review reported:

On April 8 [1913] the Kitsilano Indian Reserve of 80 acres, which had long blocked the expansion of Vancouver, ceased to exist and Mr. Bowser completed its acquisition for the Government by handing each Indian concerned a bank-book showing a balance to his credit of $11,250 - a total of $300,000. The families involved were to settle at the Squamish Reserve some distance from the City and the Minister told a meeting in Vancouver [April 8] that the profit to the Province would be $1,000,000.[31]

The Kitsilano hurdle over, the next problem for
local Tories was to win federal cabinet support
for the over-all harbour plan - a job that fell
to Harry Stevens. He easily obtained the approval
of the Department of Public Works but ran into a
snag when he saw the minister, Robert Rogers of
Winnipeg. For some reason Rogers was reluctant to
approach the cabinet and at one point asked Harry
to forget the whole idea. Rogers had misjudged
his man. Half an hour before a cabinet meeting
was to take place, Stevens presented Rogers with
an ultimatum. 'Either you get this contract signed
today ... or I'll resign my seat and tell the
public and house why.'[32] A few months later in
Vancouver, Harry had the satisfaction of hearing
Rogers inform local officials that, in addition
to the harbour improvements, a large grain storage
elevator would be built and operated at federal
expense. By 1914 this giant structure had been
completed, but for the next four years it was not
used to full capacity because of the war and also
because a huge rock slide had blocked off part of
the Panama Canal. The elevator became known as
'Stevens' folly,' but not for long. The resumption
of normal traffic through the canal, coupled with
the return of peacetime trade, brought a shipping
boom that surpassed even Harry's highest hopes.
A total of 95 million bushels of grain were handled
by the elevator in 1919.

The start of hostilities in 1914 found Harry at
home, where he soon became embroiled in the Komagata
Maru incident. This sad affair arose in part from
regulations passed by the Laurier administration
barring the entry into Canada of any immigrant who
did not come directly from his land of origin.
During the summer of 1914 a Punjabi agitator char-
tered a Japanese vessel, the Komagata Maru, and
despatched it to Hong Kong to collect 376 Sikhs
who had arrived there from India. As soon as their

22

ship docked at Vancouver, these unfortunate passengers were refused permission to land. 'Case after case came into the courts; and as the time lengthened, the rations of the Sikhs, who were no longer supplied by the shipping company, became shorter and their plight more desperate.'[33] By July 18 the final court decision had upheld the deportation order - the Sikhs had to go. But the Komagata Maru was no longer available for their return passage, so on that date immigration officials and local police boarded harbour craft and headed for the ship, intending to transfer the Sikhs to the Empress of India, bound for Hong Kong, their original embarkation port.

Harry Stevens MP was a member of the citizens' committee accompanying the 175 officials and police who headed out to the Komagata Maru. The despairing Sikhs had seized control of the ship. 'I was on board a large tug,' Harry later recalled, 'and our police force went out to the ship to restore the control by the Japanese captain.' When they got alongside, 'the Hindus [as Vancouverites called them] threw out large chunks of iron grating from the furnaces of the ship, and great hunks of coal, and bombarded us and drove us off.' A few days later, 'every roof-top near the harbour was crowded by citizens who had risen early to watch H.M.C.S. Rainbow, which had been called from Esquimalt, perform her first important function in escorting out of Vancouver harbour a shipload of British subjects.'[34]

Harry Stevens admitted that it 'was a tragic affair from the start to finish, but it was designed by them [i.e. the Sikhs] to defy Canadian law. And had it succeeded, there would have been many others follow ... Where there are Hindus, or any of the other Asiatics, we've got to remember they're different from us ... Their view of life, their philosophies, their concept of social pro-

23

cedure ..., these are different from ours.' Unlimited immigration 'would soon swamp this country and overwhelm the white race.'[35] Undoubtedly, these views were held by most white British Columbians then, and it is unlikely that any number of them, including Harry Stevens, ever changed their minds. Theirs was an outlook, however, that is common even today. Then as now, racial issues brought violent reactions. According to Francis Stevens, during the Komagata Maru affair the family's house was under police guard 'day and night' after his father had received anonymous threats against his life.[36]

When the European war broke out in August, less than two weeks after the Komagata Maru incident, Harry Stevens had immediately tried to enlist, at the age of 36. He was told he could contribute more on the home front, so he returned to his post in Ottawa, taking military training courses and occasionally accompanying Sir Sam Hughes, the energetic minister of militia, on recruiting drives. In the main, however, Harry's role during the first world war was that of a hard-working parliamentary back-bencher. By contrast, his desk-mate, R.B. Bennett, seemed destined for greater things, despite his sharp criticism of Tory railway policy. In January 1914, Bennett left Stevens' side to occupy the former seat of Arthur Meighen, the new solicitor-general, and in June 1915 Bennett went overseas with Prime Minister Borden as his parliamentary secretary. Borden's diary for the war years contains many references to Bennett and McBride and Bowser and to matters relating to British Columbia. Harry Stevens' name is never mentioned even though he was a frequent caller at the prime minister's office.

In 1915 Harry Stevens suggested to Sir Robert that a study be made of the feasibility of creating a modern civil service. Borden agreed and named

a committee consisting of three deputy ministers
plus Stevens to examine existing civil services,
notably in Britain, and to draft tentative legislation. A Civil Service Act was passed in 1919
and Harry Stevens understandably took some credit
for this milestone which did much to reduce ramp-
ant patronage in the appointments to federal
offices.

For the most part, Harry Stevens' attention during his first parliamentary term was concentrated
on the demands and needs of his Vancouver constituency. By December 1916, according to the Monetary
Times, his efforts had resulted in a two-million
dollar dredging operation of Vancouver harbour, a
grain elevator with a capacity of 1,300,00 bushels,
and a harbour commission. 'He was also largely
responsible for the scheme of the terminal railway
and wharfage extension to cost $5,000,000 to
$7,000,000 and secured a subsidy for a dry dock to
cost $5,500,000 and worked for the extension of
postal facilities and construction of postal
stations.'[37] Undoubtedly, these 'good works' were
welcomed by most Vancouverites but, as later events
were to prove, they did not enhance Stevens' already poor relations with the provincial Tory
organization. It was ostensibly led by the ailing
Premier McBride but the actual control was more
and more in the hands of McBride's lieutenant,
William Bowser. Already he was known by some provincial Conservatives as 'little Czar' probably
because he 'had always seen to it that the party
machine was kept in efficient running order.'[38]
Harry Stevens had thwarted the provincial organization when he successfully entered the federal
field. Now, after four years in Ottawa, he obviously
was more 'his own man' as he helped direct federal
spending into the growing city of Vancouver. Clearly
he was still outside the Bowser camp but when the
McBride-Bowser forces were defeated in the provin-

cial general election of 1916 Stevens probably
had less pressure from that quarter. Instead, he
was getting it from another, as the <u>Monetary Times</u>
editorial noted. 'At present he is engaged in a
controversy with the Canadian Pacific Railway in
an endeavour to release the port of Vancouver from
railroad control and bring it under the control of
the harbour board.'

In today's terms, Harry Stevens was 'bucking the
establishment' and we might wonder who his closer
parliamentary associates were by 1916. He seems
to have made few close Ottawa friends probably
because he was not a good mixer and did not frequent the MPs' special preserve, the Rideau Club,
although he later became a member. He started to
play golf but gave it up when he found that many
MPs played every afternoon and did not appear in
the House until the late evening. Probably golf
was too frivolous a game anyway for this serious
lay preacher who never missed the Sunday service
at Dominion Methodist Church. His favourite club
was the parliamentary library and the only break
in his routine came when Gertrude arrived at long
last with Sylvia, Patricia, and Douglas for a
month's visit. They would take an apartment and
Harry would gain a new lease on life as he got
first-hand accounts about Francis' and Marjory's
school work and how well his brother Will was
keeping the business going. These Ottawa visits
must have posed a great temptation for Harry to
quit federal politics and his self-imposed Spartan
existence and return home for good. On the other
hand he had a deep sense of commitment both to
his country and to his constituents. Furthermore,
he knew that other MPs, including good friends
from the other side of the House, men like Frank
Carvell, the Liberal from New Brunswick, and Hugh
Guthrie, the lawyer from Guelph, also had to
endure personal inconveniences.

The date 3 February 1916 would always be remembered by Harry Stevens and other members of the
twelfth Canadian Parliament. On that day fire
swept through the Parliament buildings, killing
six people and completely gutting the stately
Gothic structure. In his nightly letter home Harry
gave his family an eye-witness account. He had
been in his office when the blaze was discovered
and he rushed to sound the alarm on his floor.
Then he directed several people to the elevator
and asked them to wait for him while he went looking for others. They went down without him, forcing
him to run down several flights of a spiral stair-
case, amid smoke and flames. After reaching the
basement, he found a side door and rushed outside
to safety.[39]

Harry Stevens had another reason to remember
the year 1916. It marked the first time that he
crossed swords with his former Peterborough Sunday
School superintendent, now the Toronto financier
Sir Joseph Flavelle, chairman of the Imperial
Munitions Board. It had the task of finding Canadian
firms to handle British government war contracts,
and among the firms vying for these lucrative
orders was Flavelle's own Vulcan Iron Works. Like
many other politicians, Harry Stevens was attempting
to get some business for firms in his constituency.
As he later put it, 'If Flavelle had had his way,
he would [have] built a wall along the Rocky Moun-
tains and [kept] us out on the other side.'[40]
When his efforts failed, Stevens drafted a resolution to London urging the United Kingdom to
dismiss Flavelle from his post, presumably because
of a possible conflict of interest. Flavelle was
not removed but more war contracts began finding
their way to British Columbia firms. Harry Stevens
had indicated once again that he could be aggressive
in the interests of his own constituency, even to
the point of embarrassing one of the most powerful

figures in the federal Conservative establishment.
At the same time, it is worth noting that he did
not attack the social and economic system over
which a few Canadians like Flavelle wielded such
influence. Neither did he challenge the wartime
policies laid down by his party leader, Sir Robert
Borden.

Thus, during the bitter conscription debate of
1917 Stevens argued that there could be no middle
course about the war and Canada's contribution at
Britain's side. Compulsory service was 'the very
basis of democracy.' He had no sympathy for the
three groups which, in his opinion, were opposed
to conscription: French-Canadians, certain sections
of labour, and conscientious objectors. He also
dismissed Liberal demands for the conscription of
wealth. 'The Minister of Finance [Sir Thomas White]
had been doing [it] for the past two years ...
The wartime excess profits tax was the fairest
type of taxation ever brought down in this House.'[41]

Again in August 1917 Harry Stevens strongly supported the government stand in the equally bitter
debate over nationalization of the Canadian Northern Railway. He predicted 'a new era, a step forward towards the acquisition of the control and
direction and ownership of the great railway systems of Canada.'[42] By contrast, his fellow western Tory, R.B. Bennett, proposed that the debt-
ridden railroad be allowed to go into receivership,
a move that probably would have brought down the
line's principal creditor, the Canadian Bank of
Commerce, whose former president was Sir Thomas
White, the minister of finance and the sponsor of
the nationalization bill. It was finally passed,
but not before the Borden government was forced
to use closure in the Commons and overcome strong
Liberal opposition in the Senate.

These bitter Commons debates provided a harsh
backdrop for the general election called for 17

December 1917. Confusion and dissension reigned
in many constituencies, and especially in British
Columbia. According to one account, 'party and
personal feeling, Socialist and Labour sentiment,
were rife and it required all available agencies ...
to fuse the rivalries ... into a working political
relationship.'[43] Under the Redistribution Act of
1914 the riding of Vancouver City was divided into
Vancouver Centre and Vancouver South. The former
Tory premier, W.J. Bowser, as well as Sir Hibbert
Tupper, were rumoured at one point to want the
nomination in Vancouver Centre, where Harry Stevens
would run. There was a hint here of the same old
hostility from the BC Tory establishment that
Harry had faced in 1911. He was still not one of
them. In the end the nomination was his, and with
Gertrude's unhesitating approval and with the knowledge that he had a willing group of competent
constituency supporters, Harry began his second
federal campaign. His main opponent was Billie
McInnes, 'a typical old-time orator,' as Stevens
remembers him who had resigned as a county court
judge to contest not only the Vancouver seat but
that of Comox-Alberni as well. The day before the
election they met in public debate in a crowded
downtown theatre; the results were as conclusive
as the next day's voting: Harry was returned by a
majority of 8,179 votes.

  The House of Commons which reconvened on 20 February 1918 in Ottawa's old Victoria Museum was
vastly different from the assemblage of 1911. Among
the missing was R.B. Bennett, who had decided not
to re-offer; among the new faces was George Black,
Harry's campaign manager in 1911. Another newcomer
who struck Harry's fancy right away was Robert
Manion, a medical doctor and former Liberal. Like
Hugh Guthrie and a number of others, Manion had
run as a Unionist supporter of the Borden administration's conscription stand. Sir Robert himself

was back but most Tories knew that he wished to
retire. His successor, in the minds of Harry Stevens
and other Tory back-benchers, should be Arthur
Meighen. Five years older than Harry, Meighen had
entered the House in 1908 and had quickly established himself as a brilliant debater and master
of parliamentary procedure, factors which accounted
for his great popularity among Tory MPs.

'Tall, slight, austere, severely simple in his
tastes, and endlessly hard-working,' Meighen, as
characterized by historian Donald Creighton, 'kept
to the end the mental outlook of his farming boyhood, with all its sharp clarity and some of its
narrow limitations.'⁴⁴ Harry Stevens seemed to
grow less rigid as his own political career progressed, but he undoubtedly believed, along with
Meighen, 'that man is a rational animal whose conduct should be governed by reason.' Both Stevens
and Meighen saw state ownership as the logical
solution for the Canadian Northern and Grand Trunk
railways. Hence Stevens' strong support for the
Canadian National Railways bill, largely drafted
by Meighen. Stevens also shared Meighen's contempt
for what Creighton terms 'the abstract speculations
of universities' although probably for different
reasons. Stevens may have felt a slight sense of
inferiority because he had not been to university
and he had been rebuffed when he had tried to take
a degree by correspondence. Meighen's contempt,
by contrast, probably stemmed from his brilliant
success at the University of Toronto, which may
well have revealed to him the pomposity of some
academic theorists. Undoubtedly, Stevens would
have accepted the view which Creighton assigns to
Meighen, 'that most of humanity's problems could
be solved by hard work and plain living.' Finally,
for all true-blue Canadian Conservatives there
was the British connection. 'What of Britain!
Incomparable Britain!' Meighen had exhorted Harry's

Vancouver constituents during the 1917 election campaign. 'Groaning under a burden that might stagger half the world, she borrows $5,000,000 more and sends it to bind the wounds and restore the homes of your sister city (Halifax), smitten in the holocaust of war. Britain, the hope, the reliance of the Entente, faithful to the last to every ally.'[45] Little wonder that the boy from Bristol could imagine no one but Meighen to succeed Borden.

As an experienced representative of a major British Columbia constituency, Harry Stevens had a good chance of a cabinet post if Meighen were to head an administration. And, at the tag end of the session in June 1919, Harry gave another indication that he was of cabinet calibre. After several futile attempts to get the Speaker's attention, Stevens finally got the floor to discuss a subject he had been studying for weeks: a report of a special committee of auditors appointed in 1916 to investigate the operations of terminal elevators at the Lakehead. The 300-page report, costing $125,000, had dealt with the flagrant practice of the elevator companies in cheating farmers by over-charging for dockage - the waste grain the companies separated before delivery to the Lakehead.[46] The 'overages' always appeared on the firms' books, but not until the end of the season, and, as a result, the farmers usually received from these monopolistic grain-handling firms even less than they had expected. Stevens was touching on an extremely delicate situation. The spokesman for the thirty western Unionists, T.A. Crerar, had resigned as Borden's minister of agriculture only three weeks before and his group had already been meeting in separate caucus. For years Crerar had been president of the Grain Growers Grain Company and at first he implied that Stevens knew nothing about the complexities of the grain-han-

dling trade. When Stevens' answers indicated otherwise, Crerar quickly dropped his superior attitude
and settled back with the others to learn more
about this revealing report. Stevens later claimed
that his hour-long speech and the resulting debate
led to significant amendments to the Grain Act,
including measures to prevent misuse of the dockage
fee. Of more immediate significance was the fact
that his own political star was on the rise.

Just a month before this June 1919 debate on
grain handling, Harry Stevens had been named vice-
chairman of a Commons select committee to investigate increases in the wartime cost of living. In
the subsequent well-publicized hearing Stevens'
persistent questioning caused more than one witness
to squirm. At one point, he asked J. Stanley McLean,
president of Harris Abattoirs, to explain the
fact that when the Harris firm had been capitalized
in 1918 its accumulated profits amounted to
$1,200,000. Another committee member, E.W. Nesbitt,
accused Stevens of dealing unfairly with McLean.
'If a man has a brain to build up a bulk [profit]
you are going to punish him!' Nesbitt shouted
across the table.[47] The committee's report, however, seemed to support Harry Stevens' line of
questioning; it recommended that parliament pass
a Board of Commerce Act and a Combines and Fair
Prices Act. Parliament quickly complied, no doubt
mindful of the current post-war economic slump
and widespread labour unrest. Under the new legislation, 'No person was to accumulate or withhold
from sale any necessity of life, beyond an amount
reasonably required for the use or consumption of
his household, or for the ordinary purposes of
his business.'[48] These and other concepts were
made law at a time when the federal government
assumed it still had far-reaching powers under
the War Measures Act. This assumption was not
supported by the Judicial Committee of the Imperial

Privy Council when it was asked later to declare
on the constitutionality of these two acts; the
learned jurists decided they were beyond the powers
of a peacetime federal government.

Such legislation as the Combines and Fair Prices
Act and amendments to the Grain Act reflected the
Methodist morality that was so much a part of
Harry Stevens' economic and political philosophy.
It is not surprising, therefore, to find him among
the fifty clerics and laymen who formed the General
Council of the Brotherhood in 1920. This was a
Canadian branch of a British organization that had
been trying to win British and European labour
movements to 'a new socialism of Christian inspira-
tion and purpose' when the war broke out in 1914.
The honorary president of the Canadian group in
1920 was T.B. Macaulay, president of the Sun Life
Assurance Company, and, besides Stevens, lay members
of the General Council included Charles Dunning,
soon to be premier of Saskatchewan and after 1926
a prominent member of Mackenzie King's federal
cabinet. The heightened sense of 'social passion,'
as one historian has termed it, could be felt in
most parts of post-war Canadian society, and for
Harry Stevens, still a Methodist lay preacher, it
provided a larger audience.[49] 'The evil effects
of economic problems,' he told one group in 1920,
'invariably arise from erroneous moral conceptions.
An over-reaching employer has a moral defect in
his character.'[50] On 25 March 1920 he told a
Washington convention of American lumber dealers:
'You cannot supplant the priority of the state
with your own individual interest without losing
yourself and impoverishing the state.'[51] The
same high moral note was sounded in an article on
post-war economic problems that he wrote for the
June 1920 issue of Saturday Night:

I propose that this commonwealth, by the action

of its Parliament, and through the agency of its government, enter into partnership with the industrial, commercial and financial forces of the country - that we remove the spirit of antagonism and jealousy now existing between directing powers of industry and the people by replacing it with a common purpose ... Such a partnership would be attained by a taxation or profit sharing scheme, similar to the business profits tax in form, but instead of withdrawing the amount of the assessment in cash from the business, it shall be 'capitalized' and remain in the business as new capital. Such capitalized surplus earnings shall become the property of the State.

This 'partnership' would 'supply an effective antidote to the extremist demand to "nationalize industry" by securing to the public all the advantages of such nationalization while at the same time retaining private and personal initiative.'

Rapid political events during the next few months allowed Harry Stevens little time for theorizing. By July 1920 Arthur Meighen had assumed the leadership of the Conservative government, and the press was filled with speculation about cabinet appointments. As the senior member from British Columbia, Harry Stevens was a likely choice - a view endorsed by the editor of the Vancouver Daily World. He wrote Meighen that he thought Stevens had 'the trade instinct and more important, the Democratic instinct.'[52] Meighen obviously had a high regard for Stevens' campaigning skills and soon asked him to help with two by-elections.

Early in 1921 Harry returned to his boyhood haunts in Peterborough where a confusing and discouraging situation faced the party. The Conservative member for West Peterborough, J.H. Burnham, had resigned because, as he had told Meighen, he had had enough of the Union government; he wanted

to get back to old Conservative principles such
as the protective tariff.[53] Failing to win the
Unionist nomination, Burnham ran anyway, along
with the official candidate. It was a situation
that Harry Stevens could not save: the Liberals
took the seat for the first time since 1908.

In the summer recess of 1921, when Harry would
have spent his time with his family at the 'ranch,'
he responded to another request from Meighen for
help. To a Medicine Hat by-election he took along
young Francis, now in his fifteenth year and eager
to help his father with some campaigning. Unfortunately it was the Peterborough situation all over
again. The party standard bearer, Lt. Col. Nelson
Spencer, another staunch 'tariff man,' faced a
straight two-party fight. His opponent was Robert
Gardiner, of the United Farmers of Alberta, who
in reality represented Liberal interests too since
the other old party had shrewdly decided against
running a candidate. As he had argued during the
Peterborough fiasco, Harry told Meighen that pro-
tection or free trade as an issue did not amount
'to a row of shooks.' There had to be 'some new
line of action' if the Conservatives hoped 'to
hold any portion of the North West.' The result,
which Harry reported as 'a serious catastrophe,'
saw Gardiner top the polls by a resounding majority
of over 9,000 votes.[54]

Talk of a general election was much in the air
during the autumn of 1921, and on his daily walk
to his office in downtown Vancouver, Harry met
constituents and friends at every corner, anxious
for his views. He would be running again, this
time as a cabinet minister. That milestone in his
political career was reached on 21 September 1921
when he was sworn in as minister of trade and
commerce. Another member of the cabinet, destined
to be short-lived, was R.B. Bennett, who received
the justice portfolio, an indication that he would
be a candidate again in the forthcoming election.

35

Despite his continued support of the Meighen government, Harry Stevens probably had few illusions about its chances of re-election. Meighen himself had become personally identified with many unpopular policies filled with political liabilities. He had been largely responsible for drafting the bill nationalizing the Canadian Northern Railway — legislation that had angered and alienated the Montreal financiers who had so long controlled both the Conservative party and the Canadian Pacific Railway. French-speaking Quebec blamed Meighen for the hated Military Service Act. Organized labour accused him of fathering the restrictive legislation aimed at punishing the leaders of the Winnipeg General Strike. Western farmers were angry because Meighen had refused to continue the wartime wheat marketing board. These issues alone were almost enough to bring down any government, but the situation was made worse and almost hopeless by an economy unable to shake loose from the post-war slump.

If Harry Stevens had put his personal affairs first, he would have left politics in 1921 and tended to his business. Thanks to his brother Will's attention and the help of a faithful staff, the company was still a going concern, but it would have progressed faster with Harry at the helm. It needed his drive and personal contacts. There were also the growing demands of the family. Francis would soon be finished high school and hoped to go on to university, an expectation his father enthusiastically supported. Another three years and all three girls would be attending high school, bringing closer the time when major decisions about their future would have to be made. Did he have the right to spend so many of these precious years away from home? In the end there was no decision to make. He and Gertrude had made it in 1911: the annual trek to Ottawa would continue, voters willing. Harry was a politician first, a businessman second.

The general election of December 1921 brought another impressive personal victory for Harry Stevens in Vancouver Centre, in marked contrast to the Tory rout in the rest of the country. R.B. Bennett failed by a narrow margin to regain his Calgary seat, but for Harry's former colleague there were consolations. Shortly before the election Bennett had received 500 shares in the E.B. Eddy Company, through the will of his old New Brunswick friend and client, Mrs. Jenny Eddy; in another five years Bennett would control this huge concern, just a stone's throw from the parliament buildings. In the same period Harry's personal estate would suffer drastically, but he had one asset that the millionaire bachelor Bennett would never have: an intimate and wide family circle. Thus, as Bennett left his Calgary hotel suite in 1921 for his annual Christmas visit with his brother in New Brunswick, Harry could temporarily forget the political wars and enjoy his traditional Christmas in Vancouver. The festive dinner brought together Harry's family, his brother Will's, and the maternal grandparents, Mr. and Mrs. Glover. After Harry had done his usual expert carving job,and they all had eaten too much, they would reminisce about the Vernon days. Harry was in his element. He would regale them with stories about the time the train he was firing ran away, with a circus aboard; about meeting mountain lions as he drove the stage between Penticton and Camp McKinney. Throughout the Christmas week, the Stevens' living room would be filled with neighbours and relatives; in this particular year they could congratulate him on his third successive federal victory. Fortunately, the December election meant that Parliament would not begin until March so Harry could enjoy his family, attend his oft-neglected business, and mend some local political fences.

37

This latter chore was all the more necessary
now that the Liberals were in power in Victoria
and determined to establish firm relations with
the new Mackenzie King government in Ottawa. Thus,
while Premier 'Honest John' Oliver journeyed east
in February, Harry Stevens reminded Vancouverites
that not all political benefits had come from the
Grits. 'Stevens' Folly,' the grain elevator so
long a white elephant, was now 'filled to capacity,'
and the customs dues collected at the port of
Vancouver were 'annually well over the $15,000,000
mark.'[55] On 8 February 1922, Harry Stevens told a
Vancouver meeting of the Young Conservatives that
'during the past year the late government proceeded to coordinate all the railways with the
exception of the C.P.R.,' thus eliminating 'an
immense quantity of costly duplication.' He thought
much of the reason for the Meighen government's
defeat stemmed from opposition organized 'by the
chief competitor of the national railway system,
the C.P.R.' He also named the Bank of Montreal,
Canadian Cottons, Dominion Textiles, 'and other
powerful financial interests' led by Sir Lomer
Gouin and 'the French Canadian contingent of the
province of Quebec.' He claimed that this Quebec-
based corporate and political group 'absolutely
dominate the government of today' and were determined to 'discredit public ownership in Canada.'[56]
    The 1922 budget debate a few months later gave
Harry Stevens another opportunity to criticize
this powerful Montreal clique. He thought that
the big corporations such as Dominion Textiles
should pay the new 7 per cent excess profits tax
being proposed by the Liberals but that established,
family-owned firms, 'the very back-bone of the
industrial life of this country,' should be
exempt.[57] In particular, he cited one he remembered as a boy in Peterborough. It had begun making
ploughshares about seventy years ago and 'today

they have a moderately large agricultural implement business.' In effect, he was expressing his distaste for the increasingly impersonal corporate world, and, in particular, for the corporate mergers that were obliterating these small firms. Like Stevens himself, most had been born in the late 19th century, when a man could make it on his own by establishing, operating, and expanding a family business. The end of that age was coming at a speed directly proportional to the number of mergers taking place in the 1920s. Equally significant in terms of later political events was the fact that while Stevens the parliamentarian was voicing disapproval of this trend toward bigger and fewer businesses, his former desk-mate and future political leader, R.B. Bennett, was making millions from mergers. According to Max Aitken's later account, he and Bennett sold one of their joint creations in 1923, Alberta Pacific Grain Elevators, in a deal which gave Bennett a capital gain of $1,350,000.[58]

For his part, Stevens in 1922 gave no indication that he bore any personal enmity towards the new corporate giants or those who controlled them, so long as they did not oppose Meighen and the Conservative party. The same could not be said for his view of the BC Conservative establishment and its leader William Bowser. The west coast Tory leader had tried to persuade Stevens not to run federally in 1911, and before the 1917 election Bowser's name had been mentioned as a possible candidate for the Tory nomination in Stevens' own riding. By 1922 Bowser's free-wheeling political machine was probably an embarrassment to Meighen as well as being beyond his control. This may explain why Meighen prevailed upon the reluctant Stevens to challenge Bowser's provincial leadership at the 1922 Conservative convention. Harry must have realized that he had little chance of winning and

he had agreed only after an anti-Bowser faction
had approached Meighen and himself on the first
night of the convention, declaring that they would
'bolt' the convention if Stevens did not allow his
name to go forward.[59] Bowser won the leadership
easily, and Harry, probably with a sigh of relief,
turned his attention back to federal politics.
The British Columbia situation remained in a state
of turmoil. A group of young Conservatives held
their own convention in January 1923 and formed
the Provincial party, naming General A.D. McRae
as its leader. A millionaire lumberman who numbered
among his close business associates R.B. Bennett,[60]
McRae initially financed the new movement, but as
a provincial election approached in 1924, 'Vancouver business men soon rallied to the cause.'[61]

In May 1923 Meighen had asked Stevens to tour
Alberta and Saskatchewan 'to meet our friends,
deliver addresses and endeavour to have them perfect their organization.'[62] Harry thought this
effort a waste of time. What the party needed was
a full-time national organizer operating with its
'full authority and approval.' Meighen seems to
have acted on this suggestion inasmuch as he soon
appointed a committee of MPs 'to devise, provide
for, construct and maintain a federal organization.'
Harry Stevens would have been the logical chairman,
considering the interest he had already shown and
the work he had done. The job went instead to
another west coast member, Dr. S.F. Tolmie, MPP
for Victoria and minister of agriculture in the
Union government.

Harry's disappointment must have been keen, but
he remained the faithful, dependable party man,
using his debating skills against the Liberal
administration of Mackenzie King. During the 1923
examination of the Liberal government's Combines
Bill, he called the proposal 'inquisitorial' because
it would give wide powers to a registrar who could

40

conduct 'star-chamber proceedings' based upon
requests from 'six uninformed, irresponsible individuals' who might represent a business rival.[63]
Later in the same session, as a member of the
Commons Committee on Banking and Commerce, he
defended his party's position and his own belief
in the capitalist system. Specifically, he led the
opposition to a proposal from James S. Woodsworth,
the Independent Labour member for Winnipeg Centre,
calling for a revision to the Bank Act every year
instead of every ten. Woodsworth also wanted a
government audit of all banks, the granting of
organizing rights to bank employees, and limitation
of the interest rates on loans to 7 or 8 per cent.
All these amendments to the Bank Act were defeated
at the committee hearings, and as Harry indicated
long afterwards, the banking establishment felt it
owed him a debt of gratitude. About two weeks
after the hearings, Sir Thomas White, the former
minister of finance who had returned to the board
rooms of Bay Street (he was now vice president of
the Bank of Commerce and a director of the National
Trust), offered Harry, on behalf of the banking
fraternity, the sum of $125,000 'for the wonderful
job' he had done.

> And I said, 'No' - I knew him very well - I always
> called him by his first name, Tom - I said, 'No,
> Tom, I can't take that because if the banks do
> anything which I think is contrary to the public
> interest, I'll oppose them just as bitterly as
> I supported them against these radicals ... And
> I turned it down. And he told me at the time he
> said, 'There's no string attached. We did it for
> Sir Wilfrid Laurier, and we did it for Sir ——,
> former Prime Minister before Laurier's day.[64]

Turning down bankers' bribes was much easier than
avoiding the continuing squabbles of the BC Tory

41

party. Liberal Premier Oliver, faced with cries
for reform and charges of corruption within his
own party, had called an election for June 1924.
Despite strong advice to the contrary, Harry
Stevens gave in to 'the most urgent request of
Meighen'[65] and agreed to return home to campaign
for Bowser. Fifty west coast Tories refused to
accept his explanation that 'the success of Oliver
would have some effect upon the continuance in
office' of the federal Liberals. They sent him a
bluntly worded telegram:

> This is not your fight. Thousands of good Con-
> servatives are supporting the Provincial party
> in order to clean up the provincial political
> situation and they deeply resent any interference
> from Ottawa. Our advice is you better stay out
> of this mess.[66]

Stevens promptly answered F.W. Rounsefell, the
first name of the 50-odd on the telegram, explaining
that both he and Meighen took the view 'that as
Mr. Bowser now occupies the position of leader
by selection at a regularly called convention of
the Conservative Party at which we were both present, that the Federal Members from B.C. should,
unless on a point of difference in present policy,
support the choice of the convention.'[67] Stevens
dutifully toured the province on behalf of Bowser
in what proved to be one of the bitterest campaigns
in British Columbia's history. 'The public became
so badly confused that when the ballots were counted' on 20 June 1924 all three party leaders had
suffered personal defeat.[68] Oliver soon won a by-
election and resumed his premiership; Bowser
retired; McRae decided to enter federal politics.
Harry Stevens hurried back to Ottawa in time to
give a strong speech in favour of the Church Union
bill. The Rev. J.W.D. Woodside of Chalmers Presby-

terian Church in Ottawa was in the gallery to
hear him and immediately wrote in praise of a
speech which he thought one of the best he had
ever heard.[69] But Stevens had not heard the last
of the bitter British Columbia election campaign.

In mid-July 1924 the Victoria Times wrote a
post-election editorial accusing Stevens of being
a traitor to the Conservative cause and of having
'a secret alliance with the Provincial Party.'
Stevens strongly suspected that Bowser had inspired
the editorial and when Bowser's Ottawa man, Senator
Robert Green, began spreading similar stories
around Parliament hill, Harry angrily decided to
give Meighen his side of the argument. Unable to
get an appointment, he immediately sat down on 17
July and wrote a long letter to his leader. Remind-
ing Meighen of his first election victory in 1911,
achieved 'in spite of the bitter and organized
opposition of W.J. Bowser,' Stevens referred to
the next four years when he was 'constantly subjected to the most crude, unfair and unjustifiable
interference and propaganda of calumny from within
our own party, inspired by Bowser and largely
through the medium of Bob Green at this end.' He
charged that this faction had 'sought by every
conceivable means to control the patronage in
Vancouver and to discredit' him wherever possible
in eastern Canada. Stevens had 'for the past thir-
teen years been aware of their efforts' and had
borne 'in silence, without complaint their bitter,
underhand methods.' Though millions of dollars
had been spent on the harbour and city of Vancouver
'during our term of office,' even Stevens' bitterest
political enemies had been unable to point a finger
'to one single act of malfeasance on my part or
any suspicion of it.' At this point, Stevens'
account shifted abruptly, and distributed blame
for Conservative fortunes in British Columbia:

On the other hand, I cannot help but remember
that Bob Green (whose counsel is accepted within
the party in preference to my own) has a reputa-
tion which was and is one of the greatest detri-
ments to the Conservative Party in British Columbia, and furthermore, had these men succeeded
in securing the patronage in Vancouver, the Conservative Party would not have had the clear
record it now has ... My object in now writing
you is to warn you that the Federal interests
in B.C. are intimately bound up in the provincial
situation, and it is about time the Conservative
Party shook itself free from these barnacles
and brings back into its fold, and to its support,
the thousands of responsible and respectable
citizens who have been standing aloof because
of the control of this faction.[70]

The last thing Meighen wanted to hear about was
more party bickering. For months he had been
fighting off repeated attempts by Montreal Tories
to remove him from the leadership. He replied to
Stevens' letter immediately, saying he had not
known Stevens had been seeking an interview; he
would be glad to see him that day. He would want
to know how Stevens supported his charge that
Bob Green's counsel was being accepted within the
national party in preference to Stevens'. He also
wanted proof that thousands of people were 'standing aloof' from the Conservative party in British
Columbia because of the control exerted by the
Bowser-Green faction. 'After that we will have no
difficulty.'[71] Apparently Meighen and Stevens
ironed matters out to their mutual satisfaction.
    In the summer of 1924, Harry took advantage both
of the parliamentary recess and of his friendships
with several influential citizens. He decided to
make a business trip to England, in the hope of
obtaining much-needed timber orders for several

British Columbia firms. He went well armed with
letters of introduction. Sir Robert Borden gave
him one to the president of the Bank of Nova Scotia
and another to Lloyd George. Sir Thomas White
informed the London manager of the Canadian Bank
of Commerce that Harry Stevens was 'one of the
most prominent and leading members of the Conservative Opposition.' The president of the Bank of
Montreal, Sir Frederick Williams-Taylor, was more
specific: 'Mr. Stevens' services to the banks of
Canada in the Committee on Banking and Commerce
were of great value and highly appreciated.'[72]
This was Harry's first trip back to the old
country. Late in November 1924 he booked in at
London's British Empire Club. It was an unfortunate
choice, for on the 24th a fire swept through the
building. Harry was the first to turn in the alarm,
and his interview with London reporters made the
front pages:

I was asleep ... when I heard a crackling noise
behind my head. I immediately arose, switched on
my light, and went to see what was taking place.
I got as far as the lift shaft, but was then
driven back by great sheets of flame that were
rapidly licking their way along the passage
towards my own and other people's bedrooms. I
saw that escape had been cut off by the ordinary
stairway, and I realized that it was up to me
to raise the alarm.[73]

'AM ALRIGHT,' he cabled home to Gertrude. 'ESCAPED
BY FIREMAN'S LADDER. ONE WAS SUFFOCATED, FOUR
INJURED. AM ABSOLUTELY SAFE.'
Undeterred, Harry continued his tour. After
visiting the creosoting works of the London Midland
and Scottish Railway Company, he was able to cable
H.C. Hooper in Vancouver that he had a firm offer
for 250,000 eight-foot sleepers 'but must shade

price previous quotation and delivery free on rail,'[74] The best lay ahead: a state dinner at the Savoy for Sir George Foster and himself as guests of the British Empire League. Harry was soon to realize, however, that there was no escape from Canadian politics, even in London. This was the time when Prime Minister Mackenzie King was resisting British attempts to speak for a 'united Empire,' and the Canadian high commissioner in London was a dedicated Liberal, Peter A. Larkin, long-time treasurer of the Ontario Liberal party. The high commissioner did not attend the dinner, and his absence was noted. His press officer, Henry Thompson, obviously a Tory appointment, wrote to Stevens later about political implications of the banquet:

> It was a matter of comment from many that the High Commissioner from Canada was not present, but then he always played politics to the limit; and it was also a matter of comment amongst several that the gentleman whom he sent to deputize for him, Lt. Col. J. Reid Hyde, C.B.E., ... left the gathering before Sir George Foster was a quarter of the way through his speech.[75]

To give him his due, Larkin's job was to defend Canada's interests, and, like a growing number of Canadians, he abhorred British snobbishness, especially to 'colonials.' Shortly after the banquet, he wrote to Mackenzie King: 'The trouble is that in the minds of men here, we still continue in a state of tutelage; we are children and consequently troublesome instead of men on whom they can & do depend in grave emergencies.'[76] To Harry Stevens, revelling in this semi-state visit to his old homeland, such an attitude toward the British was unthinkable. But he was like Larkin in being just as partisan, and undoubtedly felt one should expect the worst from the King administration, particularly in its relations with the motherland.

A few weeks later, in February 1925, Harry was back at his old stand in Ottawa as Parliament began what many expected would be the last session before a general election. His first major speech, hard-hitting and effective, came on 6 February, the second day of the speech from the throne debate, immediately after that of James Woodsworth, the Labour member from Winnipeg, and now the recognized leader of the so-called 'Ginger Group.' Stevens accused the King administration of subsidizing a privately owned foreign shipping combine at the expense of the Canadian tax-payer. Amid repeated interjections from King, Lapointe, Crerar, and Forke, there followed one of the most heated debates of the entire session.

But Harry Stevens must have been wondering what good he was doing, for himself if not for his party and constituents. After fourteen years in the House of Commons, he was losing heart; financially, he was dying. As he later recalled in a letter to Joseph Atkinson, owner of the Toronto Star, the 'long absences in Ottawa' had forced the closing of the auditing branch of his Vancouver business and he had had to pay $5,000 to cover an amount embezzled by the former manager of his insurance branch. In 1925, Harry desperately wanted to quit politics. 'Had I done so, it would have reflected seriously on the Rt. Hon. Arthur Meighen, who was my much-loved leader, and I determined to stay with him during the forthcoming election.' The financial risks he took were serious. 'I then cashed in all my life insurance. My wife sold the home and we pooled all our resources, and I formed the company known as Vancouver Holdings Limited. The utmost we were able to gather together for that company was about $45,000. I borrowed some further funds from the bank and launched this company.'[77]

47

Harry Stevens won his fourth successive general
election in 1925, though the victory had Pyrrhic
overtones. This time he was one of ten Conservatives
from the west coast, probably the richest in political experience and the poorest in financial assets.
Among his new colleagues was General A.D. McRae,
back in the good graces of the party, with his
dissident Provincial party a thing of the past.
Another western millionaire to return to the Tory
benches was R.B. Bennett. From Montreal came R.S.
White, co-owner of the Montreal Gazette, C.H.
Cahan, a wealthy corporation lawyer from St. James
Street, and Cahan's associate, Leslie Bell. For
months this trio of White, Cahan, and Bell had been
working closely with Lord Atholstan, owner of the
Montreal Star, to oust Meighen as party leader.[78]
The Ottawa corridors carried rumours that Bennett
would be his likely successor. When Harry Stevens
first glanced around at the new Tory caucus, he
may well have felt that he should have taken his
losses and stayed home with his family in Vancouver.
He had already had cause for sensitivity toward
wealthier Tories, notably Senator Green and W.G.
Bowser. How would he fare now while those old
business associates, McRae and Bennett, hatched
schemes with their equally powerful Montreal
friends?

No doubt Meighen too was aware of these potential
pressures and enemies. In a real sense both Arthur
Meighen and his parliamentary lieutenant, Harry
Stevens, were at bay. They were waiting for some
move, not only from Mackenzie King, but from
wealthy Tories now members of His Majesty's Loyal
Opposition. Still, both Meighen and Stevens had
waited out events and their adversaries before;
they would again. Surely the 1925 election results
had shown the wisdom of this policy. It had produced a stalemate, with the Liberals holding to
power on the strength of their support from the

48

Progressives. In a letter to Harry about the best
way to woo the western Progressives away from the
Liberals, Meighen used words that could apply to
themselves: 'I more and more lean to the view that
we should not be too precipitate. We have a grip
on the situation and can only lose it by being in
too big a hurry, or by making some error in tactics.'[79] Political animal that he was, Harry
Stevens could sense victory in the offing. But it
was still four years away - and it would be directed by his first desk-mate in the House, the
millionaire R.B. Bennett. Harry had won his own
election with ease, and when his CPR train reached
Calgary on 2 January 1926 he greeted his old friend
Bennett, member for Calgary East. It must have
seemed as if life had gone full circle as they
settled down for another long trip east, talking
about their first parliamentary session together
and the exciting new one that lay ahead.

II A New Leader

The air was brisk as the CPR's transcontinental
steamed into Sudbury on 4 January 1926. Stevens
and Bennett walked quickly to the station, wondering about the messages that awaited them. Their
chief, Arthur Meighen, was requesting a meeting
in Ottawa to discuss 'the constitutional soundness
of the present Government facing Parliament as
such, while the Prime Minister has no seat.' Both
of their letters contained lengthy memoranda on
the government's legality, prepared by two Ontario
lawyers. In Meighen's view, Mackenzie King had
had at least one opportunity since the 1925 election
to contest a by-election and had declined. 'The
vote of the country was strongly against' the
Liberals and Meighen was convinced that 'a very
strong case' could be made to Parliament, and perhaps, 'if there was a forum, before the Governor-
General.'[1]

Stevens and Bennett must have spent hours dis-
cussing this question after their train pulled
out of Sudbury. Uncertainty is the stuff of politics and a great question mark hung over the forthcoming session. Meighen's Tories had won 46.5 per
cent of the popular vote and the largest number of
seats, 116; King and five Liberal cabinet ministers

50

had been defeated but 99 Liberals had been successful. The balance of power remained, as in 1921,
with the western Progressives who held a block of
24 seats. How long could King rely on their support?

Within minutes after its formal opening on 8
January by the governor-general, Sir Julian Byng,
the first session of the fifteenth Parliament began
debate on this crucial issue. The Liberal House
leader, Ernest Lapointe, in an attempt to move an
adjournment, said 'the government was justified
in retaining office and in summoning parliament.'[2]
Meighen promptly objected that two days notice of
motion had not been given and the Lapointe motion
was put aside. What followed over the next two
weeks was a lawyer's delight: amendments, motions,
and tortured legal arguments on the government's
right to hold office. Undismayed by his lack of
formal legal training, Harry Stevens plunged in
with the assurance of a veteran parliamentarian.
On 14 January he paid tribute to the excellent
legal and constitutional arguments already presented, notably by Meighen, Lapointe, Bennett,
Lucien Cannon, and Hugh Guthrie. Then, after rubbing in the Liberal failures at the polls by pointing to the personal defeats of King, Herbert Marler,
and Vincent Massey, Stevens displayed his considerable knowledge of the constitution and of parliamentary rules. He saved his most important sally
to the last:

What invisible influence is it that forces them
to cling to office? I am precluded by the rules
of the House from saying very much in that regard,
but I will say this: It is the consciousness of
the government that the moment they relinquish
office ... the moment others have access to the
files and secret information of the departments,
there will be revealed a condition which they,
if they can cling to office, would fain hide.[3]

51

The minister of agriculture, James Robb, tried to provoke him to 'proceed a little further' but Stevens would say no more. Next on his feet was G.H. Boivin, making his maiden speech as minister of customs and excise. Though he probably knew that Stevens' last remarks were aimed specifically at his department, Boivin did not take the bait.

The debate dragged on; tempers became frayed but the House maintained almost perfect attendance in case of a snap confidence vote. On 1 February Stevens asked Boivin to table 'all orders-in-council issued during the past two years for the release of alcohol from distilleries within a shorter period of time than that set forth in the Inland Revenue Act.'[4] Obviously something was brewing; indeed King had realized well before 1 February, when the House defeated Meighen's second amendment of censure, that the Conservatives were shifting their attack away from the government's right to hold office to a more vulnerable spot, the customs and excise department.

As King's biographer, H. Blair Neatby, has pointed out, the Liberal leader had known even before the 1925 election 'that a full-scale investigation of the Department was needed.'[5] To head off what might be damaging Tory ammunition for the election, King had removed Jacques Bureau, its minister, by appointing him to the Senate. The Conservative opposition had not been the only group sensing something amiss in the customs department. A group of merchants 'affected by unfair competition from smugglers' had recently formed the Commercial Protective Association and to pacify them King had tentatively agreed to establish a royal commission to investigate the smuggling allegations if the president of the association would prefer charges against any individuals. Instead the association decided to conduct its own inquiry with the help of an investigator from the customs department.

52

King himself had had a long talk with this official in December 1925 and confided to his diary that 'there is a scandalous condition which might cause us defeat.'[6] Still, he did nothing about it except to dismiss J.E. Bisaillon from his job as special inspector of customs and excise in Montreal. King's anxiety must have increased during January as from the Commons gallery (he still did not have a seat) he watched the Tories set the stage.

Harry Stevens was just as anxious for he and his colleagues had been quietly preparing for an exposé. At the start of the session he had placed a resolution on the order paper calling for the appointment of a special Commons committee to investigate 'evidence of irregular and corrupt conduct' by customs officials. On the weekend of 30 January he had travelled to Montreal for a rendezvous with one Percy Sparks, a representative of the Commercial Protective Association.[7] The throne speech debate had to be completed before his resolution could be discussed and on 1 February it began to look as if the Liberals would win a six-week recess which might give them time to prepare, and to ward off, an investigation. But time was on Stevens' side. Shortly before midnight on 1 February the intricacies of parliamentary rules enabled him to take the floor. He held it for the next two hours. It was an occasion most politicians can only dream about, and for Harry Stevens it was a rich reward for sixteen long and financially hard years as a back-bencher. His tale made the Pacific Scandal of Sir John A. Macdonald's day seem like the mildest bit of impropriety. With the tired members coming back to life and to their seats, Stevens began unravelling the tangled but lucrative activities of many customs officials. To illustrate 'the rascality and criminality' of Bisaillon, Montreal's chief customs preventive officer, Stevens charged that he had received 'tens of thousands of dollars, deposited ... to his own account,' rather than to the receiver-general. Furthermore, when Bisaillon had been brought to court in June 1925, he had been acquitted, despite the efforts of the crown prosecutor, Lucien Cannon, now the solicitor-general. Citing evidence given at Bisaillon's trial, Stevens noted that Bisaillon had denied knowing two women charged with smuggling into the country two trunks filled with narcotics; they were fined $500, but the trunks were later stolen from the police office and a man mentioned in their trial was killed in a gangland murder. There was more to this sordid saga, much more. As the clock tolled out the small hours of 2 February, Stevens never faltered; indeed, he seemed to warm to his task with the frequent interruptions from the Liberal front-benchers, who weakly tried to bring an end to this incredible story of government laxity and its implications for a gigantic smuggling operation.

Why should the honest businessmen be subjected to a veritable flood of smuggled goods brought in daily, openly, across the boundary? These great trucks, at this hour while I am talking, are crossing the boundary in a dozen places ... well known to the hon. gentlemen [opposite] - a veritable joke in the community - roaring clean across the boundary, never thinking of stopping, privileged characters, every truck loaded with contraband - all this known. Mr. Speaker, I want the public right to the revenues of this country protected. I want this defrauding of the exchequer of this country of over thirty millions of dollars ... to be stopped. I want these criminals to be brought to task. I want this government to cease its supine idleness, its ignoring of these reports. I want them to take hold, or quit and let somebody else take hold, one or the other.[8]

He concluded with an amendment to Lapointe's original
motion for adjournment, calling instead for the
House to proceed with the public business and in
particular to investigate these 'grave irregularities in the Department of Customs and Excise.'
There should be no adjournment, his amendment continued, 'until a special committee of seven members
is appointed to investigate thoroughly the administration of the said department.'

At two a.m., George Boivin agreed to the idea
of a special committee. He also revealed that the
notorious Bisaillon had been dismissed on 10 December, that is, six months after his acquittal.
Despite the hour, the weary but excited House
voted on still another Tory amendment against
adjournment which the government, supported by
the Progressives, defeated by just one vote. Two
days later approval was given to a motion setting
up a committee to investigate Stevens' charges.
His amendment to Lapointe's motion for adjournment
finally came to a vote on 5 February and again
the Progressives, 'their consciences eased by the
pledge to investigate,'[9] supported the government.
The House would adjourn once the debate on the
address in reply to the speech from the throne
had been concluded. It would reassemble 15 March,
when the customs scandal would probably be the
number one topic. Stevens had not discovered the
scandal but he had assumed a dominant role for
the Conservatives in bringing it to public attention. As he had done with the grain report ten
years before, he had worked long and diligently
to uncover the facts, and his speech indicated how
well he had succeeded. It was a logical role for
Harry Stevens. After all, this latter-day muck-
raker had begun his political career on a moral
reform platform based in large measure on his well-
developed indignation against the use and abuse
of liquor. The 1926 customs inquiry was merely

the latest chapter in the political career of
this Methodist lay preacher.

The parliamentary debate was not yet over. Stevens
remained by his leader's side throughout the Tory
filibuster, which finally ended when the Liberals
invoked closure. The House recessed on 2 March,
giving only two weeks to launch the customs inquiry before the nine committee members, Stevens
being one, had to return to the Commons. After 15
March their attention was divided as the House
resumed its sittings, now under the leadership of
Mackenzie King who finally took his seat after
winning a by-election in Prince Albert.

Stevens' brief participation in the Commons debates suggests that he was devoting most of his
time to the customs inquiry. He did not take part
in the debate on the old age pensions bill, introduced on 26 March, and for the first time in ten
years he did not contribute to the budget debate.
By contrast, R.B. Bennett, one of the four Conservatives on the committee, was almost as active a
debater as Meighen; one wonders, in retrospect,
whether the Calgary member was already preparing
for the leadership race that seemed to be shaping
up. Perhaps Stevens felt a greater obligation to
the customs investigation, considering his initi-
ating role; a growing volume of mail acclaimed
him as the public's defender. One Toronto correspondent, for example, enclosed a clipping from
the Telegram noting the extremely low prices being
advertised by Eaton's and Simpson's department
stores. Some of their goods were 'being brought in
at a much under-estimated value, therefore hurting
the Canadian manufacturer and forcing him out of
business.'[10] Stevens had no time to reply to most
of these correspondents; he was too busy helping
to prepare the committee's report. As the House
learned on 18 June, when it was tabled, it more
than substantiated Stevens' charges. Bisaillon

was a worse felon than Stevens had pictured him.
The report also named 25 firms, mostly garment
manufacturers, from whom the government should
recover excise funds.[11]

The House was given the weekend to study the
report and to prepare for debate. With the notable
exception of Bennett, who had decided he must
honour a speaking engagement in Calgary, all members of the House resumed their seats on Monday,
21 June, for what promised to be an exciting exchange. Discussion began the next day. 'Often it
became a shouting match rather than a debate and
the Speaker, whose impartiality remained impeccable,
was often hard put to it to maintain decorum in
the uproar.'[12] After the Liberal chairman of the
committee had moved third and final reading of
the report on 22 June, Harry Stevens took the floor.
He paid tribute to Percy Sparks, the special investigator for the Commercial Protective Association
who had gathered a great deal of the initial evidence over the past eighteen months.[13] Much of
Stevens' speech dealt with bootlegging of liquor,
and he ended with a skilfully worded motion calling
for the revival of the committee to investigate
allegations of political influence having been
exerted upon the department of customs and excise.
His motion incorporated the intent and some of
the words used earlier in the debate by D.M.
Kennedy, the lone Progressive member on the committee. It was a shrewd attempt to persuade the
all-important Progressive group to stop supporting
the government. Stevens himself was friendly enough
with Kennedy and other western Progressives but
he could not accept their dislike of party politics.
Outside the House, he had friends of different
political hues, from the socialist J.S. Woodsworth
to Mackenzie King himself. But he was first and
last a staunch party man, loyal to his leader and
to the majority view of caucus.

57

During debate Stevens allowed no quarter. Thus, when a Liberal committee member and a fellow Vancouverite, Dugald Donaghy, accused him of not bringing out enough evidence to support his original charges (a point probably intended to embarrass Stevens before his home-town supporters), he angrily replied that some of the evidence reflected so unfortunately on matters of personal character that certain members of the committee and the press had agreed to suppress it.[14] But it was when the Liberals tried to implicate Tory lawyers and politicians in the sordid smuggling activities, that the debate degenerated into mere mud-slinging. The Independent Labour member, J.S. Woodsworth, observed that the House of Commons, 'which is primarily a legislative body, is these days turned into a court,' with Conservative prosecutors and Liberal defendants - 'all of them revealing their partisan bias.'[15] Undoubtedly aware of Stevens' personal bias against liquor, he reminded him that A.E. Nash, the legal counsel for the Commercial Protective Association, had testified that owners of one large distillery had contributed to the campaign funds of both parties. 'Now when this condition exists, I say that we have in our midst an organized form of debauchery that ought to be pilloried before the people of this country.' Stevens did not disagree or interject, even when Woodsworth concluded with an amendment to Stevens' motion. This, in effect, would have avoided a direct censure of the King administration; consequently Meighen challenged the Woodsworth amendment as being separate from the main motion and hence out of order. It was now past five a.m., Saturday morning. The harassed Speaker requested an adjournment until Monday to study the matter.

After a few hours rest, Harry sat down to write Gertrude about what must have been his most thrilling moments as an MP.[16] What he could not know was that King had decided to avoid a vote on his amendment by requesting the governor-general, Lord Byng, to dissolve Parliament. Few could have predicted Byng's reaction: rather than dissolution, Meighen should be given the opportunity to take office.

                                    June 26 1926
Well Dearest,

This is a momentous day. Everyone has been at fever heat excitement for the past 24 hours. The House sat from 2 p.m. yesterday until 5.30 a.m. today. I never left the Chamber, except for meals, during all those long weary hours. I was compelled to remain as I was constantly under attack and it would have appeared cowardly to have left. I said 'weary hours' but scarcely a moment passed that was not pregnant with passion, excitement.

It was very trying. The galleries were packed and hundreds of people [were] walking the corridors. It is said that there has never been such interest shown since Confederation. I am of course both the hero and the villain of the hour. Utterances in the House alternate between fierce denunciation, exaggerated and bitter, and vociferous praise.

Through it all I fail to feel any great excitement - certainly no elation - no sense of triumph - only a deep consciousness of the burden of it all, not only what is past but what is likely to come.

We defeated the Government three times last night, by two votes twice and once by one vote. Yet Mackenzie King will not resign, although the rumour is that he will on Monday ...

Of course all is excitement in the corridors today - cabinets are being formed and scrapped.

Meanwhile Arthur Meighen is the man on whose
shoulders the load must chiefly rest. He will
have a hard task with no majority in the House.

By by - Lots of Love
Your Harry

Meighen's chance came sooner than he or anyone
expected. Twice on Sunday, 27 June, King met with
Lord Byng, but each time the governor-general was
adamant: there would be no dissolution. The next
afternoon the Liberal leader, after explaining
that His Excellency had refused to accept his
advice, stunned the House by announcing the resignation of the Liberal administration. According
to King, 'Meighen was clearly taken by surprise,'[17]
but it did not take him long to recover. He would
accept Byng's request to form a new government.
On the morning of 29 June orders-in-council were
passed naming the new Conservative cabinet. H.H.
Stevens would be acting minister of customs and
excise, acting minister of the interior, mines,
trade and commerce, and agriculture and superin-
tendent-general of Indian affairs. Stevens and
his new cabinet colleagues became 'acting' ministers as part of a desperate move by Meighen to
comply with a parliamentary rule which said that
any member of Parliament, upon assuming cabinet
rank and salary, had to resign and run again in a
by-election. Had they all done so, the Tories
would have lacked a majority in the House as well
as their best debaters. It was Meighen alone, as
prime minister, who resigned. He had reasoned
that seven ministers without portfolios serving
as acting heads of government departments would
not receive a minister's salary but would be able
to complete the remaining work of the session
without the need of an adjournment. Then he could
call an election on the issue of the customs

scandal. The legality of his tactics was later
upheld by Dr. Eugene Forsey in his definitive work,
The Royal Power of Dissolution, which also supported
the constitutionality of Lord Byng's decisions.

In the practical world of politics, legal fine
points took second place to tactics. Thus Meighen
could only watch helplessly from the gallery as
King challenged the constitutionality of the government and in effect seized the political initiative. His deliberate questioning of each minister
on his right to hold office and administer public
funds was enough to sway the wavering Progressives.
On 1 July, amid great noise and confusion, the
Progressives once again tipped the balance of
power by supporting a Liberal motion that Stevens
and the other Tory ministers without portfolio
should have followed the example of their leader
and resigned. Meighen had no alternative but to
advise Lord Byng to dissolve the House. For the
second time in less than a year, Canadians were
being asked to go to the polls; the new election
would be 14 September 1926.

Harry Stevens did not return home immediately
following dissolution. A sudden attack of gall-
stones sent him to the hospital for an emergency
operation. Gertrude hurried east to be with him,
bringing first-hand news of the children. Francis
had had another successful year at the University
of British Columbia and his choice of theology as
a career greatly pleased his father. Their eldest
daughter, eighteen-year-old Marjory, had been a
steady help to her mother. Sylvia and Patricia,
now active teenagers, had been keeping a close
eye on young Douglas as they all enjoyed yet another summer at the 'ranch.' Much as Harry longed to
see more of them, here he was, flat on his back
in an Ottawa hospital, with the prospect of another
election campaign as soon as he got home. He and
Gertrude must have talked many hours during this

hospital sojourn about his political future and
his business affairs. Neither of them seems to have
had any doubts about his staying in politics: a
year ago they had decided he would remain. Visits
from Meighen, Bennett, Sir George Perley, and other
political colleagues must have strengthened this
resolve.[18] Further encouragement had come in
letters from P.T. O'Farrell of the Montreal Financial Times, who relayed the opinion of Sir Edward
Beatty, CPR president, that 'there were only two
men capable of leading in the Conservative ranks,
Bennett and Stevens.'[19] The journalist implied
that Bennett had the edge, but he reassured Stevens:
'You are young and you can bide your time. You
get the credit everywhere for unhorsing King and
the country won't forget it.'
    The Liberal leader had no intention of forgetting
Harry Stevens either. On 11 September, in Ottawa,
King told a mass Liberal rally that Stevens had
used his prestige as an MP to promote stock speculation in an American oil company. He cited as
his source an editorial in the Vancouver Province.
Two days later this Tory paper gave a different
version. Its editorial summing up the several
campaigns on the west coast said they had been
'generally clean except in Vancouver Centre.' 'Here
a campaign of abuse and vilification has been
going on, during the past week, having for its aim
the defeat of the Hon. H.H. Stevens. The chief
actors in this have been the Vancouver Sun and J.C.
McRuer, K.C., a Toronto lawyer who says he is
acting on his own responsibility.'[20] The editorial
also referred to a Sun story claiming that in 1922
Stevens had used his parliamentary stationery to
support an oil company's promotion plans. The
Province attacked the Sun for publishing the story,
which had been based on a forged letter, and, on
his return, Harry categorically denied the charge.
On 13 September the Toronto Star printed King's

62

apology to the Province and another to Stevens
who had already gone ahead with a $100,000 libel
suit against the Sun. As Francis later recalled,
'Mother never forgave the Vancouver Sun (no matter
how it might change management) and until her
death in 1966 she wouldn't permit the Sun inside
her house. If Dad wanted to read it, he could ...
at the office, and he did.'[21] Gertrude had never
made a political speech and had rarely accompanied
Harry during his campaigns. Quiet by nature, she
seldom talked politics, even at home; yet, when
she pressed her lips tightly together and uttered
not a word, her family knew that 'Mother had her
dander up.' This kind of silent support meant
more to Harry than anything else, and helps to
explain how he could shake off the vicious public
attacks directed at him, particularly during
that 1926 campaign. Stevens' former campaign manager and present colleague, George Black, wrote
to Bennett in 1928:

> The Grits made a dead set at him and he smote
> them hip and thigh. The smuggling-bootlegging-
> lawless element did all they could to pull him
> down during the federal election of 1926 and
> the general impression was that they had to some
> extent succeeded ...[22]

In the end, the Liberal smear tactics came to
naught: Harry took Vancouver Centre by an even
larger majority than in 1925. His Liberal opponent,
Dugald Donaghy, who had won in Vancouver North in
1925, might have fared better in his former riding
where General A.D. McRae took the seat by a mere
692 votes.

R.B. Bennett had been re-elected in Calgary but
Arthur Meighen had made his last Commons speech.
Along with many other Tories he had gone down to
defeat, in his home town of Portage La Prairie.

Never again would Stevens and many other House of
Commons men thrill to Meighen's rhetoric and debating skill. The Meighen era had ended, and, to
some observers, the Bennett era had already begun.
Long before his defeat Meighen had become aware
of Bennett's presence in the wings, and had known
of greater support among Montreal's St. James
Street Tories for the wealthy Calgarian.[23] Harry
Stevens had had a high regard for and a warm personal friendship with Meighen, who had now fallen
in the political wars, as all might one day do.

With Meighen gone, the Conservative MPs moved
quickly to select a new Opposition spokesman.
Meighen himself had asked the party's senators
and members, as well as defeated candidates, to
attend an Ottawa meeting on 11 October to choose
his successor. It named Hugh Guthrie, the Ontario
lawyer who had left the Liberals to join Borden's
Union government in 1917. He would be the tempo-
rary leader until a national leadership convention
could be held, probably in 1927. Harry was not
being mentioned as a possibility, and the fact that
General McRae had been named chairman of the sub-
committee on organization strengthened belief in
many quarters that his long-time friend, R.B.
Bennett, would emerge an easy winner. Stevens
must have felt some bitterness. Although he never
committed any such thought to writing, he might
well have aspired to be leader instead of continuing as the ever-faithful lieutenant. It seemed
that he lacked the money or the connections, or
both, to be a member of the inner circle, on the
provincial scene as well as the federal.

Parliament was not due to open until 9 December
1926 and the late autumn found Harry back on the
coast, attending to his long-neglected real estate
and insurance business. Once again, however, politics competed for his interest. He was on hand
for the provincial leadership convention held at

Kamloops on 23 November – an event described by
the Daily Province as the 'most momentous in the
history of the Conservative Party in British
Columbia.' The big question was: would W.J. Bowser
come out of retirement and challenge for the
leadership Leon J. Ladner, who since 1921 had been
the federal member for Vancouver South. The race
was thrown wide open, however, when Bowser announced
even before nominations closed that he would not
run. The post went to another federal member, Dr.
S.F. Tolmie of Victoria. The Liberals' voice in
Vancouver, the Sun, claimed that the key role in
this selection had been played by General McRae.
'His withdrawal of support from the move to have
W.J. Bowser return to office appears to have pretty
nearly settled the fate of the proposal.'

Harry Stevens apparently played no important role
in these provincial party manoeuvres; forces and
personalities beyond his influence seemed to be at
work. An identical situation was shaping up in the
federal sphere; again Harry seemed destined to
watch from the sidelines as another leadership
struggle began. He might well have had mixed feel-
ings as he prepared for the long trip east and a
new parliament. Later, during the short pre-Christ-
mas session of the sixteenth parliament, he uttered
not a word. On December 15 the House adjourned and
Harry returned home to Gertrude, the children, the
Glovers, a host of friends and relatives. Home
now was a big comfortable place near Stanley Park
and it was now that Harry first began taking the
long walks that in his later years would become
part of the local tradition. The Christmas recess
was just what was needed to restore his vitality
and verve. Its highlight was Christmas dinner. As
Francis remembers:

It was always an old-fashioned family affair.
Mother was one of seven sisters. Two of her

sisters (one of whom married Dad's brother Will)
lived in Vancouver as did miscellaneous nieces
and nephews ... and the Glover grandparents.
Usually the three families, with a dozen children
between them, and the various cousins to the
number of twenty or thirty or more [gathered] for
a turkey dinner. Dad would carve the turkey(s)
at the table. He was good at it, and his knife
was always well sharpened. Mother cooked the
meal, with plum pudding, Christmas cake, and
mince pies - all quite traditional and delicious.
There was no liquor - but we had a whale of a
time.[24]

When the House of Commons resumed its sessions
on 8 February 1927, Harry Stevens was on his feet
repeatedly during the first hour, demanding one
explanation after another on a variety of topics.[25]
On 15 February the acting party leader, Hugh
Guthrie, informed Harry that he would be Opposition
critic of the customs estimates.[26] Bennett was
given finance to watch, but his speech opening
the budget debate was, he admitted, ill prepared.
'I have not in a busy life been able to give that
measure of attention to the business of the country
during the last few weeks that its importance
demands.'[27] Not so Harry Stevens; when his turn
came a week or so later, he obviously had done
his homework. In this first major address to the
new parliament, he carried on a running debate
with most of the Liberal front-benchers, hitting
out at the government's trade policy and ending
with a condemnation of its plan to export St.
Lawrence River power to the United States. He
could not know it but he was touching on a future
issue of major proportions, the Beauharnois power
deal, which would one day be revealed as political
corruption of a complex order. On 10 March Stevens
continued the attack when he began debate on a

66

bill to provide steamship service to the West
Indies. He charged that the bill was planned to
give financial assistance to two Montreal Liberal
supporters who had recently purchased a British
shipping firm. Charles Dunning, the minister of
railways and canals, hotly denied the allegation,
but he drew the fire of Stevens and other coast
members when he said that two of the five ships
for the service would be built in Britain.

For the Tories, the autumn promised much more
excitement. In February the party's first national
leadership convention was set for 11-12 October
in Winnipeg, and as soon as the announcement was
made the Tory front-benchers rallied around the
several candidates. From the first, Stevens supported Bennett, probably because like other Tories
in the know he could see that the wealthy Calgary
bachelor had a long lead on the other aspirants,
notably Hugh Guthrie and C.H. Cahan. He also knew
that Bennett was not only capable and a westerner
like himself but also had the necessary support
of the Montreal financiers and businessmen who had
made things so difficult for Meighen. Undoubtedly
Stevens would have preferred Meighen, but this
brilliant, analytical parliamentarian would never
again be a Commons colleague. Harry Stevens never
showed it, but he would have been less than human
if he had not had some bitter moments as he watched
the 'corporate élite,' to use a modern term, regain control of the Conservative party, as he saw
the rising hopes of an MP with only six years in
Parliament compared to his own consecutive sixteen,
assisted by a manager who had nearly wrecked the
provincial party and whose palatial home was un-
comfortable for more plain-living Vancouverites.
Nevertheless he set out, in his usual purposeful
way, to visit all the local party headquarters
throughout British Columbia informing them that
Bennett was their man. Thus even if Stevens did

wonder about the bitter irony of recent political events - and his subsequent actions strongly suggest that he did - he performed as faithfully as ever. The results of the Winnipeg leadership convention were as predicted. Bennett emerged an easy winner with 780 of the 1,554 votes cast in the second ballot. Stevens was one of the seven 'favourite son' candidates who withdrew before the first ballot; later he recalled that Bennett came to him after the victory, shook his hand, and said, 'Harry, I owe this entirely to you. You are the one who put me here.'[28] An overstatement, as Harry well knew, but he probably appreciated the gesture.

Stevens' only speech before the full convention came shortly before the end, during the debate on the party's policy resolutions. Some eastern delegates had demanded that the resolution on immigration be changed to delete the clause calling for exclusion of Orientals. In defence of the original resolution, Stevens declared, as deputy chairman for British Columbia, that it was time Canada fell in line with the ban against Orientals already enforced in South Africa, Australia, and New Zealand. In advocating such a frankly racist policy, Stevens was being consistent. His one visit to China during the Boxer uprising had convinced him that here was a culture that could never be integrated into the Canadian or British way of life as he knew it. His first experiences in municipal politics, including that memorable visit to the gambling dens of Vancouver's Chinatown; his role in the Komagata Maru affair; his abiding belief in the superiority of British institutions and white Christianity: all these reinforced his view that Canada and in particular British Columbia would be better without any more Orientals. Obviously many other delegates to the Winnipeg convention agreed with him: the exclusion claused stayed.

68

During the remainder of 1927, Harry was able to be at home, enjoying his family and tending to his real estate business. His Vancouver Holdings Limited was attempting to develop the area at the foot of Hollyburn Ridge known as the British Properties, and the project prompted him to make a trip to England in December to find financial backing.[29] Sweden was also on his itinerary; here Harry would strengthen his contacts with the Johnson shipping interests in connection with the brokerage side of Vancouver Holdings. Another Canadian visitor to the old country at this time was R.B. Bennett, who may well have been on hand to hear Stevens address the Empire Parliamentary Association on 13 December.[30] As the Opposition expert on trade and commerce, Stevens also addressed a joint meeting of committees on migration and land settlement and trade, communication and finance. He urged that British factory workers rather than British farmers should be given most encouragement to emigrate to Canada, and he deplored the growing American control of Canada's mining and lumbering industries. On 21 January 1928 he addressed the foreign and colonial affairs sub-committee of the National Liberal Club, choosing as his topic 'Empire Foreign Policy as viewed by a Canadian.' Stevens called for frank acknowledgment of Britain as senior partner in the Commonwealth, whose leaders, preferably prime ministers, should work out general principles for it, recognizing as they did so that questions of foreign policy should be non-partisan.[31]

In contrast to his trip a few years earlier, this one in the winter of 1927-28 enabled Harry Stevens to travel farther and at a more leisurely pace. He left no daily record, however. One thing is certain: the journey took him away from Canadian federal and provincial politics for nearly four months. During that time, while Bennett was quickly

establishing himself as party leader, Stevens was
mainly involved in business, his speeches notwithstanding, and it is quite probable that he gave
serious consideration at this time to quitting
politics. Moving about in the business circles of
London and Stockholm, he must have envied not only
their affluence but their anonymity. Yet he never
ceased to be a politician. It was just that his
political role was increasingly difficult with
the Conservative party under new management. The
masterly parliamentarian Meighen had been succeeded
by the wealthy corporation lawyer Bennett, who,
in turn, was leaning more and more on McRae and
others like him. The 1926 election results had
not only changed the Liberal-Conservative balance
in the House of Commons: it also had shifted the
emphasis within the Tory party, so that it was now,
more than ever before, a party of and for Big
Business. At least, so it must have seemed to
parliamentarians like Harry Stevens, to his genial
desk-mate from Fort William, Dr. Bob Manion, and
to George Black, Harry's fellow townsman and old
friend. With Bennett at the helm and McRae at his
side, an inner circle of wealthy corporation lawyers seemed to have taken over the party. Tories
like C.H. Cahan and E.B. Ryckman had been members
of the party if not of the Commons for years, but
under Meighen's leadership they and their lawyer-
colleagues from Montreal and Toronto had been
kept under control. That control had been considerable in the case of Cahan who had been forever
plotting with his St. James Street friends against
Meighen, the author of the railway nationalization
bill, the act that had checked far-ranging plans
of the CPR, with whom Cahan, White, and other
Montrealers had been closely associated. A towering
figure of a man, Cahan, like Bennett, was a Mari-
timer and a graduate of Dalhousie law school. He
had 'helped to engineer the Conservative-Nationalist

70

alliance of 1911,'[32] had made a fortune from mining speculation in South America, and more recently had been close to Lord Atholstan, the Machiavellian owner of the Montreal <u>Star</u>. Ryckman was a distinguished graduate of Osgoode Hall law school who had married a daughter of Edward Gurney, a wealthy stove manufacturer. The vice-president of the Dunlop Tire and Rubber Company and a director of many others, Ryckman had long played a leading role in Toronto Tory circles similar to Cahan's in Montreal.

Harry Stevens knew these men in the same way as he knew General McRae. He was friendly enough with them, chatted with them in caucus and at the Rideau Club, but he identified more with Tories such as Black and Manion. Neither Black nor Manion had great wealth, neither represented large eastern urban areas. Both were congenial, outspoken, and sympathetic with the interests of more average Canadians: lumbermen, railroaders, trappers, and the like. Manion was one of the most popular members of the House, known more for his wit and fund of stories than for his weighty debates. What Harry especially liked about Bob Manion and George Black was their humanity: despite their professional education and wide travel, they could still identify with the Canadians who had voted for them. So could Harry Stevens. Parliament must represent all citizens, not just the rich and powerful; he would continue to serve.

For the first time since entering federal politics, Harry Stevens was absent when the new session of Parliament opened on 26 January 1928. Shortly after he returned to Canada at the end of March he wrote Bennett giving detailed suggestions on party organization, both in the House and throughout the country.[33] Bennett began his reply of 3 May by regretting that Stevens had not been at the opening when 'you would realize the handicap

71

under which we suffered in dealing with public
matters.' Harry's proposed national secretary was
'not available for a party in view of the demands
that are being made for just such individuals by
the large business enterprises in Canada.' Bennett
promised to consider 'the whole question of organization,' but 'the party is without money, and in
view of what has transpired during the last few
years, it is difficult for it to obtain money'[34]
(apparently a reference to the problems Meighen
had faced after wealthy Montreal Tories had with-
drawn their financial support because of his railway policy). Bennett himself would provide the
solution to the party's financial problem, by
digging deeply into his own private fortune. He
agreed with Stevens about the need to improve the
party's organization at Ottawa: the day after he
wrote he had to send out a general memo urging
better attendance in the House. 'At one time this
afternoon we only had twenty odd members in their
places. The Prime Minister remained in his place
all afternoon, and may I ask you to make a very
special effort to be in your place when the House
is in Committee of Supply, unless released by the
Chief Whip, Mr. Charters. This is very important
in view of the propaganda in the Montreal Liberal
press that there is lack of harmony in our ranks.'[35]
George Black sent back Bennett's memo with the
terse comment: 'Is the whip inarticulate?'
    Stevens went back to British Columbia to assist
in the provincial election called for 18 July,
and on 11 June Bennett received a wire from him
passing on a constituency request that he lead a
Vancouver ticket. 'After most careful consideration,' Bennett replied, 'have concluded impossible
for you leave here.'[36] It appears unlikely that
Stevens was seriously considering at this time a
move into provincial politics. The BC Tory organization was constantly in a state of turmoil, and

72

each time he returned home Harry was under pressure
from Vancouver Conservatives to enter the provincial field. The fact that he simply passed on this
request to Bennett suggests that he was leaving
the decision up to him, knowing what his answer
would be. In the election, the absentee Conservative leader, Dr. S.F. Tolmie (he had resigned
as federal member for Victoria only on June 7),
defeated the Liberal administration. Among the
letters Harry received congratulating him for his
part in the victory was one from Arthur Meighen,
now a Toronto business executive. Meighen thought
that it would 'help federally to a tremendous
degree.'[37] Stevens' Vancouver friends also made
sure that Bennett learned of his efforts. George
Black, who maintained a Vancouver law office though
he represented the Yukon, wrote Bennett that
Stevens 'really led the B.C. battle of hard knocks.'[38]

British Columbia politics, both federal and
provincial, continued to occupy much of Stevens'
as well as Bennett's time for the remainder of
1928. To Stevens, it must have seemed that nothing
had changed. Five years earlier he had complained
to Meighen because Senator Green's advice had been
sought more than his. Now Bennett was doing the
same thing - consulting Green and others from the
west coast about a candidate for the federal by-
election in Victoria caused by Dr. Tolmie's resignation to assume the provincial leadership.
Shortly after the BC Tories' narrow victory,
Stevens tried but failed to get Bennett to block
an appointment as provincial party secretary
because no federal member had been consulted.[39]

Evidences of provincial division seem to have
weakened Stevens' spirit. Subdued and preoccupied,
he sat on the opposition front benches during the
spring session of the 1929 Parliament, taking little
part in the throne speech debate, a discussion of
the opium and narcotic drug bill, in which he

73

might have been expected to participate, or in a
debate on bank mergers, a marked concern of his
earlier, especially in 1923 during debates to
amend the bank act. He did speak for about half
an hour in support of a technical education bill,
and there was another glimpse of 'the old Harry
Stevens' on 5 March when, in introducing an amendment to the natural resources resolution, he
clashed briefly with Prime Minister King; but
Cahan presented the main Conservative arguments
in favour of Stevens' amendment, which of course
was defeated.[40] One other speech completed Stevens'
effort for the 1929 session. Clearly, if his political fires were not going out, they were burning
low.

By late April Stevens was turning his attention
once again to BC politics. In a letter to General
McRae, now the party's national organizer, he
passed on some criticisms he had received about
'a somewhat disorganized Conservative rank and
file' since the advent of the Tolmie government.[41]
He thought it imperative that something should be
done to educate 'provincial opinion' in anticipation
of a federal election in 1930. No reply from McRae
appeared and by June Premier Tolmie and Stevens
were both complaining to Bennett about the provincial situation, which continued to be plagued by
warring factions. By August Bennett decided to
investigate himself.

He was met in his Vancouver hotel suite by sixty
or more angry Tories who kept him late for a gar-
den party at General McRae's mansion, Hycroft.
Harry Stevens and another Vancouver member, General
J.A. Clark, had their own grievance: they had not
even been informed of Bennett's west coast itinerary, but had learned from another party stalwart
that General McRae had determined what it would
be.[42] The Vancouver Sun gleefully reported the
Tory bickering. It claimed that in his three years

74

at Ottawa McRae had reached the peak of influence,
pushing aside other federal members, including H.H.
Stevens, 'once the big noise federally in this
province ... Today the two multi-millionaires R.B.
Bennett and General A.D. McRae are running the
Conservative party for the whole of Canada.' The
Sun predicted that the pair would eventually
struggle over which would be in control. A letter
to Bennett from a writer with a strong temperance
bias claimed that 'determined efforts have been,
and are still being made, both by the liquor interests and selfishly ambitious men in our party
to drive the strongest, truest, and most dependable
B.C. Federal Member, H.H. Stevens, from public
life.'[43] He was correct. Harry Stevens had had
enough of politics.

On 31 October from Vancouver, Stevens wrote
Bennett a lengthy personal letter indicating his
intention to resign immediately. His Vancouver
Holdings formed four years earlier was going so
well that it needed his full concentration. He
also wanted to give his family 'some of the time
and attention which the duties of public life have
denied them for the past eighteen years.'[44] He had
tried to discuss the matter with Bennett in Ottawa
'but unfortunately circumstances prevented that
meeting from taking place.' Bennett telegraphed
Stevens urging him not to take any action 'until
I can communicate with you. It is impossible to
contemplate the result of such a procedure.'[45]
Stevens agreed to wait, but a second letter on 7
November gave other reasons for his decision, including his discomfort with the party's important
men of wealth:

You will appreciate, I think, what I am now going
to say, namely that there are some members of our
party in Ottawa, whom we count among the front
ranks, who while possessed of abundant wealth

themselves, do not hesitate to cast aspersions
upon me because I was unable to match them -
dollar for dollar - in personal wealth and none
of them apparently have given me any credit for
the sacrifice of my personal affairs in the interests of public duty.

I am enclosing the last auditor's report of
Vancouver Holdings ... in order that you may
appreciate what I have accomplished in the last
two and a half years, and to demonstrate to you
that I am not quite a 'dud' on business matters ...

On 9 November Bennett assured Stevens that he had
sympathy with his financial concerns but also indicated that he put political considerations first
in asking him to remain:

Nothing that has happened since I first undertook my present duties has given me greater concern than your suggestion that you desire to
resign during the present Parliament. I do not
think I would have accepted the responsibilities
I did had I thought that such a thing could happen ... I understand and appreciate your situation. I passed through it once myself, and instead of going into public life I undertook to
accumulate a competence. You have a wife and
family and it is your duty to look after them,
but on the other hand you have undertaken certain political responsibilities and I feel certain ... that you will not leave me in the
lurch ... I am sure you realize that a by-election
at the present time in Vancouver would be fraught
with the gravest consequences to the Party
throughout Canada.[46]

Bennett, about to leave for his annual Christmas
trek to New Brunswick, implored Stevens 'at least
not to resign your seat until the end of the

present Parliament.' 'I have gathered,' replied
Stevens a week later, 'that the only point to
which you take serious exception is the question
of when my retirement should take place.'⁴⁷ Therefore, to 'minimize the inconvenience,' he would
make the announcement when he felt like it, but
omit a date when the resignation would take effect.
He made it on 4 December; the reaction was widespread and revealing. His closest parliamentary
friend, R.J. Manion, wrote from Fort William hoping
he would reconsider. 'You have been one of my real
friends,' Stevens replied, whereas 'the attitude
of the millionaire group, particularly Chaplin
and Ryckman, has not contributed to preventing me
from making the announcement.'⁴⁸ He added that
'the Conservative Party's prospects for victory
would be greatly enhanced if the dollar stamp were
less pronounced, and if a man's personal wealth
were less used as the yardstick to measure his
value.' And then he declared: 'I am now determined
to show these fellows that I can do quite as well
in business as I have done in public life.' He
was taking this resolute step two months after
Wall Street's financial collapse. But there was a
great host to support Stevens' view that nothing
could really shake the economic firmament in 1929.

A veteran Conservative member from Kingston, W.F.
Nickle, sent to Stevens on 13 December a report
from the Globe, signed by 'Justitia,' which implied that Stevens' efforts during the customs
inquiry had aroused the ire of the liquor interests,
who in turn 'were largely responsible for exerting
great pressure to shove him into the background
of the party.' Nickle added his own wry comment:
'Someone, apparently, knows much of the methods
of certain groups that have influence in the national life of this country.'⁴⁹ The Toronto Star had
its own explanation for Stevens' decision. In a
story of 6 December filed from Vancouver under

the heading 'Split in British Columbia Ranks is Given as Reason ... Apparently Shunned by Bennett,' it claimed his retirement was 'a culmination of events,' and referred to his libel action against the Vancouver Sun on the eve of the last election (later dropped) which had accused him of shady dealings with a Chicago oil company. It went on to a purported history of his Vancouver business dealings:

> Mr. Stevens was a grocery clerk when he was first elected alderman in Vancouver in 1909. Two years later he went to Ottawa and has been a member ever since. He recently built and sold one of the most luxurious apartment houses in Vancouver.
>
> Since the Conservative Party assumed office provincially he obtained from the legislature in the face of bitter opposition the revival of the charter of a defunct railway project in Northern B.C. and immediately thereafter sold it to the Consolidated Mining and Smelting Company, a subsidiary of the CPR.
>
> Because this line threatens to rival the government-owned Pacific Great Eastern as a Pacific coast outlet for the Peace river area and because people do not understand why a political intermediary should have obtained this charter for the CPR, Mr. Stevens has been much criticized for his part in this transaction.
>
> He is now a wealthy man dealing in apartment blocks and railway charters. He probably is ready to retire.[50]

To refute this graft-to-riches account, Stevens wrote a private letter to Joseph E. Atkinson, owner of the Star, 'with the hope that it may appeal to you as a fair-minded man.'[51] He gave a detailed account of his business career and how

it had at first grown and then declined because
he had had to spend so much time in Ottawa. He
admitted that Vancouver Holdings had built 'luxuri-
ous apartment buildings,' thanks to money he and
his wife had raised from life insurance and from
'a few gentlemen with faith in me subscribing to
the capital stock.' Despite this help, there were
two mortgages outstanding. As for the sale of the
railway charter, Stevens argued that it had been
made 'before the present B.C. government came
into office,' and that it had netted him only
$10,000.

> After 40 years of struggle, I am forced to really
> start again to build. Had I not entered public
> life I should undoubtedly long ago have been
> wealthy with the opportunity offering in this
> province ... For a life annuity of $5,000 a year,
> I will turn over to you everything that I have
> in the world.

The last suggestion was an odd one for the proud
Stevens to make, especially to such a staunch
Liberal as Atkinson. One can only conclude that
Stevens was trying to emphasize his main point,
that he had made no money in politics. On the
other hand, he might have been aware that Sir
John A. Macdonald had received similar financial
help to enable him to carry on in public life.
Atkinson must have taken the annuity suggestion
seriously and mentioned it to business friends,
for just two weeks later Bennett wrote to Stevens:
'I have not given up the hope that something may
transpire to make' the retirement 'impossible,
but it will interest you to know that I have
received several communications from friends suggesting that we should take steps to provide you
with an annuity that will enable you to give your
service to your country.'[52] By the year's end,

Stevens appeared to be weakening in his resolve
to retire. When a Toronto back-bencher queried
him, he replied: 'I do not wish to disregard in
any way the desires of the party, but one must
consider one's own affairs to a certain extent at
least.'[53] During January 1930, Stevens and Bennett
had many opportunities to talk when the Tory
leader toured the west coast. On 16 January, with
Stevens beside him on the platform, Bennett declared that 'no matter how great the personal sacrifice [Stevens] must be encouraged to continue in
public life. Such experience as his is only gained
by years of toil and devotion to office.'[54]

How can we explain this public and personal out-
pouring? Harry Stevens had been rubbing shoulders
with 'big business' politicians ever since he
entered parliament. Why strike out against them
now? He may have been angry at those wealthier
colleagues who 'cast aspersions' upon him, but
why should this staunch Methodist, steeped in bib-
lical lore on the pitfalls facing the rich man,
say that he would 'show them' by amassing a great
fortune? Did the Stevens family suddenly face a
financial crisis at this time?

To answer the last question first, Harry's family was as close-knit and as secure as ever. Of
his two oldest children, Francis was about to
start a career that had his father's deep approval:
that of a United Church minister; Marjory seemed
to have developed a serious interest in an attrac-
tive young man, James Lovick, and a wedding was
likely. The two younger girls, Sylvia and Patricia,
were happy, healthy, close companions; thirteen-
year-old Douglas also presented no problems.
Gertrude, as she had always done, left political
decisions to Harry. She had long grown resigned
to the disagreeable sides of a politician's career:
the two three-storey apartment buildings and the
eight-mile railroad Harry had been involved with

80

naturally would become skyscrapers and multimillion
dollar enterprises in the eyes of the Vancouver
Sun.

Clearly, Harry Stevens was continuing to be the
good provider for his family but there was a financial cloud on the horizon. Stevens had been one
of the founding directors of the Manufacturers'
Finance Corporation, formed in 1925, probably at
the instigation of another director, A.E. Grassby,
a Winnipeg music store proprietor, to finance
consumer purchase of pianos made in Amherst, Nova
Scotia. The firm went bankrupt in 1928 and the
lengthy litigations and voluminous correspondence
in the ensuing months had added to Harry's trou-
bles.[55] Little wonder he wanted to quit politics
to make a fortune: he was feeling the pressure
from his creditors. Furthermore, eighteen consecutive years as an MP inevitably meant political
enemies anxious to even the score with this tee-
totalling, somewhat self-righteous, lay preacher –
politician who had laid bare the irregularities
in the customs department. In 1929 Harry Stevens
had little help in countering the mounting smear
campaign launched by Vancouver Liberals. They
were constantly trying to suggest a conflict of
interest between H.H. Stevens MP and Harry Stevens,
principal shareholder in Vancouver Holdings Limited, a firm that dealt in real estate, timber
rights, and mining claims. They never could prove
anything, if indeed there was anything to prove,
but in the 'roaring twenties' when Vancouver,
like most large cities, still had competing newspapers with their political colours proudly nailed
to their editorial mastheads, a half-truth or an
out-right smear was all that was necessary. Experienced and successful politicians such as Stevens
could and did endure editorial innuendoes, especially if they knew they had the ear of their
leader. But with General McRae's arrival on the

81

Ottawa scene and his domination of the Tory party
organization, Stevens' influence had faded rapidly.
He could not even get an interview with Bennett to
discuss his grievances; nor could he get support
from the wealthy old-style Tories - Ryckman,
Cahan and the rest - many of whom had not given
nearly as much service to the party as he had. To
Harry Stevens in 1929, the Conservative party had
to represent more than big business, and he could
take some satisfaction in the fact that he had
helped to broaden its base, to make it appeal more
to ordinary Canadians. The superior attitude that
the corporation lawyers often displayed in front
of Stevens probably annoyed him most, because he
was in such constant and close contact with them:
in the House, in caucus, and at the Rideau Club.

In the end, Harry Stevens did not retire in 1930.
Bennett undoubtedly was one reason: he could be
most charming and persuasive, as his long string
of legal victories attests, and his west-coast
tour in January 1930 was intended as much to pla-
cate the dispirited Stevens as it was to silence
the warring BC factions. For his party, Harry
proved open to persuasion. His keen political eye
could see the growing possibility of a Conservative
victory in the next federal election, for one
reason. If the provincial scene was any indicator -
and it was usually a good one - the Tory chances
looked promising. Since Bennett had assumed the
federal leadership, Dr. Tolmie had swept to power
in British Columbia, internal squabbling notwithstanding, and on 6 June 1929 J.T.M. Anderson had
won a Tory victory in Saskatchewan. Even if he
may have resented his influence, Stevens must
also have admired General McRae's energy and ability in reorganizing and revitalizing the national
party. A new newspaper, the Canadian, had been
launched and everywhere the Tories seemed to be
on the move.

The second factor that probably influenced
Stevens to remain in federal politics was the
sharp decline in the west-coast economy during
the last half of 1929. Margaret Ormsby has given
a graphic picture of the unemployment and unrest
that had reached disturbing proportions in the
very month in which Stevens was making his decision:

Vancouver was first to feel the sharp impact
of the business depression: after the stock-
market crash, the building trade ... was paralysed, and as a sequel to its collapse, the lumber industry became completely disorganized.
Soon, new tariffs, currency contraction and
fluctuations of foreign demand caused the cancel-
lation of orders for salmon, and the cannery-
operators ... were forced to reduce their staffs.
Activity on the waterfront lessened when the
great glut on the world grain market affected
sales of Canadian wheat, and shipments to the
coastal elevators fell by 17,500,000 bushels.
When, during the next few months, the basic industries of mining, lumbering and fishing suffered sharp reverses, the city became filled
with unemployed working-men. Bread-lines were
forming outside the City Relief Office by December.
    The Communists lost no time in organizing the
unemployed and in arranging demonstrations ...
    The month of January, 1930, was unlike any
previous month in the history of the city. The
number of unemployed persons increased by three
hundred per cent; the police again broke up pro-
cessions, made arrests, and dispersed a large
demonstration in the Powell Street grounds.
Civic appropriations for relief soared; a scandal
developed when it was discovered that the chief
City Relief Officer had accepted a 'rake-off'
for meal tickets; and the nervous citizens,

believing that Vancouver had been occupied by a
'Red army,' hesitated to leave home for an evening's pleasure.[56]

If the Conservatives did win the next federal
election, Harry Stevens would almost certainly get
a major cabinet post. What better way to help the
growing number of unemployed in his own city? Here
was a meaningful role that he could and would fill;
he would return to Ottawa, and he still set no
date for retirement.

Most political observers agreed, when Parliament
reconvened in late February 1930, that this would
be the last session before an election. Faced
with mounting unemployment everywhere and sagging
trade, the Liberal government was on the defensive.
In the throne speech debate Bennett declared that
Canada faced 'abnormal unemployment,' a point
taken up by A.A. Heaps, the Independent Labour
member, who criticized Parliament for wasting
time and introduced an amendment calling for immediate government action to deal with this unemployment. Heaps's action sparked the most heated
debate of the session, one that would have dire
consequences for Mackenzie King. Throughout the
three-day debate, Stevens was one of the most
active interjectors; he gave no major speech himself, but his constant needling helped provoke
King into making on 3 April what has been considered
his worst parliamentary indiscretion:

... So far as giving money from this federal
treasury to provincial governments is concerned,
in relation to this question of unemployment as
it exists today, I might be prepared to go a
certain length possibly in meeting one or two
of the western provinces that have Progressive
premiers at the head of their government -

Some Hon. Members: Oh!
Mr. Mackenzie King: - but I would not give a single cent to any Tory government.
Mr. Bennett: Shame!
Mr. Stevens: Shame!
Mr. Mackenzie King: Do my hon. friends say 'shame'?
Mr. Bennett: Yes, shame!
Mr. Mackenzie King: What is there to be ashamed of?
Mr. Stevens: You ought to be ashamed of that.
Mr. Mackenzie King: My hon. friend is getting very indignant. Something evidently has got under his skin. May I repeat what I have said? With respect to giving moneys out of the federal treasury to any Tory government in this country for these alleged unemployment purposes, with these governments situated as they are today, with policies diametrically opposed to those of this government, I would not give them a five-cent piece.[57]

Before the House adjourned for Easter, Stevens, mindful of the forthcoming budget debate, wrote Bennett endorsing a suggestion from another Vancouver member that there should be a want of confidence motion on going into supply and just before the budget debate; this would keep the government on the defensive.[58] Bennett did not act on the suggestion and the Liberals regained the initiative when they introduced the budget on 1 May. Stevens delivered his speech on the budget a week later, but it came as an anticlimax: two days earlier King had confirmed the rumours by announcing that a general election would be held later in the year. Stevens was followed by Mitchell Hepburn, who apparently was unaware of any change in Stevens' plans to retire. He expressed his regrets that 'one of the ablest debaters on the opposition

85

side' should have announced his retirement. He
hoped that the report, like that of Mark Twain's
death, had been 'greatly exaggerated.'[59]

So it seemed. On 23 May Bennett informed Tolmie
that Stevens would direct the BC campaign for the
general election on 28 July. Tolmie promised his
full cooperation, for 'Stevens and the provincial
organization have come to some arrangement concerning the handling of affairs.'[60] He also reported that Ian Mackenzie, the Liberal MLA for
North Vancouver was 'to be taken into the Federal
Cabinet and carry the Liberal banner either in
Central or North Vancouver.' As it turned out,
the capable Mackenzie chose Vancouver Centre,
where Stevens had finally decided to re-offer.
But the veteran Conservative member scarcely had
time to note his latest opponent. He was too busy
touring not only other British Columbia ridings
but the prairies as well. Stevens was one of
'three front benchers on the Conservative side of
the House besides Mr. Bennett' to cover such a
wide area, the others being Hugh Guthrie and Bob
Manion.[61] Still, Harry was not too busy to write
to Francis, on the eve of his ordination as a
United Church minister, telling him how sorry he
was not to be there.

> I think you are starting on the greatest work
> in the world. To be successful you must love
> humanity and have almost infinite patience with
> their faults. Son, don't expect too much from
> your people, and try to discover good points. I
> am amazed at the good one can find in most un-
> expected quarters. If it were possible to unwind
> the tangled skein of life, I would gladly take
> your place. I almost envy you.[62]

Stevens managed to get back to his riding for
the traditional last rally, where he outlined his

ambition for Canada. He hoped it would become a
unit of the Empire 'concerned not with a few petty
tariff items, but with all the great problems con-
fronting the Home Government, questions that would
stagger any other country in the world but Britain ...
I would like to see Canada go to the Imperial Conference in a spirit of co-operation, unity and
trust in the Motherland's statesmen.'[63] Appeals
to the 'old country' tie, however, were not enough
this time. Harry Stevens and four other Vancouver
Tories, including General McRae, went down to
defeat. The west coast was already sinking into
the great depression, but Stevens' first major
political defeat was attributable to other factors
too. The endless squabbles of the provincial
Tories, the ceaseless campaigns against him by
the Vancouver Sun, and, perhaps most damaging of
all, his announcement that he was leaving federal
politics - all contributed to his defeat. Stevens
himself regretted the time he had given to the
general campaign at the expense of his own. 'I
left that to my friends and they took the view
that I was so strong ... I didn't need to do anything and they did nothing.'[64]
    This defeat could have been a blessing in dis-
guise if Stevens had really wanted to stop. But
prolonging his departure left the impression that
he was open to persuasion. Perhaps what he really
wanted was more recognition from the party for
his years as a back-bencher and opposition work-
horse. The letters he had received urging him to
reconsider probably had an effect, but Bennett
was much more influential, especially as the new
prime minister of a majority government. He invited Harry Stevens to be his minister of trade
and commerce and urged him to meet him in Ottawa
shortly before the cabinet was to be sworn in on
7 August. Stevens consented, was sworn in with
the rest, and when the incumbent in Kootenay East

resigned to accept a position on the Vancouver
Harbour Board he was elected by acclamation.

III The Speech-maker

Personal as well as political adjustments faced
Harry Stevens upon his return to Ottawa in the
late summer of 1930. After the swearing-in cere-
monies on 7 August, he began to look for accom-
modation: Gertrude and the family would be moving
east when the regular session began early in the
new year. He found a comfortable house at 37
Lynden Terrace, about a mile from the parliament
buildings and situated on an arm of the Rideau
canal system. This personal detail attended to,
the new minister of trade and commerce eagerly
set to work becoming familiar with his greater
responsibilities and his new staff. His deputy
minister was Major T.C. Parmelee, a veteran civil
servant who had been a member of Borden's personal
staff; his executive assistant was W.H. Grant. A
methodical man by nature, Harry Stevens admired
efficient administration and he was determined to
make full use of this experienced team.

Efficiency rather than innovation was what
Canadians might expect from this hard-working,
serious politician. In his nineteen years as an
MP, Harry Stevens had always been as conventional
in his politics as in his religion. He was a Conservative Methodist rather than a radical Protes-

tant. He had always believed that each Canadian held the key to his own material well-being. Sometimes, as in the case of abuses in the operation of public utilities, the state had to exert its control and power. He had no sympathy for militant trade unionists who took matters into their own hands and caused the turmoil of a Winnipeg general strike. He had gone out of his way to oppose the efforts of the Independent Labour member, James Woodsworth, to have an annual revision of the Bank Act. Harry Stevens had always supported the two-party system, wherein members' views were democratically voiced in caucus and implementation of policy was left to cabinet and the party leader. He had served under Borden, Meighen, and now Bennett; he might admire Sir Robert most, but all leaders had received his full support. True, Stevens had threatened to resign twice in the past six years, but because of personalities rather than principles. In 1924 he had been angry at the devious ways of Senator Green and certain west coast Tories; in 1929 he had been provoked by the superior attitude of wealthy colleagues. Both times, he had decided to remain in the House of Commons, for him the most worthwhile political arena. Now, in 1930, Harry Stevens held one of the senior cabinet positions in the first Conservative government to be elected with an over-all majority since 1911, the year he entered Parliament. According to one study of the 1930 election results, 'the new government group was dominated by eastern, urban, creditor and capitalist interests to a greater degree than any previous government which had possessed a majority in the House of Commons.'[1] Stevens' new cabinet colleagues included C.H. Cahan of Montreal, secretary of state, and E.B. Ryckman of Toronto, minister of national revenue. They and several other corporation lawyers had been lording it over him while they were members of the Opposition. Would Stevens feel less sensitive toward them now that he was minister of trade and commerce? Much would depend on the actions of Prime Minister Bennett as together they faced the complete collapse of the economic system they so much admired.

Bennett had won the 1930 election largely on his image as a successful man of action. He would restore the Canadian economy by ending unemployment and by 'blasting our way into the world markets,' and he would summon an emergency session of parliament. It opened on 15 September and was dominated by the prime minister, who was also his own minister of finance and secretary of state for external affairs. He made the major speeches and introduced the two main bills: one authorized the government to spend $20 million on public works and the other raised tariffs to their highest level in history. Bennett also informed the house that it would be asked to make a general tariff revision at the next regular session; in the meantime, he predicted that this new tariff schedule would mean work for at least 25,000 Canadians. His minister of trade and commerce and the other members of his cabinet said practically nothing.

Following this emergency session, Bennett led a delegation to the 1930 Imperial Conference in London. Harry Stevens was one of three cabinet ministers chosen; the others were Hugh Guthrie, minister of justice, and Maurice Dupré, the solicitor-general. The advisory staff included W.D. Herridge, personal assistant to the prime minister, Dr. H.M. Tory, chairman of the National Research Council, and Dr. R.H. Coats, dominion statistician.[2] Stevens was the chief Canadian spokesman in the Committee on Economic Cooperation, but the other Canadian cabinet ministers headed committees. In fact, the two senior civil servants, Tory and Coats, played more prominent roles than any of

the cabinet ministers; ironically, Coats' Bureau
of Statistics was responsible to the minister of
trade and commerce. The conference was, however,
dominated by Bennett, whose proposal for an inter-
empire preferential tariff, to be considered
later at an Ottawa meeting, was one of the few
positive notes sounded.

The Canadian delegation returned home from London shortly before Christmas and Harry Stevens
set off for Vancouver to collect his family and
enjoy the holiday. He left Ottawa in grand style:
Bennett had persuaded him to take the prime minister's private railway car which would be used
to bring Gertrude and the children back and also
could be Harry's base for a brief speech-making
tour through his new riding of East Kootenay. One
of these speeches was given on the way out at the
coal-mining town of Fernie, already paralysed by
the depression. After talking with local officials,
Harry wired Bennett suggesting that the freight
rate subvention be extended for railway coal to
be used east of Kenora 'as formerly considered by
you. Would strongly urge this as useful solution
to Crowsnest district problem.'[3] At present the
subvention only included grain and flour. Boarding
the private car again, Stevens went on to Trail,
where he picked up Francis and his wife at their
first ministerial charge. They arrived in Vancouver
on Christmas eve, to be greeted by Gertrude with
a telegram in her hand. It was from the prime
minister: 'You have placed us all in a difficult
and embarrassing position. Please leave Vancouver
Christmas night ... Cabinet greatly distressed.'
Stevens did not hesitate for a moment: he would
return the next evening. But surely he must have
questioned the cabinet's concern about the contents
of a telegram sent to the prime minister's office
three days before Christmas; few ministers would
have remained in Ottawa and it would be most un-

usual for Bennett to canvass them about a mere
proposal. Most likely Bennett was the only one upset, because a cabinet minister had dared to raise
on the hustings such an explosive issue as freight
rates. It was too important a matter to be bandied
about in a remote British Columbia coal-mining
town and later to be made the subject of an uncoded
telegram. Also, Bennett may have been serving
notice that he alone must select the time and
locale for raising potentially delicate issues.
In any event, the incident was long remembered in
the Stevens household. As Francis later recalled:
'Bennett, the rich bachelor, didn't seem to understand the meaning of family life. Dad was more or
less philosophical; Mother was bitterly upset.
But we had our last Christmas together as a family,
and Dad left alone for Ottawa. And Mother and the
other four moved out later.'[4] Just what happened
when Stevens and Bennett met over this issue is
not known. Stevens left no record among his ministerial papers of having sent the telegram and
all that the Bennett Papers have is the original
message.

   In January 1931, shortly after Stevens returned
to Ottawa, he had another idea about unemployment:
why not set up a council to study it. Dr. O.D.
Skelton, under-secretary of state for external
affairs, might be chairman and others would represent labour, industries, and the universities.
'Why talk such nonsense,' retorted Bennett. 'Do
you think I want a lot of long-haired professors
telling me what to do? If I can't run this country,
I will get out.'[5] The House of Commons heard a
similar suggestion in May 1931 when Alfred Speakman
of the United Farmers of Alberta introduced a
motion to establish a national economic council
to study a wide range of social and economic problems. Having learned of his leader's view on such
matters, Stevens loyally rejected the idea, argu-

ing on 6 May that the government thought it best
to use 'trained officers of the state' rather
than go outside the civil service for experts and
advisers.[6] A few days later Bennett rather than
Stevens introduced an act establishing a tariff
board. Stevens did second the motion, but during
second reading for general debate it was Bennett
who answered all the Opposition's questions and
criticisms.

The Liberal opposition was undoubtedly aware by
this time of the dominating role in the government's affairs being played by the prime minister.
On 14 May, Fernand Rinfret, a Liberal front-bencher,
observed that a member of a mission sent to China
by the department of trade and commerce had reported directly to Bennett. Rinfret hoped that in
addition to external affairs and finance, the
prime minister 'has not taken a slice out of
[Stevens'] department because I think he will prove
to be a good minister, as good as may come from
the ranks of his party.'[7] Stevens quickly rose
to the bait: 'The Prime Minister in all his relations with his ministers acts in the most courte-
ous manner ... I do not know of anyone I would
rather have cooperating with me ... than the present Prime Minister.'

Cooperation seemed lacking in the matter of the
Australian trade agreement. It had been a thorny
subject ever since the Liberal administration had
negotiated it in 1925, only to discover, to
Mackenzie King's horror, that some sections actually raised the tariffs against Canadian goods.
During the 1930 campaign Bennett had denounced
both the Australian and the New Zealand agreements
even though they had been extremely profitable for
shipping, lumbering, and other west coast interests.
This stand was one reason why the Tories had done
so poorly in British Columbia.[8] Apparently Bennett
was more concerned about the lot of Canadian dairy

94

farmers, notably those in eastern Canada, who had been complaining loudly about New Zealand dairy products being dumped on Canadian markets. Now that they were safely in opposition it was the Liberals' turn to raise this controversial matter. On 8 June, in the House, Stevens had to inform Ian Mackenzie, the Liberal who had defeated him in Vancouver, that all statements about the treaty would be made by the prime minister 'in the course of a few days.'[9] On 16 July, Bennett introduced the long-awaited bill and promised an explanation during second reading. This he eventually gave; his minister of trade and commerce said almost nothing. Admittedly, Stevens and his counterparts throughout the western world seemed powerless to stop or change the course of the depression, but few could have been as speechless as the once-voluble Stevens.

His image was further tarnished during this dismal 1931 session by a minor flurry in June over My Creed. This was a pamphlet issued under his name and widely distributed to chambers of commerce and similar groups throughout the country. The Liberals argued in the House that it did not warrant the public expenditure of $7800, but Stevens defended it because he thought its sentiments worthy of support and because it had been 'overwhelmingly demanded' by the public. He did not elaborate and since there is no written evidence of these demands, one can only conclude that they had been made verbally to Stevens on the hustings. It said:

I believe in Canada.
I love her as my home.
I honour her institutions.
I rejoice in the abundance of her achievements.
I have unbounded confidence in the ability of her people to excel in whatsoever they undertake.

I cherish exalted ideas of her destiny as a
leader among world nations.
To her I pledge my loyalty.
To the promotion of her best interests I pledge
my support.
To her products I pledge my patronage.
And to the cause of her producers I pledge my
devotion.[10]

When J.S. Woodsworth pointed out that contrary to
the economic nationalism endorsed by the pamphlet,
Canada needed to find export markets, Stevens
seemingly could find no reply. He never referred
to My Creed again.

From every aspect, Harry Stevens' first year as
minister of trade and commerce had been as much a
failure as the national economy he was supposed
to encourage. Understandably, learning the inner
workings of a new department took time, but his
role in the House was something else. Rarely if
ever did his performance reflect a member with
twenty years of experience; repeatedly, he deferred
to his leader who monopolized the debates on all
major issues. Like the rest of the cabinet, Stevens
seemed to have been overwhelmed by Bennett's
forceful personality.

The end of that 1931 spring session must have
been eagerly welcomed by the Stevens family as
they left Ottawa and headed for home. But the
west coast would provide no respite from the deep-
ening depression; the first of the long, hot dry
summers had begun, described by Margaret Ormsby
for the Okanagan:

As the supply of water in the Okanagan Valley
became exhausted, the irrigation flumes dried
out and cracked, and in the orchards the leaves
hung limply on the trees. Every day now ... the
sun, as if reflecting the flames of forest con-

flagrations, rose and set as a mammoth ball of
fire. But still the apples grew, and in such
quantity that the disposal of the crop, particularly after the [B.C.] Produce Marketing Act
was found unconstitutional by the Supreme Court
of Canada in 1931, became an acute problem.[11]

Harry Stevens could not be blamed for the weather
or for the economic restrictions posed by inter-
pretations of the British North America Act, but
as the ranking cabinet minister for the west coast
he was expected to do something for its unemployed.
He toured British Columbia extensively, visiting
the provincial public works projects being financed
under the 1931 Unemployment Relief Assistance Act.
He also helped to negotiate an agreement signed
19 August between the federal and provincial
governments whereby local authorities would be
responsible for municipal unemployed with depend-
ents. Single men and transients (and British Columbia's warm climate attracted more than any other
province) would continue to be under joint federal-
provincial jurisdiction. By the end of August 1931,
35,842 single individuals and transients had been
registered, 20,000 of whom were considered a 'provincial responsibility.' To house them, camps were
to be set up. According to a confidential report
sent to Bennett sometime in the autumn of 1932,
'The British Columbia government was entrusted
with the organization of this whole scheme, and
it is not too harsh criticism to say that either
through incapacity or lack of faith or both they
did not justify the confidence placed in them.'[12]
Some of the early camps were 'along most extrava-
gant lines.' Furthermore, political patronage was
widespread and when federal government intervention
in October 1932 ended the BC operation, $2,873,744
had been spent on the camps of which wages had
amounted to only 66 per cent. 'The registration

was thoroughly re-examined and the number of men in camp cut down from 11,000 to about 6,000 who seemed to be bonafide cases.'[13] Clearly this scheme was not the answer, for the country as a whole and certainly not for British Columbia, which continued to attract a disproportionate number of single unemployed Canadians.

The final solution was provided by General A.G.L. McNaughton, chief of the general staff, who had made frequent tours across the country, talking with young Canadians as well as with politicians like Stevens. McNaughton's plan was that the department of national defence would establish the camps for single men, pay them a small daily wage, and put them to work at meaningful projects such as airports and road construction. By June 1934, McNaughton was able to tell R.K. Finlayson, executive assistant to Bennett, that 'up to date on the relief projects we have provided 4,805,703 man days of relief at a total cost, chargeable to the Relief Act, of $6,322,081.'[14] Under the differing auspices 237 relief camps, one third of all those constructed, were set up in British Columbia.

The other side of the picture has been painted in less flattering tones by James Gray's account of the depression, The Winter Years. He thought 'the fatal error ... was in placing the camps under the Department of National Defence and making the King's Rules and Orders - K.R. & O. - the procedural Bible.' As a result, a grievance 'would be bottled up until it reached explosive proportions.' No organization being permitted, anyone who tried to start a protest might be 'expelled in midwinter at the camp gates a hundred miles from the nearest habitation.' Camp morale, therefore, was at rock bottom most of the time and the twenty cents a day stipend was the symbol of the inmates' low status. 'It affronted human dignity as little else could have done. It was just the

98

right size to be insulting.' Gray's description of
these camps, based largely on his observation
while a reporter with the Winnipeg Free Press, con-
cludes:

> The worst thing was the hopelessness. All the
> investigators who roamed the camp - social work-
> ers, preachers, Members of Parliament, and Royal
> Commissioners - were unanimous on this point:
> the single unemployed regarded themselves as
> Canada's forgotten men. They had been filed and
> forgotten and nobody cared if they lived or died.
> But the Communists cared. In British Columbia,
> they were forever sending organizers into the
> camps to stir up whatever trouble they could
> find ... The inevitable collisions of the Com-
> munist organizers with the authorities were
> always a tonic for inmate morale.[15]

For Stevens the year 1932 was grimly similar to
1931 both in terms of unemployment and in Parliament's (and Harry Stevens') reaction to the depression. Again, in February, Alfred Speakman introduced his motion to establish a national council
of social and economic research 'to study the un-
solved problems of distribution, of purchasing
power and exchange value.'[16] Again, Stevens refuted the proposal, arguing that in his experience
the problems would be 'overcome by the age-old
method of line upon line, precept upon precept,
here a little and there a little, and in no other
way.' A planned economy like Russia's would not
work in Canada, 'peopled as it is by individuals,'
who had rooted in their natures 'the demand for
free action, the right to freedom of movement
from one part of the country to another.' Freedom
of movement there certainly would be in the spring
of 1932 as thousands of young men rode the freight
cars aimlessly and fruitlessly in search of jobs.

99

A short time after replying to the Speakman
motion, Stevens defended the government's decision
to cut civil servants' salaries. 'We do not think
that a reduction of 10% ... for this year is an
unfair contribution to the country's budget.'[17]
In March he vigorously defended Bennett against
Liberal charges of being a 'despot and a dictator'
because the new Unemployment Relief Bill would
give the government power to amend statutes and
allocate public money without further parliamentary
approval. 'There is no man in this country,' Stevens
argued, 'more jealous of the constitutional rights
of its citizens or of Parliament than is the Prime
Minister.'[18] Like many other Tories, Stevens chose
to overlook the infamous 'Section 98,' an amendment to the Criminal Code which had been passed
hurriedly by the Union government during the
Winnipeg general strike in 1919 and was still on
the statute books. This section defined 'unlawful
association' in wide terms, and thus, by it, as
A.R.M. Lower has noted, a man 'could be found
guilty of most serious offences on the weakest of
evidence.'[19] During the Liberal administration of
the twenties, the Commons had voted seven times for
repeal of this dangerous threat to individual freedom, but each time a Conservative-dominated Senate
vetoed the bill. Under Prime Minister Bennett,
Section 98 seemed more secure than ever and was
used increasingly to harass and to imprison the
most militant spokesmen for the unemployed. A few
of them undoubtedly were members of the Communist
party but it did not have anything like the numbers
among the unemployed implied by Bennett when his
government in March passed orders-in-council
strengthening the RCMP - a move defended in the
House by Stevens.[20]
    In April, Harry Stevens was praising the con-
version loan outlined in the budget. In effect,
what the government did was to move forward the

100

due date of publicly subscribed loans. Stevens argued
that the move would mean an ultimate saving of about
six millions a year. 'That is an achievement ... successful largely because of the foresight and the
skill with which it was handled by the ... leader
of this government.'[21] He also strongly supported
in the House Bennett's plans for the Imperial
Economic Conference in Ottawa in July. Stevens
played a minor role in that stormy Ottawa conference, despite the fact that it dealt mostly with
empire trade. One gets the impression that Bennett
did not trust his minister of trade and commerce
with matters of trade; he would rather have him
expending his considerable energies on the hustings,
fighting the inevitable by-elections, or in the
Commons making duty speeches. Curiously, Stevens
seemed to accept this assignment without a whimper;
apparently he was not willing to admit the possibility that Bennett wanted him out of the way
when important issues and conferences came up. For
the remainder of 1932, Stevens was one of the government's most active speakers, both inside and
outside parliament. When Bennett made an extended
visit to London late in 1932, ostensibly for his
health, Harry Stevens was making frequent forays
into Ontario constituencies. The prime minister
returned in January 1933 to chair a dominion-provincial conference on unemployment, but his minister of trade and commerce was in attendance only
briefly. Instead, Stevens was once again on the
hustings, telling a Hamilton meeting that 'this
was no time for untried experiments,' an apparent
reference to the meeting in Calgary the previous
summer of socialists, former Progressives, and
labour groups - a meeting which produced a new
national party, the Co-Operative Commonwealth Federation, or the CCF.[22]
    In the midst of this busy political schedule,
Stevens' family provided him with a pleasant diver-

sion. His oldest daughter Marjory was marrying
James Lovick at Ottawa's Dominion Church, but even
here Bennett's negative influence intruded. For
some reason - perhaps to compensate for the necessity of having the wedding far from Marjory's
many friends in Vancouver - her father had asked
Bennett to propose the toast to the bride. Bennett
would be delighted to take part; on such occasions
he could be most gracious and gallant. At the last
minute, however, he told Harry that preoccupations
with the dominion-provincial talks would prevent
him from being present. The pleasant duty was performed by Harry and Gertrude's good friend Bob
Manion.[23] In her excitement, Marjory probably
shrugged off the prime minister's decision; her
mother, remembering that Christmas eve telegram
three years earlier, might not have accepted as
easily his second disruption of their family
affairs.

Marjory's wedding helped to divert the Stevens'
attention from a growing worry: the health of
twenty-year-old Sylvia. She had developed colitis,
and increasingly 'the family life revolved about
her sick bed.'[24] Her younger sister Patricia de-
voted much of her time to her care and her mother
rarely left the Lynden Terrace house for any length
of time. In the old days, Harry's vigorous and
meaningful parliamentary duties would have taken
his mind temporarily from Sylvia's serious condition, but in the spring of 1933 he continued to
make duty speeches while his leader visited heads
of state.

In April, accompanied only by his executive
assistant R.K. Finlayson, the prime minister went
to Washington to discuss trade and other matters
with the new president, Franklin Roosevelt. The
other member of the Canadian delegation was W.D.
Herridge, the ambassador to the United States who
had recently married Bennett's younger sister

Mildred. Harry Stevens was left behind to make a major speech defending the new government budget. He also went out of his way to defend Bennett against 'a great deal of abuse' because he had not solved the depression. Stevens acknowledged the severity of the situation, but thought Canadians were leaning too much on governments at all levels. His Methodist philosophy had shown through when he had declared in March: 'Unless we can imbue the mass of the people with a sense of responsibility, there is not much hope for this Canadian democracy.'[25]

In 1933, thousands of Canadians must have found it difficult to view the situation in this light. The dairy farmers were a case in point. On 12 May the Commons' Select Standing Committee on Agriculture tabled a report on milk production and distribution. It noted that, unlike most other industries, the dairy firms were still making good profits while the milk producers 'were not receiving an equitable share.'[26] Stevens suggested to Bennett that it should be possible 'without interfering with private rights, to direct and supervise the manufacturing of our dairy products so that all our exportable surplus will be turned into by-products for the foreign market.' He was not suggesting 'that these services should be taken over by a government body, but rather that reasonable supervision should be provided.'[27] Bennett never sent a written reply and probably did not look closely at his minister's suggestion: he was preparing to leave again for overseas, this time to attend the World Monetary and Economic Conference in London. The Canadian delegation included the recently appointed minister of finance, Edgar Rhodes, and several senior advisers from the civil service. Harry Stevens and his family headed for the west coast.

The state of the Conservative party in British

Columbia was as chaotic as ever in 1933, and the
Montreal _Gazette_, still a staunch supporter of
the federal government, claimed that Stevens had
gone out 'on explicit instructions from Bennett.'[28]
Another influential Tory paper, the Ottawa _Journal_,
hinted that the minister of trade and commerce
would soon be taking over as Tory leader in British
Columbia. The Montreal _Standard_ was more explicit:
'Mr. Stevens has a call' and if he answered it,
'it would be a decided loss to the Federal Government.' This latter view was echoed by a score of
directors from some of Canada's largest firms, and
in telegrams and personal letters they urged Stevens
not to leave Ottawa.[29] He received so many such
entreaties that he finally sent out a form reply
stating that 'I will simply do the best I know
how in the general interests of the country.'[30]

There was more than a touch of weariness in
that form reply. Harry Stevens knew all too well
the hopeless state of the BC Tory party. He may
have felt that his own political future federally
was hopeless, too, but at any rate he did not say
so. He had been coaxed into remaining in federal
politics just three years before and remain he
would. It is quite possible that Sylvia's condition
was a big factor in his decision: she had had one
operation and the doctors were talking about another. Meanwhile, he would keep as busy as possible,
or as busy as Bennett would allow. In August 1933
the prime minister was back overseas again, this
time to attend the World Wheat Conference in Geneva.
Harry spent most of the summer touring southern
Ontario and, upon his return, Bennett joined him.
In September Bennett told the Montreal Board of
Trade that the Roosevelt New Deal was not for Canada: 'I do not intend to keep up with the Joneses.'[31]
Four days later in Pembroke, Stevens was saying
that he doubted whether 10 per cent of Canadians
had suffered materially from the depression; what
was needed was 'individual effort.'[32]

But privately Harry Stevens was beginning to have some doubts. On the way up to Pembroke and another meeting at Lake Couchiching, he learned from James Walsh, the managing director of the Canadian Manufacturers' Association, about the losing struggle of over two hundred small manufacturers against being 'driven into bankruptcy by certain practices of the buyers of the large department stores and chain store organizations.'[33] Walsh appealed to Stevens as minister of trade and commerce to do something. A few days later, Percy Sparks, of the customs inquiry days, told Stevens about sweatshop conditions in the clothing industry. Again, Stevens wrote Bennett, this time suggesting that 'the fair wage officer of the labour department might be asked to investigate the conditions in some of these factories now working on government contracts.'[34] Next came a letter from Mark Senn, the chairman of the Commons committee which had studied the dairy industry, reporting the discontent of some producers with trade agreements:

We need something concrete in which to make our appeal to agriculture. The political effect of the British Empire Trade Agreements is largely nullified by the suspicion in the farmer's mind that the trade reaps most of the advantages ... If we could say to the dairy and livestock farmer that a real attempt is being made to protect their interests by an organization in the same manner as the Board of Grain Commissioners supervises the grain trade, we would accomplish something well worthwhile.[35]

One wonders whether Stevens and other members of the Tory caucus also had as little hope for their leader's efforts at the international conference table. Modern economists now generally agree that the only solution to the world-wide

105

depression of the thirties would have been lower
tariff barriers and multilateral agreements. But
the many conferences Bennett attended during these
first three years of his ministry produced few
tangible results, especially for the hard-pressed
and in many cases desperate farmers. The World
Wheat Agreement in particular was useless, because
of the repeated crop failures in the Canadian
west.

Not surprisingly, when Stevens went to Winnipeg
in late October 1933 he made only a brief reference
to the wheat agreement. Clearly, he was aware that
his audience included wheat farmers who had seen
prices drop from 78 cents a bushel in 1929 to 28
cents in 1932. The western livestock farmer was
faring no better, for the worst drought in thirty
years had ruined most of the potential grazing
lands. In his speech Stevens acknowledged the difficulties in the dry terms of an accountant: 'The
trouble with agriculture is the existence of a
very low level of commodity prices and a very high
weight of debt obligations.'[36] Higher prices for
beef, butter, and eggs would help to offset the
low wheat prices. He concluded that 'if private
enterprise fails to find a solution, then the
government may have to step in,' even though the
government was not 'the best qualified party to
determine prices in view of the constitutional
restrictions.' He thought a better solution would
be to have the private producers get together and
raise livestock prices themselves.

Among the many letters Stevens received after
this Winnipeg speech was one from a Manitoba farmer,
who enclosed an official receipt from the Winnipeg
stockyards for the sale of eleven purebred Short-
horns. It read: '$103.92 less shipping charges of
$39.90, giving a net return of $64.02 or $5.82 per
head.'[37] Stevens' secretary added this comment:
'Good dope on spread of poultry and cattle.' A

106

Vancouver man thought that it was 'amazing to read in your speech' that the interest rate must be cut on mortgages 'while Mr. Bennett, in his address to the Women's Canadian Club in Ottawa the same day, stated that he was for a sound dollar and that Canada will pay what she owes. This shows that there is a difference of opinion in the cabinet.'[38]

If Stevens was receiving disturbing views on the impact of the depression, there is nothing to suggest that he was prepared to take a different course to find remedies. Like many others, he seemed to be waiting for the depression to end of its own volition. Certainly the leaders of Canadian industry appeared to be wholeheartedly behind him as minister of trade and commerce, witness their letters of concern about his rumoured departure from the Ottawa scene. More important, Bennett had every confidence in Harry Stevens, as a speechmaker. He would like him to fill in for him in Toronto early in January 1934. The occasion would be the national convention of the Canadian boot and shoe manufacturers. Ever available, Harry agreed. Neither man could know it at the time, but this speech would be the turning point in Stevens' career and in his relations with the prime minister.

iv The Stevens Inquiry

It was 3 a.m. and the light was still on in the
downstairs den of the Stevens' Ottawa residence
at 37 Lynden Terrace. Harry had been working since
midnight, writing steadily in his strong clear
hand, occasionally glancing at the clock. In a
few hours he would be taking the train to Toronto
where he would address the national convention of
the Retail Shoe Merchants and Shoe Manufacturers
Association, many of whom had already checked in
at the Royal York Hotel. Stevens had not planned
this last-minute preparation: he had had his
speech prepared well in advance but in the last
three days he had received three delegations.
They represented different groups in the economic
community, but whether needle-workers, livestock
farmers, or owners of small bakeshops, their message was the same. They were being squeezed out
by big business and they desperately pleaded with
the minister of trade and commerce for help.

They laid before me a set of facts which only
bore out what I already knew in part, and it left
an impression on my mind that I could not shake
off, and so I addressed myself to the preparation
of a speech for this Toronto group. Possibly I

should have gone there and given them a speech,
the usual stuff that is often handed out to
these gatherings, more or less innocuous, but
my mind was so filled with these conditions that
I ... [could] not remain silent.[1]

Several hundred delegates were seated before
him on Monday evening, 15 January 1934, and thousands were tuned in to a Toronto radio station.
From his opening words it was clear that he planned
to discuss more than the boot and shoe industry.
Without mentioning names, he accused the large retailers, especially the department and chain stores,
of misusing their tremendous buying power by forcing
manufacturers to give them major price concessions
or lose the business.[2] Low wholesale prices in
turn resulted in sweatshop conditions among the
workers. According to the Globe report of his
speech, Stevens declared that although he believed
in private property rights and individual initiative, 'I am getting to the point where I see that
there must be action taken of some kind.' He urged
businessmen 'to face the evils that have developed
like a canker. I warn them that unless they are
destroyed, they will destroy the system.' Specifically, he blamed the large packing firms for paying farmers as little as 1½ cents a pound for their
beef, which was later retailed for 19 cents or
more. Noting the trend in the baking industry for
large milling firms to buy out small retail baker-
ies and establish their own national chains, Stevens
said he was not objecting to their size if it
meant more efficiency, 'but I do object to such
powerful organizations being used for the purpose
of crushing or eliminating their individual com-
petitors ... or of forcing them into the purchase
of flour.' He lauded the local independent businessman as 'probably the finest expression of
democratic life to be found anywhere,' adding,

109

'It will be a sorry day for Canada when these
independent citizen-businessmen are crushed out.'
Warning his hosts that the boot and shoe industry
also had sweatshop conditions, he concluded: 'Don't
let the tremendous weight of advertising in the
public press muzzle you. Some of them [newspapers]
dare not publish these things or denounce them,
because of the advertising office receipts that
make it impossible for them to talk.' He urged his
hosts: 'Clean up your own industry first and dedi-
cate your association's strength to the task of
resisting to the limit those unfair and unsocial
practices I have described.' According to the
Globe's account, 'Those militant declarations came
with machine-gun precision, but increasing salvos
of applause met them with regimental accuracy and
the entire gathering stood to its feet like one man
as the speaker concluded.' The reporter's military
metaphor was prophetic: Harry Stevens had fired the
first shot in his war against big business.

His adversaries were quick to reply. Stevens'
speech was headlined in Tuesday's Globe. The supporting story began not with his statements but
with denials from R.Y. Eaton, president of the
T. Eaton Company, and from C.L. Burton, president
of the Robert Simpson Company. (The Globe's readers
had to turn to page 14 to find out what Stevens
actually said.) Both presidents wanted the minister
to 'name the concerns misusing their power' and
added that the allegations did not apply to their
firms. In a third statement, also on the first
page, the chairman of the Ontario Minimum Wage
Board, R.A. Stapells, denied having any knowledge
of sweatshop conditions. Even before Stevens left
his hotel room Tuesday morning to return to Ottawa,
he received a call from an Eaton's official who
'took strong exception' to the speech and 'demanded
the names of persons to whom' Stevens had referred.
This request was refused and a few hours later

Stevens told Ottawa newsmen that he would not 'enter public controversy on the Toronto charges.' The next day, Wednesday, he seemed to change his mind, for the Globe had him 'returning to his criticism of mass purchasing.' He cited an Eaton's advertisement of a few days earlier which he claimed had boasted of the low prices the firm had paid for Scottish woollens.[3]

One of the readers of this 18 January issue of the Globe probably was Prime Minister Bennett, who returned that day from western Canada. He immediately called Stevens to his office but not before he had received an Eaton's delegation which strongly expressed its displeasure. Bennett told Stevens that from the press reports the speech seemed to have gone 'further in formulating policy, without reference to the head of the government or his colleagues than a minister should go under sound constitutional practices.'[4] He requested Stevens to 'desist from further utterances of this kind.' Stevens refused and the next day sent in his letter of resignation. After referring in his letter to the three delegations he had received during the week before his Toronto speech, he went on to remind Bennett that he had described these sweatshop conditions to him shortly after Bennett's return from the World Economic Conference in 1933.[5] He had suggested then that 'the Dominion government might deal [with the sweatshops] through the control it has over sales tax licensing.' Like so many other suggestions Stevens had made to his prime minister in the first three years of the Bennett administration, this one had been ignored. He did not deny that the Toronto speech had amounted to 'formulating policy,' but he noted that he had received no adverse criticism from any other colleague. One minister had told him about 'an incident which substantially bears out the statements I had made' and another who 'has an intimate know-

ledge of the retail business stated very frankly
that he considered that I was 101 per cent right.'
Denying that he had made any specific reference
to the T. Eaton Company, Stevens cited the passage
in the speech that Mr. Eaton apparently had objected
to:

> ... the practice of mass buying of huge depart-
> ment and other chain store organizations, and
> the use of this power in the destruction of the
> small retailer (more particularly those in smaller
> towns) and the crushing of the manufacturer who
> will not accept price dictation from the mass-
> buyer ... - and a further reference reads as
> follows: The introduction of 'sweat-shop' prac-
> tices in the clothing industry which sweat shops
> are used largely by massbuyers (previously re-
> ferred to) in the breaking down of the prices
> of legitimate industry.

In conclusion, Stevens said he had done nothing
in violation of Conservative principles or 'of
the platform and policy upon which the government
was returned to power.' He promised that 'in all
matters consistent with these principles and the
best interests of the country' he would continue
to support the prime minister in the House.
    The sudden appearance of this letter of resigna-
tion must have surprised Bennett, who had received
Stevens' fullest cooperation during the past three
years. Was Stevens really serious about stepping
down or was he using the resignation as a lever
to get Bennett to act on his Toronto speech? Circum-
stantial evidence suggests that it was merely a
ploy by Stevens and two non-parliamentary advisers.
One was Warren K. Cook, a wealthy Toronto clothing
manufacturer, and the other was Percy Sparks, the
professional lobbyist who had supplied much of
the evidence of the customs scandal in 1926. Stevens

had met Cook through Sparks, probably sometime in 1933, shortly after Cook, as president of the Canadian Association of Garment Manufacturers, had instigated a study of working conditions in the men's clothing industry. The investigation had been conducted by two left-wing university professors, Harry Cassidy, already the founder of the School of Social Work at the University of Toronto, and Frank Scott of McGill's law faculty and one of the authors of the CCF's Regina manifesto of 1933. Stevens admired Cook from the start. Here was a successful businessman with a social conscience and a determination to attack poor working conditions, even when they occurred within his own industry. Percy Sparks had participated in the Cassidy-Scott study and apparently had brought Stevens and Cook together. Two days after his Toronto speech Stevens received this note from Cook: 'You may remember that I predicted it would have a definite reaction so far as you were concerned personally and I cannot tell you in a letter the remarks I have heard from many sources ... Percy will tell you some of our various plans to heap coals on the fire.'[6] This letter suggests that the trio had planned the Toronto speech in the hope that Bennett would authorize a full-scale investigation into the buying practices of the larger businesses. They probably expected that Bennett would ask Stevens to withdraw his resignation because of the political embarrassment such an unexpected act would have caused. In any case, that was what actually happened. Faced with Stevens' resignation and also with a mountain of letters supporting his speech, Bennett gave in: he would name a parliamentary committee to investigate the charges, and place Stevens in charge. No doubt Bennett had another reason for his decision. What better way to keep his restless minister of trade and commerce occupied while he, the prime minister, worked with world leaders to restore international trade.

The day after his meeting with Bennett, Stevens gave further details in a letter to Francis:

... Don't think, son, that this thing of running a country is simple or easy. Nor was it easy for R.B. When he got the letter he sent for me and said if I pressed it he would be forced to resign – that I was indispensable etc. – that it would ruin the Gov ... He then undertook to fully support me in making a full investigation into the matter with his unreserved support – & I am to draw the 'Order of Reference'.

You will likely hear and see more of this now. The letter followed an interview in which he tried to bluff me about being unfair to Eatons, etc.

I want you to know something of it all so you will not think me too indifferent to the common weal.[7]

On 2 February 1934, Bennett introduced a resolution asking the Commons to establish a select committee to investigate 'the causes of the large spread between the prices received for commodities by the producer' and the prices paid by the consumer. The prime minister noted that 'one of the trade journals has made very strong observations as to the necessity of having the business of mass buying by large organizations in some way regulated.' Whether this regulation was possible, he could not say. Stevens in his own speech added that the government was not concerned with the great industries which 'are not suffering,' but rather with the small firms being dictated to by the large organizations. He noted the absence of any legislation 'that protects or gives a chance of competitive existence to the decent small

114

industry, of which there are thousands in this country.' He thought the primary purpose of the committee was 'to find measures that are within the power of this Parliament to deal effectively with the abuses and difficulties with which trade and commerce and industry are confronted.'[8]

As Stevens and his staff were well aware, the Roosevelt administration in the United States, which had taken office on 4 March 1933, was already working on this problem of abuses in industry. Its New Deal program, and in particular the codes of the National Recovery Administration (NRA), were being studied by the Dominion Bureau of Statistics 'to see what suggestions they may have for points to be investigated and safeguarded.'[9] As Stevens' private secretary, W.H. Grant, noted in a memo to Major Parmelee, the deputy minister of trade and commerce: 'Under the N.R.A. the United States is dealing with a very similar situation to that brought to the public focus by the minister in connection with his Toronto speech. Their problems, like ours, deal with millers, sweat-shops and chain-stores.'[10] He added that Stevens was 'desirous of watching the efforts and developments of these proposals in the U.S. The Canadian Minister in Washington [W.D. Herridge] has been asked to furnish information in connection with the proposals under the N.R.A...' From his public utterances, the NRA director, General Hugh Johnston, seemed to have ideas similar to Harry Stevens'. On 31 January 1934, while Stevens was gathering together his investigators and accountants for the price spreads inquiry, General Johnston declared that he was interested 'in industrial self-government' and did not want to use the NRA code 'to run out and control an industry.'[11] Rather, he hoped industry would come forward with ideas 'as to what it thinks should be done.' In this hope both Johnston and Stevens were to be disappointed, and in Stevens'

case it was not surprising considering the make-up
and general tone of the select committee.

Besides Harry Stevens, its chairman, the Conservative members included W.W. Kennedy, a Winnipeg
lawyer; Mark Senn, the Ontario farmer who had
chaired the recent study into milk prices; A.M.
Edwards, owner of a small stove manufacturing
firm at Galt; J.L. Baribeau, a general store proprietor from rural Quebec; and Thomas Bell, an
investment dealer from Saint John, N.B. The four
Liberal members of the committee also represented
various geographic regions and, like the Tories,
seem to have been chosen deliberately from the
small rather than the big business sector of the
economic community. A Halifax lawyer and Liberal
member for the Nova Scotia farming constituency
of Hants-King, J.L. Ilsley, represented the Maritimes; another lawyer, Oscar Boulanger, came from
the rural Quebec riding of Bellechase, while a
third Liberal lawyer, Samuel Factor of Toronto
West Centre, proved to have an intimate knowledge
of the clothing industry; a farmer from the Weyburn
area of Saskatchewan, Edward Young, completed the
Liberal quartet. The eleventh member of the committee was D.M. Young of the United Farmers of
Alberta, who represented the rural area of Edmonton
West. There were no official labour members on
the committee, but A.A. Heaps, the Labour member
for Winnipeg North, was granted his request to
take part 'on behalf of labour interests' and
attended most of the hearings.[12]

The members of the Stevens Committee, as it soon
became known, held their first meeting on 15 February 1934 and the public hearings began one week
later in Room 368 of the parliament buildings,
the locale for all of the sessions during the next
eighteen weeks. They were usually attended by
other M.P.s, as well as by interested but silent
members of the big business community. The press

was always on hand and the inquiry's deliberations, played against the grim backdrop of the depression, often dominated the front pages of the large city newspapers. Bennett made no attempt to interfere with the proceedings, even when influential Tories objected to him about Stevens' choice of the committee's chief counsel, Norman Sommerville of Toronto. Arthur Meighen advised Bennett against his appointment because for many years Sommerville had been counsel for the president of the Edmonton Stock Yards, who in turn was known to have had his differences with the large meat packers, one of the major targets of the inquiry.[13] Bennett did not interfere. It was the same story when George Henry, the Conservative premier of Ontario, complained to Bennett about one of the witnesses scheduled to appear. 'A man of this type,' he wrote, 'who is definitely associated with the C.C.F. may use the information he gets for his own purposes and not for the benefit of people generally, particularly ourselves.'[14] The witness was Professor Harry Cassidy, who later spent an entire day outlining to the committee the results of the inquiry he and Professor Frank Scott had conducted for Warren Cook and the Canadian Association of Garment Manufacturers.

Many Liberals thought Stevens was too biased to be chairman, in view of statements he had made. One was tabled by a Liberal back-bencher on the day Bennett announced the make-up of the committee. It was a letter Stevens had written in reply to many he had received following his Toronto speech and it had been published in an Ottawa magazine, the Parliamentary Critic. Stevens had thanked the writer for sending illustrations 'to show the evil influence of the department and chain store system' and had added: 'We are now continuing the investigation and hope to build up a pretty strong case.'[15] According to the Liberal MP, Robert

117

McKenzie from Saskatchewan, Stevens had 'prejudged
the question' and should not be allowed 'to sit
in judgment on a committee of that kind.' Stevens
admitted writing the letter but denied that it
could be taken 'as an indication of one's mind
being made up.'

The House can rest assured that anything dealt
with in that committee will be dealt with fairly.
But I will say that as chairman of it, and having
some sense of responsibility as a member of this
house and of my duty to the country, it is my
purpose to pursue certain things vigorously and
earnestly ... to their ultimate end with the one
object of bringing out impartially the whole
truth in regard to these matters.[16]

Replying earlier to Mackenzie King's suggestion
that the problem posed by price spreads and mass
buying could be handled just as well by the combines
authorities, Stevens had argued that the Combines
Act was directed at one thing only: 'The possible
or alleged or presumed existence of a combine.'[17]
However, the government was not going to worry about
the great industries but about the small industries,
and about 'predatory price cutting' that was probably 'cutting down the wages of employees to a
starvation point.'
Any doubts there may have been about the direction
the Stevens inquiry would take were immediately
dispelled during the first days of the hearings.
While Bennett was avoiding 'all political meetings'
for some unknown reason,[18] his minister of trade
and commerce moved to centre stage. The first
witness was the Dominion Statistician, Dr. R.H.
Coats, who presented the committee with a long
memorandum referring to minimum wage legislation,
regulation of commercial houses, the Combines Act
and anti-combines legislation, and other subjects

on which expert evidence might be invited.[19] He
was followed by R.A. Stapells, chairman of the
Ontario Minimum Wage Board, who in response to
Stevens' Toronto speech had denied having any
knowledge of the sweatshop conditions Stevens had
mentioned. Formerly the president of a ladies-wear
manufacturing firm, Stapells was clearly on the
defensive throughout his testimony, particularly
when Stevens and Sommerville, the committee's
counsel, pressed him about complaints the committee
had received about 'speed-ups' in production in
several Toronto factories.[20] Stapells admitted,
when questioned by Stevens, that the wage board
could not afford to make plant inspections but
relied more on questionnaires about wage rates completed and returned by the owners.

On 27 February the third witness, A.W. Lavers,
commissioner of public welfare for the city of
Toronto, revealed through the questions of
Sommerville that at least 41 employed people in
the Toronto area were receiving city relief payments because their wages, ranging from $5 to $12
a week, were below what the welfare commission
considered adequate for a subsistence level. He
handed in a list of these people, who remained
anonymous, together with the names of the 38 firms
involved. The list was examined item by item.
Sommerville asked:

Q. What is the next?
A. Canada Packers, full time employee, $10.50
per week.
Q. That was a man?
A. That is a man.
Chairman: What would his duties be?
A. Shipper, seven years employed there ...
Q. And the next?
A. The next is a female employee of the T.
Eaton Company, full time, $10 per week.[21]

This testimony was reported almost verbatim in
the daily press and the reaction from company
officials was swift and emphatic. The most positive
reaction came from J. Stanley McLean, president
of Canada Packers, who wired Stevens objecting to
the fact that Lavers had refused to furnish him
with the names of the employees receiving welfare
payments. He asked for permission to appear before
the committee, a request that was quickly granted.

In the meantime the committee heard on 28 February from the chairman of the Quebec Minimum
Wage Board, Gustave Francq, who described the
contract system used by the larger firms in the
Montreal needle trade. They would buy material
and hand it to a sub-contractor who in turn would
give it to girls living in rural Quebec. He cited
specific cases where a company would pay its job-
bers $3 per dozen for men's pants, and the work
would be handed to families in the country for as
little as 35¢ a dozen. Stevens then posed several
leading questions to the witness:

Chairman: ... where there was keen competition
    for a large order ... [then] it is taken out
    of the hide of the workers?
A. Undoubtedly...
Q. In your experience, Mr. Francq, with these
    female workers, where they pay these scandal-
    ously low wages, do you find evidence of
    suffering?
A. Undoubtedly...
Q. Let me get that clearly; it is only the most
    efficient, experienced worker who is able to
    produce, on piece work, up to the minimum wage?
A. Well, above the minimum wage.
Q. Above the minimum wage?
A. Yes ... The piece work rate, as a rule, is
    based on the most efficient girl, and as soon
    as a certain number of girls are getting up

to a certain wage, bang goes the piece rate
again.
Counsel: Down?
A. Down.[22]

On 7 March, J.S. McLean made his first appearance
before the inquiry to defend Canada Packers against
charges of wages so low that in some cases they
had to be supplemented by local welfare agencies.
He and Stevens had met before under similar circumstances, in 1919 when McLean had appeared before
a Commons committee investigating the wartime
increase in the cost of living; at that time he
was president of Harris Abattoirs, one of the firms
that later joined the merger to form Canada Packers.
Harry Stevens, as vice-chairman of that committee,
had questioned McLean closely about accumulated
profits amounting to $1,200,000. Fifteen years
later McLean and his meat-packing empire were still
making what Stevens implied were excessive profits;
since its formation in 1927 Canada Packers had
averaged a net profit of $900,000 a year. 'Do you
consider the farmer is getting a living price?'
Stevens wanted to know. McLean admitted that the
farmer was suffering most from low prices but
thought the packer was nearly as badly off. 'The
fact remains,' argued Stevens, 'that the price of
$3.25 [per hog] is ruinous to the farmer.'[23] McLean
thought the solution lay in better cooperation
between the packers and farmers as well as in
efforts by the farmers to improve their livestock.
Although 26 other witnesses later discussed various
aspects of the livestock industry, McLean was the
only one representing the large meat-packers.
    He was followed on 8 March by Warren K. Cook,
who explained that although he was still president
of the Canadian Association of Garment Manufacturers,
he was also representing the National Fair Trade
Council, recently formed 'by those who believe

that the independent retailers are the most important factors in our system of distribution and who
regard the growth of large department store organizations, mail order houses and chain stores as
detrimental to the general interests of the country.'[24] According to Cook, his new council was
being supported by 'manufacturers, wholesalers
and others who regard the large organizations ...
as economically unsound and socially undesirable.'[24]
Judging by the seven witnesses who followed him,
the 'others' were members of the Retail Merchants'
Association of Canada. All more or less substantiated Cook's charges against the department and
chain stores: that their mass-buying techniques
were destroying the independent retailer. The
best of these briefs, presented by George Hougham,
secretary-manager of the Ontario branch of the
Retail Merchants' Association, urged the establishment 'of a department of domestic distribution
within the Department of Trade and Commerce ...
something in the nature of an economic council
should be set up truly representative of the various interests in the economic structure, with
observers from the Department.' When one of the
committee members observed that this council would
be 'practically along the lines of the [N.R.A.]
Code system in the United States' Hougham agreed.[25]
Hougham's associates from the other provinces
were not as well prepared. A weak brief from Manitoba was presented by A.E. Grassby, a music store
proprietor and along with Harry Stevens one of the
directors of the now bankrupt Manufacturers' Finance Corporation. (A few weeks after Grassby's
appearance before the committee, a well-known
Ontario Liberal lawyer, Arthur G. Slaght, instigated proceedings against Stevens for alleged
mismanagement of the firm.)
    The price spreads inquiry, by long odds the
most publicized issue in 1934, dominated all Stevens'

waking hours and from 22 February to 22 June, the
life of the parliamentary committee, he never
strayed far from its deliberations. The rare occasion occurred on 19 April when he made one of the
few major speeches he was to deliver in the Commons
in these months; significantly it was in support
of the Natural Products Marketing Bill. Introduced
by Robert Weir, the minister of agriculture, on
15 March, the bill would give the minister wide
powers to regulate the agriculture industry by
means of a dominion marketing board. At the request
of this board, or upon his own initiative, the minister could authorize investigations into costs
of products, prices, spreads, in fact almost any
aspect of the marketing of any natural product.
Speaking on the second reading of the bill, Stevens
admitted it was a departure from anything the
House had known before but he argued that it was
needed to cope with unusual circumstances caused
by high tariffs and changes in Canada's economy
resulting from many mergers in most of the major
industries. He elaborated on mergers during a speech
on 30 April in support of the budget. From 1922 to
1929, he noted, there had been 120 mergers involving
over 500 separate companies: 'The heads of these
companies vanished as leaders in business. Some
of them of course were carried into the merger
and occupied positions of leadership; but by long
odds, [most] were eliminated from the business
life of the country and no longer contributed
either their experience or their guidance to its
affairs.' Quoting from a British economist, T.E.M.
Gregory, he argued that 'we shall witness a less
blind worship of size and authority and monopoly
in business ... unless indeed the whole process
of economic adjustment' was prevented by the intervention of the state.

Parliament must ever keep before it as its dom-

inating motive, the overwhelming importance of
human values, as distinct from an ever-increasing
tendency to measure success by size and efficiency. Let Parliament hold the balance, in such
a way that genius and enterprise may receive a
just reward, but not at the cost of the happiness
and well-being of our people.[26]

It was Harry Stevens, the Methodist lay preacher,
at his best. It was H.H. Stevens, MP, enunciating
his own political philosophy. Many of his critics
in 1934 thought he was merely capitalizing on
human misfortune during the depression to further
his own political career. Rather, his role in the
price spreads inquiry was quite consistent with
his life-long concern for humanity in a rapidly
growing technological society.
Stevens' concern about mergers had been outlined
in some detail in a letter to Sir Robert Borden,
who had written just before Stevens' budget speech
about the NRA codes being drawn up in the United
States. Borden hoped that Canada would not be
'indulging in a spree of experimental legislation
in response to an unreasoning popular demand.'[27]
Stevens replied that he had no wish to 'emulate
the United States in its system of codes, but I
do realize that it is necessary that some degree
of orderliness shall be injected into business.'
Cautioning that what he had to say 'must be considered as an immature view,' he elaborated on
his fears about mergers:

Most ... were born out of the fertile brain of
a promoter who seized upon groups of existing
thrifty healthy businesses, merged them into one
great whole, and in the process, extracted large
gains for himself and a few others without actually injecting anything new into the operations,
and the net result was frankly a costly, extrava-

gant, over-weighted managerial body, supplementing intelligent and economic administration of the smaller units. In the distribution realm, the growth of the chain store and the department store is another evidence of mass without reason or form.[28]

He thought the Combines Act allowed these mergers but prevented businessmen from associating together. This act should be reversed so that independent business concerns could 'associate together for the purpose of applying broad, general principles to their industrial and commercial operations such as minimum wages, fair trading practices, etc.' There had to be 'some controlling factor that will prevent unscrupulous businessmen' from taking advantage of the farmer and the wage earner. Stevens could not say just what form such control would take but he had 'the matter in mind' and intended 'to work it out.'

As April was succeeded by May, Canadians learned through the price spreads inquiry far more than most of them had ever known about big business. It was revealed by the dividend record of the Imperial Tobacco Company, for example, that this firm had paid its president an annual salary of $25,000 from 1929 to 1933 plus additional annual bonuses from $32,000 to $61,000. At the same time a clerk in a United Cigar Store chain owned by Imperial received $25.45 for a 54-hour week selling cigars made by Toronto area workers for 75 cents a thousand and retailing for $37 per thousand.[29] The secretary of the Rubber Footwear Association, whose members were the major rubber companies, testified that four levels of discounts were given to retailers, and he added: If the 'big class A fellows' did not get their discount, they could go into the business themselves and 'then you would have a fine mess in this retail business.'[30]

125

On 5 June 1934 the committee turned its attention
to the department stores and heard the detailed
testimony of the accountant investigators who had
been poring over their books. The smaller firms
such as Woodward's and Spencer's of Vancouver
were dealt with quickly, but a 300-page brief was
tabled on the operations of the Robert Simpson
Company. It dealt with the growth of this firm
since its founding in 1872 and gave special emphasis
to the period between 1925 and 1929 when two of
Toronto's best-known businessmen, Sir Joseph
Flavelle and Herbert Cox, gradually withdrew their
controlling interest. Harry Stevens' mind must
have gone back to those Peterborough days, a
generation earlier, when he used to pick up the
family's weekly groceries at Joe Flavelle's general
store. Now, as chairman of a select committee of
the House of Commons, he was directing searching
questions into Flavelle's corporate activities
while the elderly knight watched from the visitors'
section. Stevens was particularly interested in
the store's reorganization around 1929 when, he
noted, 'there was actually taken out the sum of
about fifteen million dollars.' The committee's
counsel reported that only Cox and Flavelle had
received cash in the reorganization, amounting to
a total of $10,548,000. Simpson's employees had
been encouraged to purchase the new shares, and
they could borrow the money from the Canadian
Bank of Commerce, whose president was Sir Joseph
Flavelle. The accountants' report also showed that
in the four-year period from 1930 to 1934 Simpson's
male workers had taken an average drop in their
weekly wages from $24.68 to $19.90, while women's
wages had dropped $6.00. 'The point that I cannot
understand or cannot justify in my mind,' observed
Stevens, 'is that in the retail store they can
make such a handsome mark-up ... over 100 percent -
yet women are working for $10 and $11 a week.'[31]

Two days later, in Toronto, Stevens was making
the same kind of observations before a packed
evening service at Trinity United Church.[32] After
his talk, he rushed back to Ottawa for the Monday
morning session of the price spreads inquiry and
a continuation of the examination of department
stores.

The T. Eaton study had been conducted by a team
headed by Walter L. Gordon, son of the senior
partner in the Clarkson Gordon firm which had
supplied most of the investigators for the inquiry.
He filed a four-hundred-page report. Since Eaton's
was then, and remained until recently, entirely a
family-owned firm, this 1934 study of its financial
structure and retail history is the only material
on Eaton's operations available to the general
public. Gordon and his assistants had no difficulty
getting the information: when asked about the
investigation many years later, he said that 'as
a matter of fact, Eaton's have been a Clarkson
Gordon account ever since.'[33] As with the Simpson
report, much attention was given to salaries and
wages. The committee was told that in 1933 forty
Eaton directors had received salaries averaging
$35,000 while their 25,736 employees took home
for that year an average of $970. Furthermore, in
1932 factory piece-workers had been paid for nine
statutory holidays plus one to two weeks of annual
vacation; those still working at Eaton's in 1934
received two statutory holidays and no paid vacation.[34] When the wages of about 50 employees,
identified only by numbers, were revealed, Stevens
asked for an explanation of 'these extraordinarily
low examples.' By way of a reply, Gordon read
from the company brief:

[A few had worked only part-time, two others]
who had slowed up considerably were let out on a
short-term pension ... As to the balance of the

group, we can only put it down to good operators but slow and who could not be replaced with any better help on account of the shortage of experienced help in the garment trade in Toronto.

Stevens could only come back with an incredulous 'What?'[35]

By 14 June, after Walter Gordon had been answering questions and elaborating on statistical tables for three days, a committee member asked the chairman: 'When are we going to have Eaton's come here and answer to all this?' 'I do not know,' Stevens replied, 'They are sitting here.' He could have subpoenaed them to testify but he thought having the evidence of some small manufacturers would be more valuable. He was to be disappointed. 'I would be tickled pink,' he wrote to one Toronto correspondent, 'if we could get some of the manufacturers to come forward' but 'they have absolutely and positively fallen down.' He had been told that 'they are all cowed by the big buyers ...'[36] Despite this setback, the committee received considerable evidence of sweatshop conditions in the report of Grant Glassco, who had investigated several factories, mostly in Quebec, which supplied the large retail stores. For example, a Quebec shoe factory which sold 70 per cent of its output to department stores paid its 107 workers an average of 12.9 cents an hour. Other evidence revealed speed-ups in production and low wages to an extent that prompted one committee member to comment: 'A shocking picture.'[37]

On 22 June, the last day of the hearing, Percy Sparks returned to the stand. He had appeared earlier on behalf of the Commercial Protective Association, which had been formed to prevent price-cutting in the drug trade. This time he appeared as the legal representative of the National Fair Trade Council, which had been formed as

recently as March 1934 'to represent and to protect
the interests of the independent retailers before
the Select Committee on Price Spreads.' The council
had grown out of a meeting held in Ottawa and
attended by representatives of retail trade associations from all provinces. On behalf of this
organization Sparks had sent out 1,000 questionnaires to independent retailers, asking for statistics on their sales and mark-ups and other data
for the period 1930-1933. Only 206 replied, because,
as Sparks explained, they 'were afraid to complete
the letters that would go before the Committee.'
He also revealed what some committee members had
suspected, that Warren K. Cook and fifteen other
witnesses had been associated with the National
Fair Trade Council, suggesting close cooperation
of these witnesses in preparing their testimony
before the inquiry. Sparks' own brief apparently
was intended as a summary of the council's findings.
He cited statistics from the briefs of these earlier witnesses and emphasized the dominant place
occupied in the retail trade by Eaton's. In 1929
Eaton's had 7.5 per cent of the total retail sales
for Canada, compared to 0.9 per cent for Sears
Roebuck in the United States, that country's largest
retail organization. By way of emphasis the committee's counsel, Sommerville, added: 'That is to
say, it has a larger percentage of sales in this
country than any other store?' Replied Sparks:
'Than any other store in the world.'[38]
   Sparks recommended amendments to the Combines
Act giving trade associations such as he represented
the power to control wages, prices, and trade
practices. He also wanted a trade board similar
to the Board of Railway Commissioners. In his
final statement Sparks revealed under close questioning from E.M. Young, the Liberal free-trader
from Saskatchewan, that he had been a clothing
manufacturer himself for thirty years and that

129

department store orders had enabled him to keep
going. This information also helped to explain
Sparks' close friendship with Warren K. Cook,
another clothier, and the seemingly unrelated
events which had persuaded Stevens to make his
shoe convention speech touching off the inquiry.
The Liberals later claimed that the whole affair
had been carefully worked out beforehand by the
trio.

Whatever the immediate reasons of the inquiry,
the resulting testimony and evidence had revealed
to the general public some glaring inequities in
the Canadian marketplace, and all eleven committee
members realized that their work was far from over.
They unanimously agreed that the inquiry should be
allowed to continue beyond the legal life of the
select Commons committee, due to expire with
Parliament's prorogation, expected the first week
of July. Stevens had already recommended to Bennett
that the committee carry on as a Commission under
the Inquiries Act and his request was promptly
granted in an order-in-council setting up a royal
commission, passed by cabinet on 7 July, the day
of prorogration.[39] Undoubtedly this cabinet action
stemmed from the favourable publicity in the daily
press. The 'Stevens Committee' had become a household name and letters by the thousands had poured
in over the last few weeks of the inquiry, most
of them urging the chairman to carry on. 'No one
would be happier than I to see you someday Premier
of this fair land,' wrote a United Church minister
from Toronto.[40] Perhaps he had heard the well-
founded rumour that Prime Minister Bennett, who
had avoided public appearances since January 1934,
was planning to retire to a lordship and an English
manor. The mayor of Winnipeg thought he noted a
definite swing towards the Tories; a Quebec resident
was sure Harry Stevens had saved the party; a
Saskatoon lawyer sent along a clipping from the

Canadian Forum which suggested that Stevens should join the CCF and rid that new socialist party of its radical flavour. Liberal as well as Conservative MPs sent their congratulations and enclosed favourable clippings from local newspapers. Organizations were responsive: Orange Lodges, the Catholic Association of Commercial Travellers, the Restaurant Owners of Ontario, several ministerial associations, and many boards of trade and district ratepayer groups all forwarded copies of resolutions sent to Prime Minister Bennett. By far the most active was the Retail Merchants' Association which used its monthly magazine to induce hundreds of members to inform Stevens of local support and often to supply more information. At one point, Bennett sent Stevens a memorandum he had received from the Alberta Retail Merchants' Association. 'It was very kind of you,' replied Stevens, 'but as a matter of fact it was I who got them to circulate this.'[41]

Bennett could not have ignored Stevens' role as the central figure in the price spreads inquiry: there could be no doubt about who should be the chairman of the royal commission. Even before cabinet had passed the necessary order-in-council Stevens was preparing for the next stage. The mountain of mail he had received had convinced him, if he needed any convincing, of the value of publicity, and he gladly consented to speak to the Conservative members' study club just before they departed for the summer recess. As was his custom, he spoke without notes, but a stenographer was on hand to take down his speech verbatim so that it could be typed and distributed to any Conservative wishing it. The study club speech was in the event to receive much wider distribution. After paying tribute to Bennett for his efforts to correct the external causes of the depression, and to the members of his select committee, Stevens turned

to recent political developments in Europe and
the threats to constitutional government. The
United States, despite 'all the magnificent efforts
that Roosevelt' had made, was 'not under a democratic form of government.' The only major country
that had 'really survived' was Great Britain, 'and
the progress they are making is certainly wonderful.'
Then he turned to the Canadian scene and to strong
criticism for recent mergers and public stock offer-
ings in connection with General Steel Wares and the
Burns meat-packing company. But 'the classic' was
the Robert Simpson Company. It had been 'practically
an ideal institution, profitable, and well-managed
because part of the profits had been ploughed back
into the business.' Then, in 1925, Sir Joseph
Flavelle and his associates had taken out $5,000,000
from the operation. 'Not much cause to complain
there' - but in 1928 had come re-financing. Quoting
from committee evidence, Stevens described how the
store's employees had invested $2,000,000 and the
public another $10,000,000 on the assumption that
the company planned to expand. Now Sir Joseph and
others left the company, taking with them $10,000,000
in invested earnings.

> ... In its place they left $12,000,000 of mort-
> gage bonds. But the tragedy of the thing is this,
> that the bonds were not secured by the assets
> of the Robert Simpson Company, they were secured
> solely by the common stock ... The $2,000,000
> that the employees got is not worth a snap of
> the fingers ...[42]

In the event, Stevens explained, the firm had
been forced to raise its average mark-up by about
18 per cent to cover 'the added load of the over-
head.' This increase could not be passed on to
the consumer, so Simpson's applied pressure on
their suppliers to sell for less. The net result

132

was the sweatshop, particularly in the needle trade, the boot and shoe factories, and furniture plants. 'In these industries,' Stevens continued, 'men and women are living on a basis that is a disgrace to Canada, and as far as I am concerned, I will never rest until something is done to remedy it. I do not care what happens.'

Toward the end of his talk, Stevens revealed for the first time some of the effects of the wide publicity the inquiry had received. Both Simpson's and Eaton's had increased their employees' wages and the tobacco firms and the growers had signed a three-year contract giving the farmers a guaranteed price. Two Montreal firms had contributed $4,000 to their employees as compensation for their evasion of Quebec's minimum wage law. Stevens went on to lay down certain principles for Conservatives.

Real conservatism in politics in my mind does not consist of being allied with or dictated to by large financial influences, but rather, if it is to survive, it must find its influence in the home and on the farm where real opinions are formed ... I believe that this Conservative party must readjust itself, get a new orientation of its views on some of our political policies and fix them upon the well-being of the farmer first, and on the large body of industrial workers in the second place. The real health of the nation depends upon the success of these two groups. It cannot be otherwise.

Here again was the crusading Methodism that was so much a part of Harry Stevens: the spirit that had taken him into the moral reform movement and into the hurly-burly of Vancouver politics a quarter of a century ago. He had never given up, and now, in June 1934, the tremendous response

133

from the price spreads inquiry must have told him
that the message was getting through, penetrating
perhaps even a few of those conservative Conservatives seated before him. He knew the fight would
never be won, but the knowledge that by autumn his
investigation would be underway again, this time
as a royal commission, gave him strength.

He needed encouragement in these days. Within
the week Gertrude would be taking Patricia, Douglas,
and Sylvia back to their Vancouver home and it was
a question how many more times Sylvia would be able
to make the long trip. He had already arranged for
her to see Montreal specialists later in the summer.
The prices spreads inquiry, however, had to take
precedence over his wish to join his family. He
must find more accountant investigators, acquaint
the royal commission's secretary, L.B. Pearson,
with what had already been covered and what lay
ahead; he must edit the study club pamphlet for
mimeographing and distributing to those MPs who
had not heard his speech. The hot July days swept
by in a torrent of activity. Instead of his noon
walk to Lynden Terrace he ate a hurried lunch at
the Rideau Club. And then back to work again. But
he was never too busy to write his daily letters
home. He knew how eagerly Gertrude and the family
watched for them; she never failed to send daily
replies.

On 2 August 1934, Stevens and Grant, his private
secretary, boarded a train for Vancouver. At Winnipeg on 4 August, an urgent message awaited
Stevens. His deputy minister, Major Parmelee, told
him on the telephone that Bennett was very upset
about quotations from the study club pamphlet which
had appeared in both the Ottawa Citizen and the
Toronto Star, two staunch Liberal papers. Moreover,
C.L. Burton, president of Simpson's, had wired
Bennett threatening to sue for libel if further
publication was not withheld. As Bennett's subse-

quent investigation was to reveal, 3,000 copies
of the pamphlet had been printed at government
expense by James Muir of the Dominion Bureau of
Statistics, a former member of the Parliamentary
Press Gallery. 'In accordance with the usual practice carried on under arrangements with Mr. Stevens,'
Muir later explained to Bennett, 'I sent copies
marked 'personal' to a few of his special friends
who are editors of the daily newspapers in Canada,
the general idea being to keep them in touch with
the trend of events, but not for publication.'[43]
Muir was implying that Stevens, as minister of
trade and commerce for the past four years, had
been using the facilities of the Dominion Bureau
of Statistics, which was under his jurisdiction,
to publicize the efforts of his department - a
common if perhaps slightly unethical practice that
politicians still follow while in power.

On 5 August Stevens phoned Bennett who told him
that six copies sent to newspapers had been recov-
ered, but two days later John W. Dafoe's Winnipeg
Free Press, an unrelenting critic of the Bennett
administration, published the pamphlet in full. A
prominent Winnipeg Tory, John T. Haig, immediately
wrote Bennett, expressing his view that perhaps
publication should have been withheld 'until after
the [Royal Commission] investigation was completely
finished'; nevertheless he praised Stevens for
bringing out the facts. He also enclosed a copy
of a letter to him from the president of the University of Manitoba, Dr. Sidney Smith, who thought
'that our mutual friend Stevens owes the Free Press
a big advertising bill. Tell him from me that that
was a superb statement, whatever it was prepared
for.'[44] Bennett also received an anxious letter
from W.W. Kennedy, Winnipeg lawyer and one of the
six Tories on the price spreads committee. He was
concerned over Ottawa reports that Stevens might
be replaced as chairman. These probably stemmed

from the visit C.L. Burton had paid to Bennett's office on 8 August, when he presented sworn testimony from the price spreads committee's records. Burton argued that these showed that Stevens' remarks about Simpson's in his speech had been untrue. It was after this meeting that Bennett had attempted to prevent the pamphlet from being published. Kennedy wrote Bennett that if Stevens were replaced, 'the results politically would be disastrous. The commission might just as well fold up ... The feeling here and the feeling throughout the whole west is so strong against such action that I cannot refrain from writing you.' George Matthews, secretary of the British Columbia branch of the Retail Merchants' Association, wired the prime minister to the same effect. A letter from W.D. Herridge in Washington did not mention Harry Stevens, but urged Bennett to 'declare for the new Toryism, for it means government in business.' The people wanted action, 'and if government does not give it to them, action they will nevertheless have, and it will be action of their own making.'[45]

As for the prime minister, he apparently had no intention either of replacing Stevens as chairman of the commission or of changing the role of his government. Uppermost in his mind was the forthcoming Geneva meeting of the League of Nations; he was scheduled to leave Canada with his delegation on 1 September. He needed Stevens to maintain a positive image of a Conservative government deeply concerned about the depression; he also had named him and R.J. Manion as the principal cabinet spokesmen for five by-elections in Ontario ridings on 25 September.

The evening of 4 September found the ever available Stevens addressing a meeting in Kenora in support of the Tory candidate. Ten days later the Kenora voters heard from Mackenzie King, who had some free advice for the minister of trade and

136

commerce. 'If I was Mr. Stevens, I would defy Mr.
Bennett, leave his cabinet, and stand up and fight
for the principles in which I believe. But no, Mr.
Stevens is going to be chairman of the Commission.'[46]
A few days later, in Toronto, Stevens replied to
the Liberal leader's remarks in a fighting speech
in support of the Tory candidate in Toronto East,
former mayor Tommy Church:

I notice Mr. King said this to the electors in
Kenora: 'It is a choice between Bennett and
Stevens'. When has it become Mr. King's prerog-
ative to speak for the Conservative Party? ...
This solicitude for the imagined and concocted
differences between the Prime Minister and myself
really is most touching. The question one naturally asks is: When did Mr. King become so concerned about what happens in the Conservative
Party? I am certain of this, that if he were
assured that there was something wrong ... nothing
would please him more.

In contrast to his Kenora speech, which barely mentioned the price spreads inquiry, Stevens now dealt
with it at great length:

I am condemned for seeking to know too much. I
am considered to be a busy-body. Some of my
friends of the so-called 'large interests' would
scarcely look at me. They hold their hands in
holy horror. I am an Ishmaelite. Well, it does
not worry me very much. I have been criticized
for talking too much to the public. I am [doing
that now because] I found after talking to business organizations for two or three years there
were no results.[47]

By now it was clear that this 'little general
election,' as it was being called, had developed

into a straight fight between King and Stevens.
No doubt the wily Liberal leader realized the political threat posed by a Conservative party aroused
and in fact being led by the man who had launched
the price spreads inquiry. Even as Stevens was
speaking in Toronto, King was reading parts of the
pamphlet to '5000 wildly enthusiastic supporters
at St. Thomas.' King claimed that the inquiry had
originally been a Liberal proposal during the 1933
session of Parliament. Harry Stevens arrived in
St. Thomas two days later and promised a meeting
of 3,000 citizens that 'the shocking conditions'
revealed by his committee's investigations would
be the subject of legislation at the next parliamentary session. He again repeated his warning
that if the businessmen did not 'put their affairs
in order, they could expect more and more government interference.' He also defended Bennett's
efforts to promote empire trade. These St. Thomas
speeches marked the end of the by-election campaigns. In summing up, the Ottawa correspondent
for the New York Times observed on 23 September
1934:

  The hope of the Conservatives is that Trade
  Minister Stevens in his latter day role of David
  defying the Goliaths of the Canadian banking and
  industrial world, will be accepted by the electors
  as a sign that the Bennett government has the
  people's interests at heart ... There are many
  who believe that unless the situation changes
  greatly before the next election [Bennett] will
  retire from politics and realize an ambition he
  has sometimes dallied with in fancy - that of
  buying a house in England and living there. Mr.
  Stevens may be one of those who holds this view.

Considering the ever present depression and the
by-election score since 1930 (the Liberals had

won six, the Tories three, and Labour one) the
Conservatives' hopes in the five ridings could not
have been high. In four the Tory candidates were
decisively defeated; only the colourful Tommy Church
was victorious in Toronto East. Liberal newspapers
such as the Winnipeg Free Press and the London
Advertiser were jubilant. The Montreal Gazette,
usually a Conservative supporter but acknowledged
as the voice of St. James Street financiers, thought
that the decision to play up the price spreads
inquiry and Stevens' role in it was 'anything but
a strategic masterpiece.' The Saskatoon Star-Phoenix
thought the results would 'have a very definite
effect on Mr. Stevens' career in the immediate
future.'

This last observation was astute but to understand the critical decisions Harry Stevens made
in the month following the by-elections a much
more important event must be considered. On 15
October 1934 his twenty-three year old daughter
Sylvia was operated on at Montreal's Royal Victoria
Hospital. For the next few hours and days the life
of this courageous girl hung in the balance as
she fought to win the grim battle she had been
waging for three years against colitis. Her mother
never left her side and her father was in constant
touch by telephone from Ottawa. By 19 October the
worst seemed to be over. Stevens did his best to
concentrate on the forthcoming royal commission
hearings, slated to begin 30 October. On 19 October
also Bennett returned from Europe and on 25 October
he held his first cabinet meeting in four months.

Ordinarily the proceedings of cabinet meetings
remain secret but this session on 25 October was
widely publicized from several sources. Harry
Stevens rather than the prime minister was the
immediate centre of attention. Bennett had little
to say, in contrast to the elderly Sir George
Perley and C.H. Cahan, generally regarded as the

cabinet's St. James Street spokesmen. They demanded a statement from Stevens 'in the light of complaints that had been made by those who claim to have been injured by misstatements contained in the pamphlet,'[48] an obvious reference to the charges made by C.L. Burton. Stevens answered briefly, then Cahan returned to the attack and demanded that a public apology be made to Sir Joseph Flavelle at the start of the royal commission hearings, scheduled to begin in four days. On this note the cabinet adjourned until the next day, Friday. Bennett emerged in an affable mood and chatted amiably with newsmen for fifteen minutes.[49] Cahan had his news conference too, with one lone reporter, Charlie Bishop of the Ottawa Citizen, which released the details of the cabinet meeting in its next issue, including the ultimatum issued by Cahan: Stevens must apologize or resign.[50]

That Thursday evening Harry wrote a long letter to Francis. No mention was made of the hectic meeting that afternoon. Instead he described Sylvia's operation and her present condition.[51] In the past his letters to his son had been filled with views and speculations on federal politics, and the complete absence of political topics strongly suggests that on 25 October 1934 Harry Stevens had one problem uppermost on his mind: Sylvia's illness. His anxiety over this family crisis almost ruled out the possibility of a rational decision about his political future. The next morning found him in the office of his friend Harold Daly, an Ottawa lobbyist who had had a falling out with Bennett. Also there was Bob Lipsett, another disenchanted Tory who had lost his job as the party's publicity director and now worked for the arch Liberal paper, the Toronto Star. Why Stevens should have found himself with this pair at such a critical juncture in his career is a mystery. There is no evidence to

140

suggest that he sought them out; apparently he
simply ran into them on the way to his office or
they were waiting for him when he arrived. In any
case, Daly and Lipsett tried to convince Stevens
that he would be asked to resign when cabinet met
that afternoon. Their arguments, which were never
recorded, might have gone in this fashion. After
all, Bennett had not come to his defence when
Cahan and Perley lashed out at him; therefore he
must have agreed with them. Why not beat this
millionaire clique to the punch, write out his
resignation, and send it immediately to Bennett's
office? Whatever Daly and Lipsett said at this
fateful meeting, bitter memories of indignities
suffered at the hands of these 'colleagues' must
have flashed through the worried Stevens' mind.
Politics must have appeared trivial and malicious
at such a moment, with Sylvia probably dying. Perhaps Daly and Lipsett were right: he would resign,
and not just from the cabinet but also from the
chairmanship of the commission. A letter of resignation was sent to Bennett before the cabinet met.[52]
    That afternoon, Friday, 26 October, Prime Minister
Bennett again faced his cabinet, but, as one
reporter put it, he 'played Hamlet without the
Prince of Denmark. Mr. Stevens did not attend.'[53]
Instead Bennett had to read out his minister's
resignation, his second in ten months; it was
accepted. On Saturday, 27 October, Stevens issued
a statement to the press, outlining his position,
denying Cahan's charges, and explaining why he
had resigned. On Monday, 29 October, the day the
price spreads hearings were to be resumed, Bennett
made public Stevens' letter of resignation and his
own reply. Understandably, the prime minister made
no mention of the cabinet fight but dwelt instead
on his reasons for trying to suppress Stevens'
pamphlet. It had been 'fundamentally unsound' for
Stevens to discuss the price spreads proceedings

141

publicly before the final report, and some of the
pamphlet statements 'were without any basis in
fact.' He did pay tribute to Stevens' 'industry
and zeal as a minister.'

The tone and emphasis of the newspaper editorials
were predictable. The Montreal Gazette gave a long
account of Stevens' parliamentary career, which
read like an obituary. The Ottawa Citizen's editorial was typical of the Liberal press: 'The process
of disintegration of the Bennett Cabinet is plainly
underway. It is most unlikely that Bennett would
have accepted [Stevens' resignation] but for the
probable alternative of having to accept the resignation of some other ministers.' The Hamilton
Spectator, Calgary Herald, Edmonton Journal, and
the Saint John Telegraph-Journal all sided with
Bennett, saying in effect that Stevens had deliberately forced the government's hand. The Vancouver
Province admitted that Stevens probably had 'sinned
against the rule of cabinet solidarity,' but thought
that in view of the conditions 'he finds in industry
and business he considers his responsibility to
the people greater than his obligation to consult
his colleagues.' The Vancouver Sun, never a Stevens
fan, almost gleefully noted that the Tory party
was split 'right down the middle' and that Stevens
had 'created a situation which only an immediate
election will clarify.' After reading the press
comments, Francis Stevens wrote his father from
Vancouver a prophetic letter:

When I think about the situation, I always see
you leading out a new party drawing from all
three of the old parties - not getting a great
deal of support from the hacks and politicians ...
but winning popular approval. Perhaps it might
be a reform party pledged to clean up things ...
setting up fair standards, nationalizing some of
the great public utilities, giving the farmer

142

and labourer both a square deal by means of
federal laws as to wages, conditions, hours, etc.,
using the tariff to protect the country and not
the industries ... I believe the country needs
a change, and ... you are the only man in sight
that would have a ghost of a chance to do it. I
shudder to think of King in again, and that's
what we are doomed for if you are subdued.[54]

An astute appraisal, based on the closest of family
ties. Francis Stevens knew well his father's high
regard for the principles of the Conservative party –
the party of Sir John A. Macdonald and Sir Robert
Borden. Harry Stevens was still a member of that
party as well as the key member of the Royal Commission on Price Spreads. He would press on. If
his work meant a direct confrontation with Bennett,
so be it.

v The Waiting Game

'What is the reason that these large fish companies with 90 percent of their catch handled by
trawlers and about 10 percent handled by these
fishermen, what is the reason that they cannot
pay ... an additional cent a pound and thereby lift
them out of penury and poverty?'[1]   The questioner
was Harry Stevens. The scene was the east block of
the House of Commons on 1 November 1934, the opening day of the hearings of the Royal Commission
on Price Spreads. It would sit until 2 February
1935. The new chairman was W.W. Kennedy, the lawyer
and a Conservative member for Winnipeg, but it was
clear from the start, as one newsman wrote, 'where
McGregor sits is the head of the table.'[2] Harry
Stevens continued to dominate the proceedings.
There was one significant difference from the earlier inquiry: because he was no longer chairman
and a cabinet minister, Stevens had more time for
outside speaking engagements. He was much in demand.
Local branches of the Retail Merchants' Association
were particularly anxious to hear him, and so too
were church groups.
   On 4 November, Stevens told a meeting at St.
James Church in Ottawa that 'it matters little
what sort of a social or economic system you have;

144

if it has not a real sound moral background it
cannot contribute much to the happiness of the
people.' He cited Woodrow Wilson's comment that
society could not afford to have individuals 'wield-
ing the power of thousands' and be inaccessible to
law. Because corporations could not be put in jail,
they were doing what individuals could not do.[3]
But this lifelong crusading Methodist and latter-
day Populist did not need a church audience to get
a favourable response. The next night, 5 November,
in Toronto, addressing 3,500 members of the Ontario
branch of the Retail Merchants' Association, he
was hailed as a leader, although 'whether as a
leader of thought or of a party,' as the Toronto
Globe put it, 'could only be surmised.' In a lead
editorial in the same paper, Stevens was depicted
as 'not a hero or demagogue, but a Crusader.'
Drawing on a recent survey made of Ontario weekly
newspapers, the Globe noted 'a thread of thought
indicating that the Canadian people, like Mr.
Stevens, are determined "to see the job through."'
The St. Mary's Journal seemed to sum up the situation best: 'It appears to us that Mr. Stevens'
campaign is bigger than any leader, bigger than
any political party.' The Globe concluded: 'Are
either the cabinet members or the Opposition chiefs
giving sympathetic attention to the facts that have
been brought out at the inquiry? ... The public
will not wait indefinitely for an answer.'

At least one cabinet minister was concerned. On
6 November Bob Manion sent a short letter to Stevens,
who had sent him a clipping to show that he 'had
been loyal to Bennett to the last.' 'The only thing
I can say,' replied Manion, 'is that I am sorry
about the whole show. Miss you very much and really
do not see where you and we are going from here.'[4]
The Ottawa Journal later that month also recorded
this mood of uncertainty:

145

Politicians are quick to admit that Mr. Stevens'
position at the moment is favourable with some
of the voters, but they also declare that some
of his theories on economic problems are not
practical, particularly as illustrated by the
failure of the N.R.A. in the United States. What
the politicans want to know is what Mr. Stevens
has in mind ...[5]

C.H. Cahan undoubtedly was thinking of Harry
Stevens when he told a Montreal meeting on 27 November that 'political and social propagandists,
blind leaders of the blind,' were trying to get
the federal government to exercise powers belonging
to the provinces. 'One of these [probably R.J.
Manion] to whom I recently suggested that a certain
course of action was unconstitutional made reply:
"To hell with the constitution."'[6] Speaking two
days later to an Ottawa meeting, the secretary of
state was more specific in his legal references:

Judicial opinion is to the effect that the Parliament of Canada is not vested with jurisdiction
to interfere with the management of particular
trades nor to prohibit practices in local or particular undertakings which enhance costs or profits ... Furthermore, the authority of Parliament
does not comprehend the power to regulate the
contracts of employment in industry and trade.

The press report concluded:

Before closing, in a few words addressed to the
younger men and women present, Mr. Cahan remarked
that he had seen many depressions when people
had to live on porridge and oatmeal scones and
the boys and girls grew up just as strong and
healthy as they are doing today under higher
standards. This depression will go like a mist
before the summer sun.[7]

146

Understandably, newsmen quickly sought Harry
Stevens' view of these remarks. Stevens thought
that the lawyers had 'almost invariably steered
Parliament to evade the real issue, rather than
see a means of overcoming it.' He added: 'Both Mr.
Bennett and Mr. Cahan are sticklers for the 'Solidarity of the Cabinet.' One must naturally imply
that Mr. Cahan was voicing government policy.'
Stevens feared that his remarks indicated the government intended to 'do nothing to carry out the
findings of its own Royal Commission.' It planned
to throw up 'a few legal scarecrows' and to rest
its case there, but he warned, 'The public will
not be content.'[8] On 3 December Stevens carried
the debate into Cahan's home riding, when he told
a Montreal meeting sponsored by the Quebec branch
of the Retail Merchants' Association that Parliament had more powers than it had yet used. Dismiss-
ing recurrent rumours that he was after the Conservative leadership, he declared his intention
was to propose to the Commons when it reconvened
in January that it establish a federal trade and
industries commission with 'unprecedented powers.'
It would administer an amended Combines Investigation Act, and, in much the same way as the board
of railway commissioners, would 'stand between
business and industrial associations and the public.' Stevens also promised to introduce amendments
to the Combines Act 'so as to define a monopoly
or quasi-monopoly and to permit business or industrial groups to form associations'[9] – an apparent
reference to organizations like the Retail Merchants'
Association, which had so strongly supported his
inquiry and in fact had helped him to carry it out.
   Two days later, on 5 December 1934, in Brockville,
Prime Minister Bennett ended his self-imposed ban
on his own public appearances by announcing that
he would not be retiring. He would lead the Conservative party in the next general election. As

for the Royal Commission on Price Spreads, 'it is
going on with its work, and when its report is
made the government will take such action as is
within its competence to do ... The government has
provided the money for the commission - no one else
can initiate anything that involves the expenditure
of public money.'[10] Clearly, he was answering
Stevens' Montreal speech and attempting to head
off any move on the part of his former colleague
to challenge his leadership. Bennett told a Halifax
meeting on 9 December that an unemployment insurance plan would be introduced shortly, and on 14
December he told a Toronto audience that 'beyond
question the government will come more and more to
regulate business.' The next evening, in Montreal,
he said that given a choice between socialism and
capitalism he would still prefer capitalism, which
must be regulated but not destroyed.

On 16 December 1934, Prime Minister Bennett, Sir
Robert Borden, Mackenzie King, and Chief Justice
Sir Lyman Duff were among the special guests of
the Ottawa branch of the Canadian Club. The speaker
was W.D. Herridge, Bennett's brother-in-law and
Canada's minister to Washington. In many respects
Herridge had missed his calling: he should have
followed his father into the pulpit. Dr. William
T. Herridge had been pastor of Ottawa's St. Andrew's
Presbyterian Church for 46 years; he had given his
son all the advantages of moral commitment as well
as a keen appreciation for the spoken word. Bill
Herridge also could have been a successful soldier:
he had come out of the war with the rank of major
and with an MC. He chose instead law, which soon
proved materially rewarding. The depression and
his marriage to Bennett's young sister Mildred
gave him a unique opportunity to use his skill
with words and his colourful, engaging personality.
By 1934 he had become convinced that Roosevelt's
brain trust had found the solution to the depres-

sion, and for the past few months he had been trying to persuade Bennett to launch a similar program.
His wealthy and influential friends (Harry Stevens
had never been one of them) were familiar with Bill
Herridge's religious background but they were dis-
tinctly embarrassed by his remarks this December
evening:

> If we looked more to spiritual leadership and
> less to capitalist leadership; if we made busi-
> ness less our religion and religion more our
> business; if we proclaimed by deeds the eternal
> truths of the Christian faith, we might find
> that this system did not work so badly after all ...
> I am well disposed toward capitalism ... but ...
> let us search through this system ... and see
> what is wrong ... The form is unimportant so
> long as it responds to the one true test of its
> effectiveness: the greatest good of the people
> as a whole.[11]

Had he heard this speech, Stevens would have
agreed. It struck an evangelical tone that Herridge
would repeat over the next few months during increasingly frequent letters to and meetings with
Bennett. However, on that December evening, Harry
and Gertrude were with Sylvia in Montreal, keeping
vigil as her end drew nearer. She died on 21 December. Two days later, her father wrote to Francis:

> It was very kind and thoughtful of you to write
> as you did about Sylvia. I am constantly think-
> ing of her and do miss her so much. I long for
> her, she was so human and so understanding ...
>   Two years ago on Christmas day I carried her
> down and we fixed her up in my big chair. She
> seemed to be improving. She entered into the
> spirit of Christmas so fully. There was no hint
> of being a special person at all.

We had our presents from the tree and she
smiled and was so interested. Then after about
two hours she said quietly 'I think I will go
upstairs now.' ... Francis, she was a great
soul. We will never know how wonderful she really
was, and I like to think of her now as having
her part in the great economy of heaven ...
    Sylvia was very wise and I think she saw into
the future. She was sure. It was as natural a
thing to her to pass on into a fuller and more
lovely life, as to arrive at Vancouver on a trip
from Ottawa ... I am sad, not because of Sylvia
for her memory thrills me, but because I have
made such little progress in life. I fail every
day and to such a degree that often I say to
myself that Christianity is not for me as I make
such an awful mess of it ... Get the vision of
Jesus as God's Son. Men do not believe that any
more, they are too scientific. It is the only
hope of the world, otherwise bedlam ...[12]

Christmas 1934 was grim for Harry Stevens and it
was with great difficulty that he returned to the
somewhat unreal world of politics. However, political wrangles were forgotten as MPs of all political sides extended their personal sympathies. Only
Bennett failed to do so. According to Francis
Stevens, his father mentioned Bennett's 'lack of
normal courtesy once or twice. I don't think it
preyed on him or made him bitter.' Gertrude Stevens'
reaction 'was typically feminine: she was bitter,
and never forgave Bennett.'[13] Harry, on the other
hand, may at this time have been ready to consider
a political reconciliation with his former leader,
or so it seemed from events during the first few
weeks of the new year.
    On 2 January 1935, when Stevens returned to the
price spreads commission, Ward Pitfield, a Montreal
broker, wrote Bennett of discussions he had had

with Stevens. 'In none of our conversations did
he indicate that he proposed to sever connections
with the party. He expressed determination to proceed with the work of the so-called 'Stevens Committee' and my thought is that he will do everything possible to push its activities further, to
the point of making speeches within and without
the House.'[14] Bennett's letter in reply on 8 January indicated a continued resentment against
Stevens, but on the evening of 2 January the tone
and content of the first of five national radio
broadcasts seemed to indicate that he had patched
things up with his former minister of trade and
commerce. Bennett began by explaining why he 'had
to defer reform until now.' One false step 'might
have led us to disaster.' But reform must come:

... if you believe that things should be left
as they are, you and I hold contrary and irrecon-
cilable views, for I am for reform. And in my
mind, reform means government intervention ...
government control and regulation. It means the
end of laissez-faire. There can be no permanent
recovery without reform.[15]

This was too much for the Montreal Gazette. 'The
Prime Minister has shocked and startled the Canadian
people, especially those of Conservative leaning.'
In Ottawa rumours claimed that Perley, Cahan, and
Matthews would leave the cabinet because they had
not been consulted beforehand about the broadcasts.
Stevens told reporters (including one from the
Toronto Globe) that he welcomed the speech as being
'recognition of the existence of problems to be
confronted' and hoped to continue a useful and
active member of the Tory party.
    As Bennett's amazing words resounded across the
nation during the next week, it must have seemed
that Stevens had rejoined the cabinet. Bennett

151

called for a better tax plan to end the inequality
of incomes, a uniform wage, a maximum work week,
the abolition of child labour and sweatshop conditions, a permanent system of 'sound and scientific
unemployment insurance,' new health and accident
insurance, and a new old age pension. He also promised a bill to 'protect producers against monopo-
listic purchases and certain types of middlemen
who are economic parasites.' Another bill would
extend the Dominion Farm Loan Act and still another
would establish an economic council 'to investigate
and advise on matters of economic account.' All
this sounded like Harry Stevens, but he was not
the author any more than Bennett. The Press Gallery
knew that it was Herridge:

> The voice on the radio is the voice of Bennett
> but the hand that writes the speeches is the
> hand of Herridge ... Rod Finlayson is the adju-
> tant-general while Herridge is the Prime Minis-
> ter's chief of staff. He digs up the raw mate-
> rial ... and is consulted more ... than any mem-
> ber of the cabinet.[16]

Finlayson later revealed that he and Herridge drew
up Bennett's New Deal in the summer of 1934 while
the prime minister was in Europe, and that Herridge
had spelled out the program in a series of long
personal letters to his brother-in-law. In his
broadcasts Bennett used phrases and sometimes entire
paragraphs from this correspondence without changing
a word.[17]
On 10 January, the day before the fifth and final
broadcast, Warren Cook wrote to Stevens from Toronto
about possibilities for action on this new program:

> Supposing that the most influential factions of
> the younger and more modern sections of the party
> were to make representation to Mr. Herridge ...

152

who has perhaps more influence than anyone else
with the P.M. ... suggesting that the P.M. carry
through his Recovery Program at the present
session, implementing as much of his legislation
as possible in the name of the Conservative Party.

If this suggestion were followed, Cook reasoned,
at the proper time Bennett should resign and go
to the House of Lords, 'calling upon you to carry
on.' In this way, 'the Party would be vindicated,
he would go out in a blaze of glory, his brother-
in-law's ambitions would be satisfied and the country would be saved.' Stevens replied on 12 January
that he could see no hope of a reconciliation
because 'the gentleman to whom we are both referring
is so vain that he does not react at all favourably
to that sort of course.'[18]
On 14 January, Stevens took time out from the
price spreads inquiry to tell a Montreal service
club that a federal commission of industry and
commerce should be established 'to administer all
laws pertaining to these matters.' What was wrong
he declared, and the Gazette reported, was 'not
so much over-production as under-consumption. The
inability to buy, that is the problem.' On the
next night, the eve of the resumption of Parliament,
8,000 people jammed into Montreal's Atwater Market
to hear Bennett declare that he had no desire to
wreck the capitalistic system; he only wished 'to
make it decent and clean ... Mergers and combines
had destroyed the market place and it exists no
longer.'
On the following afternoon, 16 January, in the
House of Commons, Harry Stevens took a seat in the
front rank on the government side, indicating to
at least Marchington of the Globe 'that he is still
a Conservative in good standing.' If ever there
was a time for reconciliation, it was now - the
last parliament before a general election. A major

153

effort towards it was underway. Bob Manion and
Stevens' successor in the cabinet, R.B. Hanson,
were chosen as mediators because they 'had been in
the past pretty good friends of Stevens.' On 14
February they reported to Bennett that they had
found their former colleague 'willing to cooperate
with the rest of the [price spreads] committee'
on its forthcoming report and that 'his whole
demeanor was one of conciliation,' except that he
was still quite bitter toward Cahan. A short time
later Bennett and Stevens met, and the latter
agreed to outline his ideas in writing. He wrote
promptly, on 25 February, that he was expressing
his views 'as though I were writing them to a close
and fast friend, and for that reason I know that
you will consider them in the light of staunch
amity. Otherwise you and I shall fight on the hustings of country against each other, John L. Sullivan
style.' Stevens 'yielded to nobody in Canada' in
his knowledge of economic problems, but he was
'always ready and glad to discuss them with an
open mind with people who are competent to do so.'
The rest of his letter dealt in great detail with
international finance and a solution to the depression based upon 'a currency stabilization agreement
between the principal exporting nations.'[19]
  Bennett apparently did not reply. A few days
later he was confined to his suite in the Chateau
Laurier with a respiratory infection. His sister
Mildred rushed up from Washington, but Herridge
remained behind. As Finlayson later explained it,
Herridge was as much in Bennett's 'black book' as
Stevens. Shortly after the New Deal broadcasts the
trio had been in Bennett's office preparing the
throne speech. Finlayson had put into the draft a
vague promise, 'in keeping with the spirit of the
New Deal,' that legislation would be introduced
placing hydroelectric power under public ownership.   Bennett objected strongly, complaining:

154

'Oh, leave me alone. I'll write this speech myself.'
Herridge testily replied: 'You couldn't write a
speech; Finlayson and I prepared all your throne
speeches.' Bennett thereupon turned his back on
Herridge, left the room with Finlayson, and refused
to speak to his brother-in-law for several weeks.[20]
It is difficult to escape the conclusion that he
remained incommunicado in his hotel suite, from
about 27 February to 18 April, because he was sulk-
ing in his tent, angry at the world and convinced
that only he had the ability to lead and to make
decisions. Ironically, the decision he really wanted
to make was to quit politics and retire to England.
As he later told his old friend Max Aitken, he
would have resigned in 1934 'but Stevens' action
made that impossible.'[21] Did he have a forlorn
hope that the gathering support for Stevens within
the Conservative party would die away? Only his
ego and his love of office seemed to prevent him
from deciding on retirement.

Herridge was familiar with Bennett's piques and
continued to write long letters as if nothing had
happened. On 8 March 1935 he talked 'about Harry
Stevens' and his essential part in any movement of
reform:

> You are the leader of a movement which has the
> power, if it has the will, to safely guide this
> country through the coming perilous years. This
> movement stands for progress, for the better
> functioning of the capitalistic system, for a
> fairer distribution of its benefits, for social
> justice, for fuller individual liberty ... Stevens
> is naturally and necessarily a part of this
> movement. His support of you will ensure its
> success. His defection may well shatter it ...
> What then remains but to accept him and use him
> as an integral part of this movement ... I pro-
> pose myself as the one who can talk to Stevens

155

and may be able to adjust this tragically foolish situation.[22]

Herridge's offer to attempt reconciliation was to no avail. The days stretched into weeks and Herridge gradually lost hope, not only for a reconciliation but for his New Deal. By the end of March he wrote to Manion that 'the colour has faded from the reform picture. The promise of performance is gone.' Manion had become just as gloomy, noting on 11 March in one of his regular letters to his son James that Stevens was 'still making speeches' - not critical ones but embarrassing. 'If R.B. dropped out, there would be a majority demand that Stevens be put in as leader. This would certainly be a queer turn of the wheel of fate if a man who really deserted his colleagues and more or less betrayed them without any just reason that I know should receive that reward.'[23]

Manion's bitterness and frustration were understandable, especially since he felt that his Roman Catholicism effectively barred him from the leadership. But Harry Stevens had not really betrayed the party. Since the current session had begun, he had not made a single Commons speech, probably because it could have been used by Mackenzie King. Rather, Stevens was playing a waiting game, attempting to influence the other ten members of the Royal Commission on Price Spreads so that the report now in preparation would contain strong recommendations. It was true, as Manion stated, that he was 'making speeches,' but outside the House. On 20 February, at a Toronto meeting jointly sponsored by the Retail Merchants' Association and the Ontario Retail Lumber Dealers' Association, he had outlined the structure of a possible federal commission of industry and commerce and a federal mortgage loan corporation to provide credit for 'a gigantic national building and rehousing program.' Two weeks later he had told a meeting of the Hamilton Advertising Club that the businessmen's main task was 'to restore industry to the control of practical men who understood' it. The history of amalgamation during the twenties 'was that of monumental incompetence, not one single merger having made earnings equal to the claims in the prospectus in which it was floated.' And he added: 'Thank heaven I am not hampered by the restrictions placed on my lips several months ago, although I admit it was of my own choice then.' On 10 March, the day before Manion's letter to his son, Stevens gave a nationwide broadcast, sponsored by the Canadian Federation of Youth. Urging 'commonsense amendments to existing laws and then a fearless enforcement,' Stevens said Canada had laws 'with holes big enough for millionaires to crawl through and company laws that permitted the fleecing of the public on the one hand and sweatshops on the other.'[24]

What did the public think of it all? Mail continued to pour in; the full-time secretary Stevens had hired after his resignation from the cabinet, Harold E. Betts, made a careful survey of the views expressed in over 400 letters received up to 1 March 1935. Retailers were the most responsive and enthusiastic. But few endorsed the editorial suggestion of the Simcoe Reformer that Stevens had no alternative 'but to start a new group of his own.' On 15 March, apparently to exert pressure on his own party as well as on the other members of the price spreads commission, he gave to the Ottawa Journal a summary of his recommendations 'for establishing fair and just practices in the marketing and distribution systems.' He would abolish all discounts, rebates, and allowances over 5 per cent, apply dumping duties in domestic trade to overcome special prices to mass buyers, and amend the income tax regulations to compel holding companies to pay tax on the earnings of individual

157

units instead of upon a consolidated balance sheet.
In a second Ottawa _Journal_ instalment the next day,
Stevens recommended a fixed profit level for corporations, with everything over that level to be
divided equally among the state, the employers, and
the employees.[25] Profit levels would be regulated
by a new federal trade commission, which would also
administer the Combines Investigation Act, the
Meat and Canned Food Act, the Food and Drugs Act,
the Proprietary or Patent Medicine Act, and, finally,
a revised Weights and Measures Act.

What did the other commissioners think of their
colleague's recommendations? William Marchington
wrote in his _Globe_ column of 16 March that 'a majority of the members favoured them except for
Stevens' 'share-the-profits' scheme.' And the Conservative voice in Toronto, the _Mail and Empire_,
reported on 21 March that the Tory members of the
commission 'were prepared to go a long way to meet
the former minister's views.' The Liberal members,
on the other hand, while 'agreeing with the principles set forth, differed with him on important
details.' On 15 March, Mackenzie King, who had
been needling the government about tabling the
report of the Royal Commission on Price Spreads,
read out the headlines from the Ottawa _Journal_ to
the House, and then directed a question to C.H.
Cahan, who 'apparently is leading the House at the
moment.' Did the government regard this commission
as a judicial body or a publicity bureau? Cahan
thought it was generally agreed it was a 'quasi-
judicial body' but 'it would appear that there are
bureaux of publicity outside ... from which reports
are emanating to the public press.' King obviously
was hoping to provoke Cahan into launching a verbal
assault against Stevens. A few minutes before this
exchange, Cahan and Stevens had had a lengthy
although restrained debate in the House on the
legality of a minimum wage resolution, during which

Cahan seemed to have reversed his position of a
few months earlier that the Canadian parliament
had no jurisdiction over wage legislation. Stevens,
with his wide practical knowledge of the law, expressed his view that 'parliament has failed to
occupy the field properly given to it by the British
North America Act,' namely trade and commerce.
There would 'be no challenge to its right at the
present time,' had Parliament 'twenty or ... fifty
years ago set itself to the task of reasonable regulation of trade within Canada.'[26]

As the spring session dragged on, with no sign
of Bennett's return, King continued to play the
devil's advocate, but of greater importance was
the growing support for Stevens among Tory back-
benchers. On 2 April Brigadier-General A.E. Ross,
in a speech accepting re-nomination as Conservative
candidate for Kingston-Portsmouth, said he supported Bennett's reform program but in the same
breath named Stevens 'as the founder or father of
these reformers.' 'Some think Stevens will withdraw
and start another political movement, but he won't,'
Ross assured the Kingston Tories. The Globe commented that this speech was the first time any Conservative MP 'has publicly linked Bennett and Stevens
as reform leaders and publicly declared himself
a supporter of both'; this 'militant and somewhat
independent-sitting man,' the Globe thought, had
'started something. He has virtually told the Prime
Minister to get Stevens back if he wishes [Kingston-
Portsmouth] support. In case his action is widely
copied at other Conservative conventions, Mr.
Bennett will have no alternative.'[27]

Bennett was still absent from the House on 12
April, a day when Harry Stevens dominated the debate. Mackenzie King had given him the excuse the
day before when he had implied that Stevens had
been responsible for still another press leak on
the price spreads report. Stevens had freely admit-

ted his responsibility for the reports that had
appeared the week before, but contended that he
had not violated his commissioner's oath or contra-
vened the Inquiries Act. The wily Liberal leader
had then referred to the study club pamphlet and
the circumstances surrounding Stevens' resignation,
and now, after asking the House's indulgence,
Stevens proceeded to give his side of that story.
He had no apologies to make to anyone. 'To whom
have I been unfair?' According to his accusers,
he had been unfair to J.S. McLean, Sir Joseph
Flavelle, the Robert Simpson Company, the T. Eaton
Company, the National Fish Company, 'as well as
to some others.'

> Has anyone during the last fifteen months ...
> charged me with being unfair to the workers, to
> the farmers, to the growers of vegetables and
> fruits, to the small merchants ... or to the
> cattlemen who appeared before the Committee? If
> anybody is prepared to point out a single instance
> where I failed to give fair treatment to him,
> then I should be alarmed and ready to make amends.
> But these, sir, are not my accusers. The accuser,
> in regard to the quotation read a moment ago, was
> Mr. Burton of the Robert Simpson Company ...

Stevens adamantly defended the pamphlet, both its
content and the fact that it had been given wide
circulation. He admitted misunderstanding between
Bennett and himself, but said he had resigned from
the cabinet because 'I felt it was desirable that
the chairman of the Commission should be in harmony
with the views of the government' and after his
study club speech and Bennett's reaction to it,
they no longer shared that harmony. Certainly he
had made speeches 'regarding the work being carried
on in the Price Spreads Committee' but he had made
them purposely. 'I knew very well that as a general

160

rule matters of this kind referred to a committee
of the House of Commons were born to die, and I
made up my mind that it would not die. And it did
not die ...' The resultant publicity had done something 'to mould public opinion' along the lines he
had suggested for remedial courses.

There are viewpoints that are widely divergent.
I respect their views but I hold tenaciously to
my own and I refuse at any time, as I have always
done for the twenty-four years I have been in this
House, to be a mere rubber stamp; if I have views,
I will express them ... No, I have no apologies
to make ... I may have made mistakes, but I certainly have tried to do my duty as fearlessly
and as frankly as I could do it.[28]

As he took his seat, desks were thumped and his
colleagues 'cheered him to the echo.'[29]
    After five long depression-ridden years the Con-
servative administration was being challenged to
seize an opportunity triumphantly. But its reactionary forces refused to budge. Their representative
was C.H. Cahan, known in parliamentary circles as
'Dino,' short for dinosaur.[30] Slightly stooped,
Atlas fashion, with a look of disdain on a face
touched off with a trim white goatee, Cahan spoke
in the measured, heavy terms of the successful
corporation lawyer that he was. Harry Stevens was
a bantam by comparison, a Cockney beside Poobah.
His friendly, smooth-shaven face, his quick, penetrating gaze, and his rapid but precise manner
of delivery suggested a fighter. Stevens had spent
most of his first nineteen years in Parliament
defending the order Cahan represented, but his
colleagues had been seeing a new Stevens in the
past fifteen months. Spurred on by the public interest aroused by his Toronto shoe convention speech,
exhilarated by the crusader's role he had assumed

161

in the price spreads inquiry, and to some extent
martyred by his resignation, Stevens now stood
firmly on the side of the common man, speaking
for those average Canadians who had voted Tory in
1930. He watched intently as 'Dino' slowly rose
in the House to make a brief statement.

In the absence of the prime minister, the Hon.
Member for St. Lawrence - St. George wished to
read his leader's letter of 26 October 1934, replying to Stevens' letter of resignation. No sooner
had Cahan done so than Stevens was back on his feet,
a letter in his hand. Into the parliamentary records
went his long letter of 30 October to Bennett,
stressing that his pamphlet had only dealt with
evidence that 'had already been exhaustively reported and reviewed in the press.' He could not
make a public apology after he had been 'publicly
spanked in the press' - a pointed reference to the
Ottawa Citizen's detailed account, supplied by
Cahan, of the cabinet meeting of 25 October. At
this point Stevens was ruled out of order, but
when the ruling was put to the House he was urged
to continue, and went on to tell the story he had
told to the Conservative study club concerning
Simpson's and General Steelwares. Then he sat
down once more, only to get back on his feet again
after Hanson, the minister of trade and commerce,
tabled the long-awaited report and evidence of the
Royal Commission on Price Spreads. Stevens moved
the report's adoption, a privilege traditionally
reserved for the chairman of the commission. No
one seconded his motion and it remained on the
Commons order paper for another six weeks.

The next speaker, J.A. Fraser, the Conservative
member for Cariboo, wished to present a petition
signed by about '30,000 retail merchants, praying
for the creation of a fair trade board ... to function
under continuous federal government supervision and
control, [and] to adopt and maintain fair trade

practices throughout Canada.'³¹ This board, urged
by Stevens over the past weeks and months, was
among the recommendations in the 500-page price
spreads report. As he must have known, the Fraser
petition was the direct result of the 30 March
edition of the monthly bulletin of the Retail
Merchants' Association, which had requested its
members to give their complete backing to Stevens
and his reform program. Here was further evidence
of the widespread support that Stevens' campaign
had engendered. And he had many friends in the
Commons too, as Manion indicated to his son, although
they were concerned about party unity:

> Our crowd cheered Stevens, as against Cahan,
> though unfortunately Stevens' action was a little
> like tearing open R.B.'s wounds and pouring in
> acid. Had Stevens refused to discuss the Prime
> Minister and merely gone after Cahan, he would
> have come off in splendid shape. As it is, it
> makes it a little more difficult to know what
> the final working out will be.³²

The wounds to Bennett's ego probably remained
open, but his physical health had nevertheless
improved. Two days after the Stevens-Cahan clash,
the prime minister left his hotel suite and returned
to the Commons, where he received a warm welcome
from all the Tories except Stevens, who sat silent-
ly at his desk. Bennett then adjourned the House
for a long Easter recess, and, accompanied by Dana
Wilgress and Lester Pearson, set sail for London
to attend the Silver Jubilee celebrations, where
Pearson would receive the OBE from King George V
for his work as secretary of the Royal Commission
on Price Spreads.

Harry Stevens was not looking for an OBE. He
wanted legislation implementing the commission's
recommendations, which closely followed his own

well-publicized views. The report called for a
federal trade and industry commission, and even
endorsed his controversial profit-sharing plan and
unit taxation of multiple-unit organizations - at
least to the extent of saying that they were 'worthy
of investigation' by the proposed commission among
the possible methods to regulate monopolies. The
three Liberal MPs in their 'Memorandum of Reserva-
tions' dealt with the sticky question of constitutionality by suggesting that the proposed trade
and industry commission be referred 'to more competent authorities in the belief that what is necessary from the point of view of economic and social
policy' could and would 'be made constitutionally
possible.'[33]   They themselves did not question the
legality of the proposed commission but they thought
others would. To emphasize their point, obviously
for Stevens' edification, they recalled the fate
of the Board of Commerce Act and the Combines and
Fair Prices Act, passed in 1919 upon the recommen-
dation of the parliamentary inquiry into wartime
price increases, of which Stevens had been co-chair-
man. These acts had been declared <u>ultra vires</u> and
so the Liberals recommended that the trade commission be cleared 'by the proper authorities.'
    The more immediate question of whether the govern-
ment would implement the recommendations could not
be answered until the prime minister returned from
England. While the royal festivities were being
held in London, more ominous events were happening
back home. In Montreal, Mayor Houde was telling
thousands of idle citizens that they had two alter-
natives: remain in the city and run the risk of
becoming involved with communists or return to the
land. In Toronto, Premier Hepburn announced on 25
April that his government would provide 20,000 new
mattresses for those on relief. The next day forty
children from Welland marched on Queen's Park,
shouting 'We want bread.' Hepburn ordered their

parents to take them home or be charged under the truancy regulations. The situation was even more explosive in Stevens' home town of Vancouver. On 24 April more than 2,000 men from provincial labour camps gathered in the city, demanding jobs and better living conditions. Suddenly they stormed up Granville Street and on to Hastings. Employees at Spencer's department store saw them coming and hurriedly locked the doors. The mob swept by to the Hudson's Bay store; hundreds of angry men charged through its open doors and smashed everything in sight. Police finally gained the upper hand, but not before Mayor Gerry McGeer read the riot act from the steps of the city hall. A few days later McGeer and another 'famous son' received further publicity. C.L. Burton, president of the Robert Simpson Company, told a meeting of Vancouver businessmen that there were 'too many Harry's and Gerry's who are damaging our credit and not giving the businessman a chance ... They were worms raising their heads to crawl about, leaving a slimy trail behind them that was putrefying and destroying the country.' 'Gangsters,' 'racketeers,' and 'bloody liars' were other terms he used, and although they were not linked with the names of individuals, the Vancouver newspaper account added: 'There was no doubt in the minds of those present to whom he was referring.'

Burton was more specific when he talked about the price spreads commission, the main topic of his speech. He said that statements before the commission could have been refuted by Simpson's if it had been given the opportunity. He claimed that Stevens had dominated the inquiry and had brought out only the evidence he desired. 'No shareholder, employee or customer of Simpson's had come forward to testify against any action of the company.' Furthermore, some of Stevens' statements were 'libellous.' Burton would have sued long ago 'had

it not been for the fact that it would make a
martyr of [Stevens].' Two of Stevens' friends
among Burton's audience immediately sent him clippings of the speech and urged him to sue, but he
would not do so.[34] He had more pressing problems
to face. As a Globe editorial put it: 'Who is to
go? Cahan or Stevens?' It also summarized the views
of other newspapers. The Windsor Border Cities
Star thought that an important segment of the Conservative party 'wanted Stevens back in the cabinet,
and if necessary, Cahan had to get out.' According
to the Brantford Expositor, 'the people admire an
outspoken man'; the Sydney Post Record said that
'Stevens has stolen the show and wants to speedily
carry out the will of the people.'[35]

Stevens' heavy mail continued to reflect broad
public support. A letter from A.R. Mosher, president of the Canadian Brotherhood of Railway Employees, outlined the hardships being caused by the
CNR's efficiency campaign, and Stevens immediately
wrote to Manion, the minister of railways and
canals, who promised to talk with CNR officials
'at once.' A railwayman from St. Mary's, Ontario,
wrote that he and his fellow workers were 'looking
to you to carry the party to victory as they are
satisfied you will do all possible to give a square
deal.' A doctor from Smiths Falls who had been an
active Tory wrote that 'if it should so happen
that you should be chosen leader, I would be more
inclined to enter the fray.' Stevens replied that
he hoped the government would pass legislation
'to make the Commission report really effective'
and he told a New Zealand correspondent that while
he wanted to support Bennett, he would do so 'only
if he comes through 100 per cent.'

On 10 May, as Bennett was about to leave London
for home, Stevens told a Toronto meeting of accountants that 50 per cent of the nation's commercial
and industrial wealth was in the hands of twelve

men, and he could 'name every company they were
in.' He predicted Canada was heading for rule by
'a super-financial or Fascist state or a destructive
revolution unless something was done to stop this
concentration of wealth.'[36] He probably was using
as his source a monthly called The Instructor,
published by Dr. W.L. Goodwin and the Community
Study Club of Ste Anne de Bellevue, Quebec. The
November 1934 issue had been sent to Stevens asking
him to investigate the price spread maintained by
a 'Power monopoly.' It listed the names of some of
Canada's best-known businessmen, including Sir
Herbert Holt, its wealthiest citizen, Sir Charles
Gordon, president of Dominion Textiles, and R.B.
Bennett, who 'owns 51 percent of the Eddy Company
and is also one of the largest stockholders of the
Royal Bank.'[37] Even though Stevens in his Toronto
speech did not name any of the twelve, the Globe
thought he was 'an outstanding man unafraid to
say what he thinks.' By way of a rebuttal, C.H.
Cahan assured a Montreal meeting that 'ninety per
cent of big business is handled honestly and businessmen do not deserve recent unjust and unveiled
denunciations.' On 13 May, while Bennett was on
the high seas, Stevens attended a nominating rally
in Windsor in support of Dr. Raymond Morand, deputy
speaker and member for Essex East. Stevens repeated
his charge that the nation's wealth was in the hands
of a 'half dozen or so'; another speaker, Eccles
Gott, member for Essex South, told the rally he
was 'for Stevens because Stevens is for Bennett,
and Stevens and Bennett are for Canada.' The
Border Cities Star noted that Stevens in his Windsor
speech had made no reference to his own position
in the party and the Globe editorial thought that
although Stevens remained loyal to it, 'the Stevens
problem would confront Bennett on his return.' Or
as Manion put it, Stevens' support was so great
'with the masses and the asses' that 'we could not

count on winning' without him. 'Harry must be taken in, or at least' Bennett had to agree to 'some arrangements whereby he will follow.'[38]

Bennett's first press statement when he landed at Quebec City on 17 May only added to the uncertainty. He would 'test his strength and then decide on his course.' If he was unable 'to carry on, a new leader will be chosen.'[39] This remark was in answer to questions about his physical health, but it could have applied more accurately to Stevens' strength in the caucus. When Parliament reconvened three days later, Bennett seemed very much the captain of the Tory ship and he soon made it clear that he planned to introduce legislation implementing both the price spreads report and the New Deal broadcasts. Herridge was firmly opposed to this strategy, arguing in a letter to Manion that 'parliament should dissolve and we should go to the country for a mandate to implement that report.' Now he feared the worst. 'The Price Spreads legislation will be emasculated. The Housing bill will lack utterly political significance, the public works bill will be laughed out of court.' He told Manion as his 'close friend' that he would not 'sit by and see my conception of what should rightly be done at this time wrecked because of prejudices and disabilities which have no rightful place in government or in the personnel comprising a government.'[40]

If one judges by his public speeches at the time, Harry Stevens had the same fears about the new legislation, but, in contrast to Herridge, he thought it should be introduced immediately. He continued his silence in the House of Commons as Guthrie, the minister of justice, introduced on 23 May three New Deal measures, but he made a mental note of Guthrie's bald admission that three proposed amendments to the Criminal Code might be in 'some constitutional doubt.'[41] Outside the House, Stevens

told reporters that in his view 'these reform bills
are inadequate.' He had 'no patience with this
government's attitude of waiting for legal opinions.'[42] Three days later, in Washington, one of
the mainstays of the original New Deal, the National
Recovery Act, was declared unconstitutional by
the United States Supreme Court. 'Extraordinary
conditions do not create or enlarge constitutional
powers.' Within a week President Roosevelt was to
state that he would amend the NRA so that it would
be legal. The Canadian government remained silent
and continued to unveil its own New Deal legislation.

On 28 May, Stevens broke his Commons silence by
disagreeing with Cahan over amendments to the
Patent Act. Yet he also did his utmost to sound a
note of conciliation: 'If there is any language
that I can use that would disabuse the mind of
the Secretary of State of the thought that there
is any desire on my part to embarrass either him
or the government or to delay the committee, I
should be very glad to use that language.'[43] He
added that he 'was not placing any blame upon the
government' but 'if this bill is pushed through
without notice being taken of these facts, then
those who are responsible' must take the consequences 'for what injustice may have been done.'
When the bill came up for second reading a few
days later, Bennett supported Cahan - a move which
prompted a Globe reporter to suggest that the
Bennett-Stevens 'gulf was widening.' Manion gave
a similar impression in a letter to his son, as
well as frustration over Bennett's refusal to discuss election plans. 'Most of the chaps in Council
do not pass any opinion on anything, and a number
of them are just waiting to get jobs before dissolution.' As for Bennett, 'he is so bitter towards
Stevens that that beclouds every thought.' He still
had not said definitely that he would lead the
party in the next election and Manion predicted

that he would 'stay until the end of the session,
then withdraw and permit caucus to choose his successor.' If that happened, Manion thought the most
likely choice would be Harry Stevens. 'There are
three or four very strong Stevens men - notably
Dr. Morand - who are carrying on a regular campaign
for him. He and I are still good friends and I
imagine that if he is chosen he will want me to do
a good deal of the fighting for him.'[44]

Manion's continued friendship with Stevens may
have been the reason for a remarkable exchange
that took place in the House on 5 June, the day
after Bennett had supported Cahan on the Patent
bill. Manion had just taken to task Donald
Sutherland, the minister of defence, for charging
that not enough ex-servicemen were employed by
the Montreal Harbour Commission, which was under
Manion's jurisdiction as minister of railways and
canals. Hansard did not record the next exchange
but it was loud enough for others to hear it and
pass it on to the press:

> Bennett: How dare you make a fool of the govern-
> ment that way. If you had told me I would have
> stopped you. You have no right to make such a
> statement.
> Manion: I have every right to make such a state-
> ment. I am not taking orders from you or anybody
> else when I am making a personal explanation.
> Bennett: If you had told me I would not have
> permitted it.
> Manion: I would have done it anyway.
> Bennett: And you would have been out of the cab-
> inet tonight.
> Manion: You can have my resignation anytime.[45]

According to Anderson, the editor of the Globe,
'It may have been a tempest in a tea cup ... but
so many tea cups are sizzling here in Ottawa.'

170

Bennett and Manion had had sharp exchanges before, albeit in less public places, and they had left no bitterness. Harry Stevens was another matter as far as Bennett was concerned.

One can imagine the anger of 'the Chief' when he read of Stevens' public speech on 5 June before an audience of 3,000 in Toronto's Massey Hall. They had turned out in response to a challenge by George Hougham, the Ontario secretary of the Retail Merchants' Association, who had demanded a show of support for Stevens. Stevens was in top form, criticizing the federal trade and industry bill introduced earlier that day. He objected strongly to the government's declared intention to place the proposed trade and industry commission under the Tariff Board, which he thought had too much to do already. Chairman Hougham denied Ottawa reports that the Association had been petitioning MPs to persuade Stevens to form a new party. 'For the moment, we are not concerned with political parties ... Stevens is the man who stands behind our principles rather than behind parties.' The next day Stevens declared that a report in the Toronto Mail and Empire about his leading a third party stemmed from that Conservative newspaper's 'campaign to discredit' him. He did not comment on a Financial Post story predicting a bitter debate in the Commons between himself and Bennett.

A clash seemed inevitable, but Stevens was working hard behind the scenes, partly to avoid it and partly to strengthen his support in the caucus. On 10 June he wrote a long letter to his cabinet successor, R.B. Hanson, outlining his suggestions for a federal grain board. Bennett had already placed a notice of motion to create such a board on the order paper. Stevens' letter concluded: 'I submit these suggestions in this way because I do not wish to openly discuss them on the floor of the House or embarrass the government in what is at present a very serious position for them.'[46]

171

Stevens faced a serious dilemma himself. Undoubtedly he was being pressured by people outside the Conservative party, people such as Warren K. Cook, George Hougham, and unknown correspondents, all urging him to form a new party. At the same time, Dr. R.D. Morand, Frank White, General Ross, C. W. Bell, and Tommy Church - to name some of the Tory back-benchers who had spoken out for him - were urging him to wait Bennett out. What better chance to make the Conservative party a truly democratic and reform party. He had come far, endured much, and finally had gained a hearing from that 'average Canadian.' Unfortunately, the initiative remained with Bennett, who continued to sit, 'dog in the manger,' refusing to declare his intentions about retiring or leading the party in the next election, now less than six months away.

At length, however, Bennett made his move. Shortly after he had sent his letter of 10 June to Hanson, Stevens was barred from attending caucus upon Bennett's explicit instructions.[47] An open clash came on 19 June when Stevens rose to speak during the third reading of the bill establishing the trade and industry commission. As he did so, Cahan immediately left the chamber, to be followed shortly after by Hanson and Perley. Bennett remained, sitting as he so often did these days, his head on his hands, now and then taking notes.[48] His head jerked up to attention when Stevens announced that he wished 'to express some views in connection with the manner in which the report of the Price Spreads Committee and Commission has been implemented.'[49]

... I am going to speak for the moment as a member of the Conservative party ... I was elected as a Conservative, and I take it that the very essence of the economic policy of the Conservative party is to be found in what is known as the national policy ... I wish to say, sir, that in

holding the views I do now, in light of the
studies revealed in this report, I am not depart-
ing one iota from the economic principles of the
Conservative party.

Reading from a speech by Sir John A. Macdonald,
Stevens urged that the National Policy was not 'for
the creation of monopolies or for the creation of
powerful corporations to operate without law and
with a selfish disregard for the rights of others.'
The price spreads investigation had demonstrated
how 'these great industrial organizations have
developed,' defying government as well as competition and achieving their power not through efficiency but by 'the power of massed capital.' He
made a detailed analysis of Bennett's New Deal
broadcasts, reading out some of the more spectacular
parts and signifying his agreement. He paid particular attention to Bennett's reference to the price
spreads commission, which had been appointed to go
into the whole question 'of the exploitation of the
defenceless primary producer and equally defenceless
ultimate consumer.' But, asked Stevens, 'Will any
one say that by the wildest stretch of the imagin-
ation the bill to amend the livestock act is in
any remote degree a correction of what were found
to be exploitations of the defenceless producer?'
As for the amendments to the Companies Act, they
were weakened by Cahan's qualifying statements
made when he introduced the bill. The bill now
before the House, regarded as the most important
of the New Deal legislation, Stevens said was
'drafted and confined to the narrowest interpretation of constitutional law.' Anticipating the
argument that the question of jurisdiction should
be left to the courts, Stevens had claimed this
recourse was both futile and weak. 'Private citizens
cannot possibly appeal to the courts against great
corporations. It cannot be done, and it will not

be done.' What was needed was a new set of rules, to be laid down by the House of Commons, rules to govern 'an entirely new method of trading ...; yet we are unprepared to meet it by reason of the fact that no use has ever been made of the power conferred upon the dominion parliament.' He ended on June 19 with these words:

> I admit the force of the argument that we must not invade provincial rights; no man has ever heard me advocate that but ... if parliament is to be handcuffed by the British North America Act, in heaven's name let us at least attempt to unravel that problem. But we have not done much in regard to it. We have been drugged into quiescence by a few ill-considered bills that were damned when they were introduced by those who introduced them.

As he sat down, the scattered applause came mostly from the Liberal benches.[50]

Now it was Bennett's turn. As he began to speak, Cahan, Perley, and Hanson quickly resumed their places. From his first words Bennett made it clear that he intended to deliver a lecture on constitutional law.[51]

> Mr. Speaker, in 1867 the provinces were united together under a statute known as the British North America Act. This constitutes the constitution of the Dominion of Canada. It contemplated a federal, not a legislative union. Under the provisions of that statute, whether we like it or not, we are bound until such time as the statute has been changed, by proper authority.

Next he referred to a select committee of the House, set up in 1919 to investigate charges that excessive profits had been made on foodstuffs, clothing,

fuel, and 'other necessities of life.' Its vice-
chairman 'was the Honourable Member who has just
taken his seat.' One of its recommendations had
been to establish a board of commerce to regulate
trade practices and to advise on 'questions of
policy where trade tends to combinations and restrictions.' Subsequently, Prime Minister Meighen had
introduced two bills, but within a year the Privy
Council had declared that 'both of them were bad.'
As for the recent price spreads report, Bennett had
thought that the commission would at least have
recommended legislation that it knew could be dealt
with by Parliament and that 'it would at least
take some cognizance of the report made in 1919'
and of the fate of the subsequent legislation. He
admitted that the constitution needed changing,
but reform could not be done in a single day. The
recent judgment declaring the NRA unconstitutional
had its 'relevancy' in Canada. After quoting from
some of Stevens' speeches, Bennett continued:

> The first step towards dictatorship in Europe was
> ... a prejudicial appeal to the little man ... Then
> followed the inevitable utter disregard of con-
> stitutional limitations ... In the end, if we
> are a law-abiding people who believe in reform
> and not in revolution, we must proceed precept
> by precept, line upon line, to the end that in
> an orderly and legal manner we may accomplish
> the ends we have in mind ...

The applause was loud and long. As one reporter
observed, 'the boom for Stevens was in eclipse.'
That evening the Conservative caucus held a dinner
for Bennett and heard him declare that he would
lead the party in the next election. Of course
Harry Stevens was not there, but neither was Manion.
Bennett had sent him out to Regina to deal with
relief camp strikers who had been moving eastward

175

from British Columbia. They had planned 'A March
on Ottawa' to demand government action. Bennett
had ordered the RCMP to stop them at Regina and
then dispatched Manion and Weir, the minister of
agriculture, to arrange for the strike leaders to
meet with him in Ottawa. Did Bennett have another
motive for sending Manion out of Ottawa at this
critical juncture in the party's history? If he
had been in the House on 19 June, would Manion
have spoken up for Stevens? Bennett might have
thought so, but the action was unlikely, judging
from Manion's views expressed in a letter to his
son two days later:

> There was a dinner to the chief by the party, at
> which dinner he announced his retention of the
> leadership. Rather strangely, the day of the
> dinner he and Stevens crossed swords in the House
> and I think ... Stevens came off very much second
> best and the Chief got all the cheers, while
> poor old Stevens at the moment seems to be out
> on the end of a limb. However, it would appear
> that he has burned the bridges and that whatever
> we do in the election will be without Stevens'
> help. I had sincerely hoped, had the chief de-
> cided to stay on, that I might have got Stevens
> in behind us ... Unfortunately Stevens has a
> pretty heavy following among the masses. It does
> not improve our chances of success ...[52]

What was left now for Harry Stevens? His price
spreads inquiry had revealed the evils of the economic system, but the old guard had stood firm
against the necessary changes. Tory back-benchers
also had remained silent - not one had dared to
challenge party discipline and speak out at the
crucial moment in support of Stevens. All those
weeks and months of turmoil, heartache, and finally
of dashed hopes! But he could not and indeed would

not forget those thousands of 'little' Canadians.
He had reached them; he had done his duty both to
them and to his own conscience; and they in turn
continued to express their gratitude, respect, and
encouragement. 'You will never know how much the
public wholly approves your attitude. The impression
is that you are an honest man who will never be
swayed by offers of money nor flowery speeches.'
'The people are fed up with both parties,' wrote
a Nova Scotia man. 'Head a new reform party and
I am sure you would get both Liberals and Conservatives.' In the opinion of a Winnipeg doctor, 'the
people are behind you and not Bennett. He is trying
to drown all your thunder with a compulsory wheat
pool ... Head a party and go to the people. They
will support you.'[53]

His own family must have been thinking along these
same lines. As far back as October 1934, Francis
Stevens had an idea his father might lead a third
party, and Gertrude had great difficulty containing
her anger whenever the name Bennett was mentioned.
She had unhappy memories of this arrogant bachelor,
ordering her husband to leave home Christmas night,
refusing to send even so much as a sympathy card
when Sylvia died. And yet she knew as did Harry
that Canadian political parties were more than mere
reflections of their current leaders. Harry had
been a faithful and extremely hard-working Conservative member for the past 24 years. And he had
served not out of blind faith but because the Tory
party had stood for some of his deepest beliefs:
for firm ties with the Old Country, for the national
principles welded together by Sir John A. Macdonald
and Sir Robert Borden. If only Sir Robert had stayed
at the helm, but now he had to stand with Stevens,
outside the fold, watching the party slowly sinking.
On 30 June Stevens wrote to Francis, about the
pressure to leadership being exerted upon him:

I am not as yet sure what I shall do as regards
the election, etc. But I expect that this week
will tell the tale. I have been under pressure
from all parts of Canada to head a new party. To
one and all I have replied that I was not looking
for leadership of either new or old parties; that
I wished to finish my job, and if I could get
good and effective legislation I would feel bound
to support the Gov. that put it in force. But
the legislation is not effective. It is not good,
so I am now faced with the necessity of making
a 'Decision'.

I told a strong group the other day that I
will not seek a leadership. If it seeks me I might
consider it. But in any case they must choose
their own leader, etc.

They apparently took me at my word and have
organized a meeting for Hamilton next Friday. I
will have men there from all over Canada and
they intend to force the leadership on me. I may
accept.

If I do I would like to have you with me here
in the East until the election is over ... Could
you get leave for a few months without pay? ...
Attached is a very rough and incomplete draft
of my policy.[54]

Obviously forces were in motion that would not
be arrested. Their prime mover was Warren Cook,
who had been in constant touch with Stevens ever
since the now-famous Toronto speech. Sometime in
the ensuing months, Cook had concluded that Stevens
would be unable to get the Bennett administration
to pass worthwhile legislation implementing the
findings of the price spreads inquiry. Like Stevens,
Cook was a life-long Tory, but being a businessman
with a social conscience rather than a politician
without a caucus, he was primarily concerned with
getting modern social and economic legislation.

If achieving it meant forming a new party at the expense of the Conservatives, so be it. Harry had great admiration for Cook's business success, his sincerity, and his organizing skills. At the moment, Cook was on a coast-to-coast tour under the auspices of the Retail Merchants' Association. He wanted to test the political climate and to ensure that the forthcoming Hamilton meeting would have national representation.

If Cook had had any doubts about the urgency of the situation, his stay in Regina would have convinced him. There he saw thousands of relief workers who had left their west-coast government camps to march on Ottawa. They had encamped in Regina while their leaders went on to see Bennett; the prime minister had delivered a brief and stern lecture, telling the spokesmen to return to Regina and order their followers back to the regular camps. On the evening of Dominion Day, several hundred strikers gathered in Regina's market square to hear one of their leaders, James Winters, appeal to local citizens for funds to keep the men from starving. Suddenly, at 8:20 p.m., the police appeared 'swinging batons freely.' About twenty strikers were arrested. The crowd angrily dispersed, but only as far as nearby lanes where they collected stones and clubs. Truckloads of RCMP were rushed to the scene and by 8:45 they had the situation under control.[55] In those 25 minutes, a grim price had been paid for the maintenance of law and order: a local policeman was dead; a striker was dying and several hundred others had been injured. In many respects, it was the Winnipeg General Strike all over again.

In 1919, Harry Stevens had not taken part in the Commons debate on the government's handling of the Winnipeg affair. He had been preoccupied with the Committee on Living Costs and with preparations for his exposé of grain-handling operations.

179

His Commons speeches throughout the twenties, however, had emphasized his conservative, almost reactionary approach to civil unrest of this kind. He
took particular delight in matching wits and words
with James Woodsworth, the socialist member and
after 1933 the CCF leader in the House. More than
once Stevens had sharply criticized Woodsworth for
his anti-British, pro-Russian views, although by
1935 their Commons relationship had mellowed considerably from the days in 1923 when Stevens accused Woodsworth of belonging 'to that particular
group of economic freaks who owe allegiance to the
Third International in preference to the British
Crown.' On 2 July 1935 Woodsworth's son-in-law,
Angus MacInnis, the CCF member from Vancouver,
introduced in the House the subject of the Regina
riots. He was answered first by C.H. Cahan, who
saw the whole episode as a Communist plot. Stevens
then defended the government for setting up relief
camps four years ago. He urged the Commons 'to be
extremely lenient in its judgment of the boys'
since they had been led astray by Communist agita-
tors 'or other persons evilly disposed.' He also
revealed that he had sent reports on the British
Columbia situation to Sir George Perley, the acting
prime minister, in April, and on 23 May he had
written again, this time to Bennett, urging prompt
action. He concluded this, his final speech of the
sixth session of the seventeenth Parliament, by
recommending that the men be put to work on highway
and park construction.[56]

Hardly the words of a radical. Rather, they reflected the views of a simple politician swept
along by the worst economic storm Canada has endured.
'Looking back over the whole picture,' he wrote
to an English correspondent on 4 July, apparently
referring to his role as cabinet minister, 'I do
not see that there is any other course which I
might have pursued that would have been any better

for the country or for the party.'[57] Whatever
Bennett might do to try to alleviate the depression,
Stevens thought the result would be 'the ruination
of the party. I do not think the Conservative Party
under his leadership has the remotest chance for
success in the coming election.' Stevens admitted
that there was a 'very strong demand for me to lead
a third party.' He had resisted so far because he
was not seeking the leadership, but he mentioned
the possibility that he might be conscripted for
the position.

On 5 July, as Parliament was winding up its business, 31 people meeting in Hamilton signed a petition. It requested H.H. Stevens to form a new party
'to reestablish Canada's industrial, economic and
social life to the benefit of the great majority.'
The first two signatures were those of Warren K.
Cook and Thomas Lisson, owner of a Hamilton printing firm, and the next day, 6 July, they personally
presented the request to Stevens in Ottawa.[58] That
same day Harry Stevens made known his decision:
he would lead a new Reconstruction party, dedicated
'to the plight of youth.' An accompanying statement
from Cook, the new party's chairman and treasurer,
said that his recent nation-wide tour indicated
that the party would have strong support, especially
in Quebec.[59]

The timing of this event suggests careful, long-
range planning. Stevens always maintained, both in
1935 and a quarter of a century later, that he had
never sought the leadership; the party had sought
him.[60] He also was careful to point out that he
had been 'as true a Conservative over the years'
as Bennett and that Bennett himself 'had instructed
the Chief Whip to notify' him that he would 'no
longer be allowed to attend the Party Caucus.'
But Stevens' personal secretary, H.E. Betts, was
hired, he himself states, 'about the middle of
January, 1935, right after Bennett's New Deal

181

Broadcasts, when Stevens saw the impossible coming up.'[61] Tom Learie, Cook's assistant and his Ottawa go-between with Stevens, later claimed that Stevens 'was out to form a party immediately following his resignation in October, 1934.'[62] A new party surely was one of the possibilities that Stevens and Cook had toyed with at that time, but, for a dedicated Tory and party man like Stevens, a better solution would be to wait Bennett out. This is the inference one gets from the letter Gertrude wrote to Francis on 27 October 1934, the day after Harry had resigned from the cabinet, but, significantly, not from the party. 'Bennett just wants to keep everything quiet, and hang on till he gets a title - maybe at Christmas. Daddy is right, and knows it and the majority of people are behind him.'[63] Unfortunately for Stevens, and for the Conservative party, Bennett refused to leave at the expected time and instead made his New Deal Broadcasts. They convinced no one and Bennett's half-hearted attempt to introduce meaningful legislation in the spring of 1935 merely served notice that he would not be retiring to England just yet. Harry was bitter. After the founding of the new party, in reply to a back-bencher who had urged him to make known the fact that he 'had not bolted' from the Conservatives, Stevens placed some of the blame on the spinelessness of Tory MPs:

> [Bennett's] action was one of pique and personal pettiness ... [but] private members of the Conservative Party have been very derelict in their duty ... in not long ago resisting the domineering attitude of their leader. They will talk, as most of them did, very freely behind his back, but for some reason or other, with a few exceptions, were afraid to express their views to his face. Had they done so things would have been much different today.[64]

182

Obviously Stevens was not happy about the prospect
of leading a minor party in 1935 - or at any other
time for that matter. However, as his friend Manion
had put it a few weeks earlier, 'Poor old Stevens
at the moment seems to be out on the end of a limb.'
The Reconstruction party was largely an act of
political desperation; it had no ideological base
to compare with that of the CCF or even the Social
Credit, soon to sweep into power in Alberta. It
was led by a dissident Tory, who, somewhat late
in his career, had championed the cause of the
hard-pressed producers, small business owners,
and thousands of nameless Canadians caught by the
depression. The party had no long-range plan other
than to force through enough broad legislation to
protect the little man. Although he never said so,
Stevens had some reason to hope that a solid block
of Reconstructionist MPs might force a realignment
of the Conservative party and perhaps gain him
the leadership. Everything depended on the forthcoming election; now that he had made the big decision, Harry Stevens gave his full attention to
the campaign.

VI The Campaign

An air of excitement hung over the large conference room of the Royal York Hotel on the hot summer
evening of 11 July when Harry Stevens spoke to the
press. He and the executive of the Reconstruction
party were drafting a manifesto 'to grapple with
pressing problems with the purpose of improving
conditions of the masses.'[1] On the desk beside
him were two books: a biography of Lord Shaftesbury
and another called Forgotten Men by Claudius Gregory.
When asked how the party would get candidates,
Warren Cook, the party's chairman and its national
treasurer, explained that four groups of ten citizens each would select candidates for their own
ridings. After the interview the executive began
examining a draft manifesto brought along by Stevens
and Cook. Everyone on the executive was 'keyed up,'
they worked far into the night before the document
was ready for next day's public unveiling.[2]
   Fifteen points summarized the 'New National Policy of Reconstruction and Reform.' The first, dealing with youth, promised 'to open up an avenue of
opportunity for all who are willing to work in all
branches of industrial and commercial activity.'
The second point, on public works, called for the
completion of the trans-Canada highway, the removal

184

of all level crossings, construction of highways
from the United States border to the national parks,
the opening of the northland to tourists, and a
reforestation program. The third point would invite
insurance, loan, trust, and mortgage companies to
use their 'reservoir of capital' for a national
housing program; if they refused, a federal plan
would be started, financed by the sale of self-
amortized bonds guaranteed by the federal treasury.

Much of the manifesto followed the recommendations
of the price spreads report. A Reconstruction government would establish a federal trade and industry
commission, an economic council which would make
an immediate and complete investigation of monetary
problems, and a federal agricultural board 'to
formulate a democratic scheme for the control of
direction' of marketing. Ordinary mortgage rates
would be restricted to 6 per cent. The national
debt would be 'ultimately liquidated' by three
means: first, the great 'gold shield' in federal
territory would be developed, 'with profits from
production accruing to the Dominion government';
second, a new policy would make it possible to
use Canadian fuel by means of federal transportation
subsidies and would also utilize the peat bogs of
central Canada, 'all of which activities will
absorb thousands of men now on relief'; third,
Canadian oil production would be encouraged 'by
opening up the vast oil fields of the northwest
Territories under federal government supervision.'
In order to balance the budget, a Reconstruction
government would administer federal taxes 'through
a single set of auditors' and would invite the
provinces to cooperate in the system which would
divide the returns on 'an equitable and agreeable
basis.' Taxes on higher incomes would be increased
and corporations operating 'on a multiple unit
basis' would be assessed on each unit.

Stevens and his executive did not have time to

draw up any concrete proposals on the complex
railway problem, but the manifesto promised to
submit 'a reasonable and sane solution' before
election day. In the meantime, they warned against
'seductive suggestions that a solution can only
be found by a national government, for the proposal of both a national government and amalgamation
of the railways emanates from St. James Street.'

Essentially, the Reconstruction manifesto was
written by Stevens, with some help from Cook. Over
the past year, in the price spreads inquiry, in
Parliament, in letters to his many correspondents,
Stevens had been making these and similar suggestions. There was not a radical idea among them
because their author was a most conventional politician, his cabinet resignation notwithstanding.
He had always upheld the basic features of the
capitalist system, and even now, when an economic
paralysis gripped the nation, Stevens believed that
the system could be made to work if the people at
large and the financial institutions would cooperate with a sympathetic federal government. Yet,
because of his attacks on big business, Stevens
could not expect much sympathy from some of the
institutions, notably from the Montreal financial
community.

The Montreal _Gazette_ agreed with only one of the
fifteen points in the Reconstruction manifesto.
Its editorial thought Stevens was 'on solid ground'
when he called for Ottawa and the provinces to
work out constitutional amendments. As for the
rest, the new party was trying to 'steal the C.C.F.
thunder.' Furthermore, the proposals would make
the individual 'a puppet of the state' and 'set
back the clock of progress for generations.' As
for the proposals to liquidate the national debt,
'these were palpable absurdities.' For that matter,
nothing was more absurd than the _Gazette_'s implication that the Reconstruction party was akin to

186

the CCF. Each had a manifesto, and there the similarity ended. A Reconstruction government would invite mortgage, insurance, loan, and trust companies to use 'their reservoir of capital'; a CCF government, according to the 1933 Regina manifesto, would socialize 'all financial machinery - banking, currency, credit, and insurance, to make possible the effective control of currency, credit and prices.'[3] The Gazette was no doubt well aware of Stevens' pro-capitalist views, but in striking back at him for his attacks against the abuses by big business, this influential voice of old-style Toryism made use of a potent weapon: the political damage from an implication, however unfounded, that Stevens was in league with the 'reds,' with the CCF - a smear tactic almost as common today as in 1935.

A better indication of Stevens' public image is the reaction of the liberal-minded Toronto Globe. This newspaper, which had given Stevens strong endorsation during the past year, now came out strongly in favour of the manifesto. So too did H.H. Hannam, secretary of the United Farmers of Ontario, although that organization left the responsibility for definite political action to its individual locals. On the other hand, the United Farmers of Alberta issued a statement saying that 'it had definitely decided not to follow the new leader.' In an editorial which was later incorporated into the Reconstruction party's campaign literature, the Monetary Times thought the new program aimed at radical reform of the capitalist system in order to give 'the little capitalist and the worker a better chance.' It saw Stevens occupying a position 'somewhat between the Bennett Reform policy and the C.C.F., but closer to the present Prime Minister.' The Simcoe Reformer thought the new party 'would draw thousands of supporters from Conservative, Liberal and C.C.F. ranks, and

187

elect numerous candidates, but unless it can command a substantial majority in the House, it can never carry out a reform program.'[14]

On the day this editorial appeared, the mayor of Simcoe, Percy Carter, offered himself as a Reconstruction candidate in Simcoe North, even though he had been president of the local CCF group. In the riding of Simcoe East, W.M. Cramp resigned as president of the local Conservative Club to become a Stevens supporter and, later, the third Reconstructionist to be nominated. In the riding of London, the Conservative incumbent, Frank White, was not renominated by his party, apparently because of his outspoken support of Stevens; he strongly hinted that he might run as a Reconstructionist, which he eventually did. On 15 July, at a Tory rally in the Toronto riding of York East, 'applause greeted every reference to the new party, and the Conservative candidate R.H. McGregor, M.P., declared that he would support any legislation arising out of the Price Spreads Committee.' A few days later, in Leamington, the Young Canada Conservative Club was formally dissolved, every member but one promptly joining a 'Stevens Club.' The exception was the Tory incumbent, Eccles Gott. Ontario ridings continued to give Stevens his strongest support, but Quebec too sent encouraging news, confirming an earlier prediction by Warren Cook. On 16 July, Jacques Cartier, the provincial Tory organizer in 1930, announced his resignation as vice-chairman of the Radio Commission; he would be the provincial organizer for the Reconstruction party.

The 'tory raft' was breaking up, said the Meaford Mirror and so it seemed. E.N. Rhodes, the minister of finance, had already indicated his retirement, although he was only 58; on 12 July, R.C. Matthews, the minister of national revenue, and J.A. Macdonald, who held the fisheries portfolio, announced their imminent departure from politics. In the end only

eight members of the original Bennett cabinet
were on hand to help him fight the election. Four –
Bennett, Perley, Cahan, and J.S. Stewart – would
be successful in their constituencies.

For Harry Stevens, the die had been cast. Though
the election date was not known (many predicted
mid-October), he began his campaign at a furious
pace which never slackened for the next three and
a half months. A thousand people greeted him and
his wife on 19 July when their flag-draped limou-
sine arrived at a Hamilton auditorium. In a speech
headlined in next morning's Globe, he declared
that the real election issue was between the people
and a handful of economic dictators. On 23 July
he spoke in Toronto, the party's national headquarters, and the next day he and Gertrude headed
west for a whirlwind tour. Going directly to British Columbia, they were joined by Francis, who had
obtained a ten-week leave of absence from his
church to help with the campaign.[5]

As so often in the past few years, politics would
take precedence over family matters. Once again,
there would be no time to spend at the 'ranch,'
and scarcely a moment to greet their first grand-
child. Marjorie's daughter, Patricia Lovick, was
born in August, the 'youngest member of the Reconstruction Team.'[6] This family phalanx was a strong
contrast to the two bachelors, King and Bennett,
celibates by choice whose most faithful companions
were their dogs. Bennett still had not made any
start at a campaign and in fact waited until 6 September, when he announced in a national radio broadcast that the election day would be Monday, 14 October. While the Stevens team headed for Victoria
and their first big western rally, King opened his
campaign with the first of several national broadcasts. 'You cannot reconstruct on quicksand,' he
declared, adding that an election giving either
Stevens or Woodsworth the balance of power 'would

lead to chaos.' Like Stevens, King was opposed to
a national government, apparently for the same reason. It would mean 'sacrificing democracy to serve
the ends of plutocracy.'[7]

More than a thousand supporters of Stevens attended the Victoria rally on 4 August. It reflected the
evangelical zeal and strong support from Protestant
church groups. The chairman, Rev. E.F. Church, told
his audience: 'We are looking to Mr. Stevens and
he is looking to God.' Stevens spoke for ninety
minutes, delivering a vehement attack on 'banks
and money powers' whom he accused of prolonging
the depression and strangling business. According
to the press he was well received by a capacity
audience, although not all present were on his
side. 'You were a member of the government,' a
heckler called out, 'Why didn't you provide work?'
'Yes, I was a member,' Stevens replied, 'but I got
out.' 'You were too long in getting out,' yelled
the heckler. After his speech, and while a collection was being gathered, the chairman reminded
those present that Stevens 'had cleaned up the customs scandal in 1926 which told of evidence that
the two old parties in B.C. had received over
$200,000 in campaign funds from their liquor inter-
ests.'[8]

Campaign funds presented a serious and continuing
problem for the Reconstruction party. What money
it did receive was handled by Warren Cook at the
national headquarters in Toronto. According to
Stevens' friend and professional lobbyist, Harold
Daly of Ottawa, Cook had convinced Stevens that
$500,000 would be available if he agreed to lead
the party. This sum never materialized. Cook's
assistant, Tom Learie, who was also permanent secretary of the Canadian Association of Garment Manufacturers, later estimated that the total amount
raised was about $35,000 and that this had come in
'in dribs and drabs.'[9] As Stevens wrote to a Sas-

katchewan correspondent, he had nothing like the resources of the Conservatives:

> We have no funds as the other parties have them. Mr. Cahan is reported as saying that he is ready to spend $80,000 on his campaign... Mr. [Denton] Massey has stated he will spend $50,000 in Greenwood. Our party won't spend that on all the candidates we put up in Canada, and we won't have to. Behind us we have something that is infinitely more valuable than all the party funds, and that is the goodwill of the people.[10]

The goodwill Stevens relied on was plainly evident when his entourage held a rally in Vancouver on 5 August. Once again Stevens explained why he had broken with the Conservatives: "The government legislation to remedy sweatshop conditions was anaemic, inadequate and ineffective." He had resigned from the cabinet because he refused to apologize "for treating financiers, magnates and shopgirls alike." The Reconstruction party was founded "on the suffering of the people," and he listed "nine tragic facts" to prove the emergency. These included "Canada failing to support ten million people; stocks of food while hundreds of thousands are hungry ... garment workers all out of jobs while workers in other industries could not buy clothes." At the end of the speech, the Rev. Andrew Roddan, chairman of the meeting, could not remember, or so commented the Vancouver _Province_'s story, that "it was not the service, for he even announced the offering."[11]

Critical press comments did not dampen the ardour of Stevens' supporters. They turned out in large numbers as he swung into the British Columbia interior, making short speeches to appreciative crowds in Kimberley, Corbin, Kamloops, Field, and Creston. Then he moved into Alberta, where William Aberhart's

191

new Social Credit party was about to sweep to a
resounding provincial victory on 22 August. On 12
August, Stevens was in Bennett's home territory.
Three thousand Calgarians "filled every seat and
blocked the doorway of the Victoria Park pavilion."
They were introduced as well to Mrs. Stevens, described as a "real westerner" whose parents had
homesteaded at Qu'Appelle, Saskatchewan, and later
in Vernon, BC, where she met her husband. "Knock-
out meeting in Calgary," Stevens wired his secretary in Ottawa. "Packed arena. 2000 turned away."[12]
It was the same enthusiastic story at Red Deer,
where the Stevens party was met by the mayor and
the chairman of the noon-day meeting, R.B. Willivery, "a one-time Conservative candidate for Red
Deer." After another mass meeting in Edmonton,
they entered Saskatchewan, receiving a big welcome
12 August from 2,500 who took up "all available
space at the Saskatoon auditorium." The chairman
was Dr. R.A. Wilson, professor of English at the
University of Saskatchewan; the provincial organizer,
W.L. McQuarrie, who was also secretary of the Saskatchewan branch of the Retail Merchants' Association, described Harry Stevens as "a new Martin
Luther of Canada's problems."

Another 2,000 turned out the next day in Regina,
scene of the Dominion Day riots, but the biggest
welcome was yet to come. On 19 August, 5,300 packed
the Winnipeg arena, and according to the Winnipeg
Free Press another thousand were turned away.
Stevens' theme was familiar: he denounced the
handful controlling Canada's wealth and credit.
The Reconstruction party favoured regulations by
a nationalized central bank rather than by men
selected by the Chamber of Commerce. Mrs. Stevens
spoke as well, describing the difficulties encoun-
tered when her husband had to give up his cabinet
position and his $10,000 a year salary. Also on
the platform was H.B. Scott, provincial secretary

192

of the Retail Merchants' Association, and the
meeting's chairman, the Rev. P.I. Pilkey, of St.
Paul's United Church. The Free Press described
Mr. Pilkey as "a long-time friend of Stevens and
a member of his advisory committee." The chairman
told the crowd that the $300 they had contributed
was a record for any political meeting. Unfortunately, the expenses on that occasion amounted to
$500. For the entire western trip, Stevens drew
$530 from party funds; one can only speculate how
much more had to come out of his own pocket.

Back in Toronto, at the national party headquarters at 57 Bloor Street West, Warren Cook was
trying to cope with mounting expenses and with the
growing number of people wishing to run as Reconstruction candidates. Each had to supply his own
election deposit of $200 but Cook had to decide
on the suitability of each aspirant and to dole
out whatever expense money and campaign literature
were available. The latter was in good supply,
thanks in part to two printing firms represented
on the national executive. Most of the 174 candidates who ran were political novices, although
ten had had some experience, including three who
had been active with the United Farmers of Ontario.
The largest single group by occupation was made
up of farmers, who supplied 33 of the candidates.
Next came 24 merchants, 12 doctors, 12 advocates,
11 managers, 7 manufacturers, 6 lawyers, 6 clergy-
men, 5 reeves, 3 aldermen, and 2 mayors. Most were
well educated and, even more important, all had
jobs - an important qualification in 1935, when
the $200 deposit would have been too great an
obstacle for most Canadians. At the constituency
level, the party's organization centred around
Stevens Clubs, which were formed with the help of
a directive contained in "Bulletin No. 1" issued
August 12 by W.S. Hunter, a Toronto journalist who
became the party's national publicity director.

The Davis-Lisson printing company of Hamilton also
produced a weekly newspaper, the Reconstruction
Party, which sold for ten cents a copy and made
great use of Stevens' campaign speeches.
Two days after his Winnipeg appearance, Harry
Stevens was speaking in Sudbury, with a truck as
his rostrum. From there he and Gertrude, together
with Patricia, Douglas, and Francis, went to Ottawa
to prepare for the Maritime campaign. On 22 August,
William Aberhart's Social Credit party took 56 of
the 63 seats in the Alberta election and for some
time rumours flew about a possible Stevens-Aberhart
combination. They were well founded. Two weeks
earlier, in Vancouver, Stevens and Aberhart had
met at the Hotel Vancouver; after a lengthy discussion they had gone their separate ways "to think
it over." According to Stevens' secretary, H.E.
Betts, his leader saw "a germ of truth in the
Social Credit platform, although he was not sure
what they really wanted."[13] On 28 August both
parties issued formal denials of any alliance.
Stevens continued, however, to have difficulty
refuting reports that the Reconstructionists had
made a deal with the Tories - reports that usually
originated with Liberal newspapers.
Mackenzie King kept referring to this possibility
when he launched his Maritime campaign early in
September but Stevens was in a good position to
deny the charge because his itinerary closely
followed King's. On 3 September he and Gertrude
and Francis left Ottawa for a quick tour of Quebec
and then on to the Maritimes. Besides making
speeches, they had to reconcile differences that
had arisen between Jacques Cartier, the party's
Quebec organizer, and other provincial members
who had been complaining that he was devoting too
much time to the Montreal area. By this time the
Ethiopian crisis had emerged to dominate the front
pages of the newspapers, and during his Montreal

194

rally Stevens was asked what his stand would be. "I think it is an unthinkable thing that Canada be dragged into a war involving obscure things in Europe or Africa. I would not consider Canadian participation ... without first consulting the people."[14] Almost the same position was taken by Mackenzie King a few days later in Quebec City when he said he favoured a plebiscite if a war started. During the first of a series of broadcasts on 6 September, Bennett declared that "the Conservative stands for Canadian rights and against economic aggression of any foreign power" and that Canadians "would not be embroiled in any foreign quarrel when the rights of Canadians were not involved." During his second broadcast, on 8 September, Bennett announced his "New Reconstruction Policy" which would include universal old age pensions for all workers over sixty. It was not until his fourth broadcast on 11 September that he mentioned his former colleague:

All his political life long, Mr. Stevens has endorsed the fundamental principles of Conservatism even when Conservatism might fairly have been called reactionary... How can Mr. Stevens hope to effectively operate upon a plan untested, untried and only a few weeks old? It doesn't look at all safe or sound or hopeful in this stormy weather... I feel it is my duty to warn you to reject [his policies]. And insofar as his success may mean a division in the forces bent upon progress [it will be] a bad thing.[15]

More free publicity came three days later when Mackenzie King spent most of his time on a national broadcast attempting to minimize differences in policy between the Reconstruction party and the Conservatives. The long-distance debate carried on by Stevens, King, and Bennett continued when

195

the Stevens group toured the Maritimes. In Halifax
Stevens argued that Bennett's old age pension was
not the answer. Instead, he pleaded for the man of
forty-five "ploughed out of employment by mechani-
zation." Francis Stevens also spoke, denying that
the new party had any connection with the Tories.
The campaign progressed through well-attended
meetings in Sydney, New Glasgow, Charlottetown,
and Moncton; several times Harry and Francis addressed meetings separately. They arrived back in
Ottawa on 21 September, and after a two-day rest
Stevens announced that he would spend the remaining
three weeks in Ontario, the province which had
provided two-thirds of his candidates. He would
travel over 2,000 miles, hold from two to twelve
meetings daily, and make at least a hundred speeches.[16] Meanwhile Francis went back to his father's
home riding of Kootenay East, where he campaigned
with Sherwood Herchmer, a Fernie lawyer and Stevens'
campaign manager.[17]

On 23 September eleven Reconstruction candidates
were on the platform in the Ottawa Coliseum when
Harry Stevens spoke to over 2,000. After promising
to restore "the outstanding five percent salary
cut for civil servants," he referred to the unemployed marchers and Bennett's charge that they had
planned to kidnap him. Stevens admitted that there
had been two or three communists among them, but
most of them were "a nice bunch who couldn't kidnap
a rat."[18]

The next day, at the wheel of his Buick, with
Gertrude at his side, Harry Stevens headed west-
ward in this last and most important stage of his
campaign. Smiths Falls, Peterborough, Oshawa, and
smaller centres heard him direct most of his attention to Bennett. To a thousand people in Aurora,
he promised to quit the campaign "if only Bennett
could show" him that the recent housing bill was
a real measure of reform. A similar crowd turned

196

out at Midland despite a heavy rain, but they did
not hear Stevens: he had lost his voice. Gertrude
took over, saying that Bennett had never spoken
to her husband since his resignation. "We can never
go back." Another speaker and candidate, W.M.
Cramp, reeve of Orillia, urged the voters "to put
Christianity into politics and humanity before
gold." At Owen Sound, R.J. Scott, president of the
United Farmers of Ontario, declared that he was
"proud to be associated with the movement." At
Kincardine, Stevens said men were being fired from
their jobs "because they dare line up with me" -
a charge later substantiated in letters he received
from defeated candidates.[19] Pointing to evidence
in the price spreads report that Canada Packers
was the largest Canadian shareholder in Dominion
Stores, he said that as a result "Canada Packers
have you from the cradle to the grave." When they
reached Sarnia, Stevens' voice gave out again, but
according to the Globe's account Mrs. Stevens and
Dr. Sam Atkinson, a Toronto author and economist,
"made good pinch-hitters". Mrs. Stevens appealed
to the women "to understand the man attempting to
better conditions of the common people, for he
would work and is sincere."

In Windsor, Stevens defended his association
with the now-defunct Manufacturers' Finance Corporation. This matter was raised again by A.G. Slaght,
the Liberal candidate for Parry Sound, even though
the charge had been dismissed by the Ontario Secu-
rities Commission just two months earlier. In his
defence Stevens called the investigation "a political inquiry from beginning to end," adding that he
had issued a writ for slander against Slaght, "the
power behind the Liberal throne in Ontario."[20]
The suit was not carried forward, for, as Francis
Stevens put it long afterwards, "libel suits are
notoriously expensive and Dad just didn't have the
resources... Besides, people tend to remember the
charges, not the vindication!"[21]

When the election campaign entered its final two
weeks, it almost seemed as if the one issue was
Harry Stevens. While Slaght was attacking him on
the radio, King was telling Winnipeg voters that
he was a one-man party. During King's campaigning
in western Canada his Ontario campaign was helped
by three Liberal premiers - Mitchell Hepburn of
Ontario, James Gardiner of Saskatchewan, and Angus
L. Macdonald of Nova Scotia - and the last had no
doubts about the Reconstruction leader: "This man
Stevens, who is going around the country enlisting
the support of an odd minister and an occasional
Sunday School teacher, this man who is getting
people to sing hymns for him is not fit to be Prime
Minister."[22] On 28 September, the day before this
comment appeared in the press, Bennett launched
what the Liberal voice in Toronto, the Star, called
"his first personal attack on Stevens." Speaking
at a Winnipeg rally, Bennett "angrily condemned
as deconstructionists leaders of the so-called
reform parties who sought to ferment popular preju-
dice against Canadian institutions and businesses."
The Star's report of the meeting continued:

> Mr. Stevens' party was seeking to tear men down.
> 'I recommend that the leader of that party put
> his own house in order before he starts telling
> other people how to run their business', the
> premier flared, obviously nettled by persistent
> heckling.
> 'Why is Sir Herbert Holt not in jail!' shouted
> someone. 'For the same reason you are not in jail.
> Oh, my friends, when I think of men going around
> the country making the charges Stevens makes,
> appealing to prejudice and ignorance ... at times
> I almost despair of my country.'[23]

Bennett's reception did not improve when he spoke
on 30 September in Hamilton. Five thousand packed

into the local arena, and before the meeting had
ended it was being conducted amid what the Globe
reporter called "impossible conditions." The trouble
broke out after Major-General Newburn, in introducing Bennett, said that the prime minister had
made one serious mistake. "That was when he took
into his cabinet that self-appointed self-annointed
leader of the Reconstruction Party." When Bennett
rose to speak, he was greeted with "Heil Hitler!"
"You're through, Bennett!" "Twenty cents a day!"
"Section Ninety-eight!" As these hecklers were
hustled out, others took their place. It was one
of many bad nights Bennett faced in this campaign.[24]

He had a better time of it on 2 October in Mont-
real, when 12,000 heard him give "an orthodox Tory
appeal." On the platform with him were Cahan and
Perley, and in nearby box-seats sat Sir Charles
Gordon, president of Dominion Textiles, and Sir
Edward Beatty, president of the Canadian Pacific
Railway,[25] with Morris Wilson, successor to Sir
Herbert Holt as president of the Royal Bank, a
company in which Bennett was still a major shareholder. Stevens' name was never mentioned in
Bennett's speech, but he compensated for this
deliberate omission on 3 October in Saint John when
he made what the press called "a vigorous attack"
on his former colleague. "What about Stevens,"
someone yelled at Bennett during his Bridgewater,
N.S., meeting. "Mr. Stevens - he's like Lenin,"
was Bennett's quick reply. "He's dead."

With only a week remaining before election day,
King, Bennett, and Stevens, in rapid succession,
converged on Toronto's Maple Leaf Gardens. On Monday, 7 October, King marched in "at the skirl of
bagpipes." The Globe, now a strong Liberal supporter,
estimated the crowd at 17,000. On 9 October, 15,000
turned out for Bennett, who was piped in by the
band of the 48th Highlanders. Two days later, on a
Friday night, Harry Stevens also rated a pipe band

and an audience of 10,000. He spoke for ninety minutes, and the few hecklers were booed into silence when he struck at election expenditures, at the profits of department stores, at banks, and at the salaries of corporation presidents. On a national budget of $35,000 how and where had Stevens found the money to hire the Maple Leaf Gardens? According to Tom Learie, the party's Ontario organizer, it had been put up personally by Warren Cook and a friend who was president of a Toronto grain elevator company as well as a Gardens director.[26]

For King and Bennett, the campaign was now over, but not for Harry Stevens. He ended it where he had begun, in Hamilton, speaking on 12 October, a Saturday night, before a thousand "wildly cheering party workers gathered at a large hotel." At eleven o'clock, in a coast-to-coast broadcast, he accused Mackenzie King and Sir Edward Beatty of conspiring to defeat him in Kootenay East where the CPR's largest subsidiary, Consolidated Mining and Smelting Company, was the area's major employer.[27] Francis Stevens has vivid memories of that radio speech:

> The closing rally in East Kootenay was held that night in the mining town of Fernie. The old opera house was packed to the rafters. We started the meeting in a normal way (with normal heckling) at 8 p.m. M.S.T. and at 9 p.m. we stopped the proceedings to listen to Dad's broadcast over loudspeakers. There was a hushed silence as he spoke. They didn't miss a word. His voice was hoarse with fatigue, but electric in its challenge and dedication. He concluded with a strong appeal to the voters in his home constituency. When the hour-long broadcast was over they rose and gave the unseen speaker a standing ovation. There were tears in my eyes as I shared their emotional response.[28]

200

On 14 October, election day, as the first results began coming in from the Maritimes, the enthusiasm which had sustained Harry Stevens and his supporters over the past fourteen weeks quickly changed to despair. Ontario and Quebec really told the tale: many thousands of votes but not enough to elect even one Reconstruction candidate. When the final results were tallied, the Reconstruction party had received more than 389,000 votes, the third highest total, but only Stevens had been elected to the House. (For a breakdown of the election results see page 205.)

"Why did they do it?" "Why did they do it?" Stevens kept asking Tom Learie on election night. After all those enthusiastic meetings, after 174 Canadians had fought as Reconstruction candidates, why had the electorate turned its back? Part of the answer must have been that most Canadians still identified Harry Stevens with the Conservative party, the party of the Depression. They knew that he had been a close colleague of Bennett's for four of the past five years. Furthermore, Stevens had been an unwavering and unapologetic Tory for all but the last of his 24 years in Parliament. The voters hardly needed Mackenzie King to remind them of these facts. From the start of the price spreads inquiry, Stevens had worked hopefully and unceasingly to make the Conservative party the vehicle for the economic and social reforms so obviously needed. Herridge had been working toward the same goals. If they had joined forces they might have been able to convince Bennett, despite his well-known sensitivity to unsolicited advice. But Bennett would scarcely allow Stevens' name to be uttered within his presence, and with Herridge's wife Mildred staunchly supporting her brother, a Herridge-Stevens alliance was out of the question. Also, both had political ambitions, and after 24 years of faithful service to the Tory party Stevens must

have considered himself a logical successor to
Bennett.

Why did Stevens not wait Bennett out? The answer
seems to lie in the chain of events and the unusual
circumstances prevailing during the last week of
October 1934. Stevens could have ridden out the
storm over his pamphlet: he knew that Cahan had few
supporters in caucus and did not rate highly with
Bennett. What prompted Stevens' resignation was
his despair - but despair not over his political
future but for the health and life of his daughter
Sylvia. At that particular point, politics looked
shallow and useless. Had he fallen in with Manion
after that crucial cabinet meeting, instead of
two disenchanted party followers, he might well
not have written out that second resignation.

Once he had resigned from the cabinet, Stevens'
old crusading Methodist zeal and Bennett's intran-
sigent attitude propelled him towards the creation
and leadership of the Reconstruction party. His
political instinct and experience must have told
Stevens what the result would be, but at least he
could carry on the fight and spread the message
of the price spreads inquiry, so that, if not in
1935, then in some future election the changes
would come. And for Harry Stevens, the campaign
had brought a satisfaction in the support of his
son that only a father could know. He wrote to
Francis two days after the results[29]:

Your disappointment must be equal to my own. I
am old and know something of the vagaries of
human nature, but you, I think, did trust your
fellow man and expected more of them.
I am not bitter. I do feel a bit helpless.
What I want to do, though, is to tell you how
greatly I appreciated your wonderful assistance.
I am very proud of you. In the Maritimes, I learned that you were possessed of excellent judgment

and indefatigable devotion to duty. Your work in
East Kootenay saved my seat. I know I could not
have won except for your splendid work. It was
wonderful.

Now son, forget it all, and devote yourself
to your work. Teach your people the Laws of God.
Learn all you can about them yourself. The time
will come when you will be needed, so be patient
... My love to Annie and God bless you both.

Your old Dad

VII The Return Home

To federal politicians, Ottawa is a small world
in itself. To Harry Stevens, immediately after
the 1935 election, it must have seemed both a
lonely and an angry world. His first and his favourite Conservative leader, Sir Robert Borden,
wrote to Manion: "Mr. Stevens' action during the
past six months has profoundly astonished and disappointed me. In destroying for the time being the
Conservative Party, he has thoroughly eliminated
himself."[1] "My only regret," the angry Manion wrote
to Herridge, "is that Harry won his own seat, as
I think he is a despicable cad." A week later, in
a letter to Bennett, Manion almost gleefully noted
that at the Rideau Club, "Stevens is about as close
to being a man without a country as the original
of that part of the American classic. He is receiving his desserts."[2]

Manion, Borden, and other members of the Conservative party naturally placed most of the blame
for its defeat at Stevens' door but as one observer,
Escott Reid, wrote in 1936 theirs was not a valid
explanation:

> ... the competing policies of the Liberal and
> Conservative parties had little influence on the
> voters, for the issues in the campaign were most

204

obscure. Nor is it enough to say, as some Liberals do, that the election was in the main little more than a devastating protest against the personality of Mr. R.B. Bennett ... A shrewder politician might, however, have kept Mr. Stevens within the ranks of the Conservative party and thus have prevented the loss of a considerable number of seats and votes. It would appear, in fact, that the election did not constitute a decision on issues or personalities, but merely demonstrated the wisdom of the Liberal party's policy of having no policy. The Liberals counted on the depression defeating any government, and the depression did what was expected of it.

How many seats did the Reconstruction party cost the Tories? Manion put the figure at between thirty to forty; Harold Daly said long after that "Reconstruction party candidates in Quebec cost Bennett ten seats" but Stevens himself would not give any figures.[4] The statistics of the table are revealing.

The Election of 1935

Party	Provinces					Total elected	Votes polled	% polled
	BC	West	Ont	Que	Man			
Cons.	5	4	25	5	1	40	1,308,688	29.6
Lib.	6	29	56	55	25	171	2,076,394	46.8
CCF	3	4				7	386,484	8.7
Soc. Cr.		17				17	187,045	4.2
Reconst.	1					1	389,708	8.9
Others	1	2	1	5		9	104,356	1.8

Sources: Hugh Thorburn, Party Politics in Canada, pp. 216-24; Canadian Parliamentary Guide, 1936.

According to Reid, "the Reconstruction Party turned out to be an Eastern party," getting 90 per cent of its votes from the east, especially in Ontario and in the largest cities. His description is more than borne out by the writer's own analysis. In 62 ridings, more than half of them in Ontario, Conservative rather than Liberal candidates would have won if the Reconstruction vote had been added to the Conservative; in 10 ridings, including 7 in Quebec, Reconstructionists placed second and the Tories third; in 68 three-way contests, the Liberals won 57, the Tories 11 (the Tories did not oppose Stevens in Kootenay East); in 32 ridings, the Reconstructionists beat their CCF opponents, but in 46 other contests the opposite resulted.

The phenomenon of the 1935 election was not that the Liberals won and the Conservatives lost, but that over 750,000 Canadians rejected both these old parties in favour of either the Reconstruction party or the CCF. In the writer's view, both Harry Stevens and James Woodsworth represented vital, historic, and separate streams of Canadian conservatism. Woodsworth was the red tory in Canadian politics, Stevens the tory democrat or populist. The 1935 election brought out these two conservative elements to full public view for the first time. As many predicted at the time, Harry Stevens would quietly return to Tory ranks. It was just as predictable that Woodsworth and his democratic socialists would remain outside the conservative fold from that day to this. But as Gad Horowitz has pointed out, "the tory and socialist minds have some crucial assumptions, orientations and values in common, so that from certain angles they may appear not as enemies, but as two different expressions of the same basic ideological outlook."[5] Both Stevens and Woodsworth in 1935 - and Diefenbaker and Douglas thirty years later - admired the British parliamentary system and had a deep concern

for the 'little man.' They also revered the British
monarchy and were suspicious of American domination.
The tragedy was that Stevens and Woodsworth regarded each other as being in opposing political camps,
representing irreconcilably different ideologies.
There is no denying that if in power Stevens would
have kept the capitalist system and Woodsworth
would have introduced the socialist state. But
there were possibilities for compromise in Stevens'
(and Bennett's) willingness "to use the power of
the state for the purpose of developing and controlling the economy"[6] and Woodsworth's concept
of economic socialism; those possibilities the
two Canadian tory forces refused to recognize.
The Conservative party remained out of office from
1935 to 1957 not because Stevens, or Bennett for
that matter, had wrecked the party or because of
the cleverness of Mackenzie King. It was because
the Conservative and CCF leaders failed to see
that they represented two continuing forces of
Canadian toryism.

After the 1935 election Harry Stevens had no
choice but to continue for the time being his un-
enviable role as the lone Reconstructionist MP.
In mid-November he met with Warren Cook and several
other members of the party's executive in an attempt to maintain the impetus and the support
generated during the campaign. A press release
after their meeting indicated a determination to
carry on, and to hold a "Dominion-wide conference
in the course of the next few months."[7]

On 6 February 1936, at the opening of the new
parliament, Harry Stevens was in his place on the
Opposition side, but in a far corner, well removed
from his former colleagues. A week later, in the
throne speech debate, he advised the new members
that they would be able to contribute so long as
they did not allow their better judgment, their
convictions, and their conscience to be dominated

"by the exigencies of the party whip."[8] He promised
to cooperate with the new Liberal government, but
it soon became apparent that he intended to be an
active member of the Opposition. By the time the
session ended in June he was almost as active a
critic as Bennett, although he had no illusions
about his former chief. Writing to a correspondent
in March, Stevens described Bennett's performance
in opposition as "erratic and irresponsible."
"When his efforts are bitterly and strenuously
bent to interfere with the progress of things it
naturally has considerable effect. In fact, he has
been pretty much that way through the whole session
but last week was the worst I have ever seen."[9]
Stevens' judgment might have been clouded somewhat
by the fact that Bennett had been circulating
malicious rumours about Stevens' business activities. In essence, he had been saying that those
involved in the First Narrows Bridge project in
Vancouver had assisted Stevens in paying his personal debts. With the help of his former associate
in the price spreads inquiry, Norman Sommerville,
Stevens drafted a letter to Bennett in April,
strongly denying the charges and threatening legal
action if his "private and family affairs were
dragged into public and subjected to innuendo and
bitter personal attack."[10] The letter was never
sent, the libel action was not initiated, but their
relations never improved. R.K. Finlayson has recalled the day in 1937 when he and Bennett passed
Stevens in front of the parliament buildings.
Finlayson gave Harry a cheery greeting. "What did
you speak to that fellow for?" Bennett wanted to
know.[11]

As for the Reconstruction party, its empty coffers
and debts told the story. "We have tons of advice
but no support financially," Stevens wrote a Peterborough friend in May. "I have been amazed and
stunned at the refusal of people to part with a

few dollars. That is our trouble and that is our problem." He never mentioned the payments on notes that he and Cook were still meeting; by the end of 1936 this financial indebtedness was the only tangible proof of the party's continued existence.[12]

Inside the House of Commons, Harry Stevens was sounding more and more like a former Conservative cabinet minister. Speaking in the 1937 budget debate, he defended the 1932 Ottawa trade agreements and described the Liberal budget as about as barren as any he had listened to in twenty-six years. Later in the same speech he commented on the Privy Council ruling handed down on 28 January 1937 that the Bennett New Deal legislation had been ultra vires. In Stevens' opinion, these references "never should have been made." The only way "properly to test a law is to put it into operation with the force and influence of the government behind it. Then let a citizen challenge the law in the courts on its merits."[13] He made no other major speech in the 1937 session. After spending a pleasant but vigorous summer at home, Stevens embarked on an extensive business trip to England and Sweden. He seemed to wish to put politics aside and tend to his tenuous private affairs. The Manufacturers' Finance Company still hung over his head. On 24 January 1938, Norman Sommerville, who was acting as his solicitor in the litigation over the firm, informed him that the balance owing was $5,650, and that his own obligation amounted to $500. Presumably he settled this account in the next few months, and, seemingly undeterred by this lingering reminder of a business failure, he began looking for capital to launch a mining venture in the Harrison Lake district. He and several Vancouver associates had acquired control of the Starr group mining properties, amid rumours that he planned to resign his Commons seat to become president of British Properties Limited, a real estate firm with

extensive holdings in Vancouver. It was partly in
connection with this venture that he made his overseas trip. He returned home in March 1938, in time
to give away his third daughter Patricia, who was
marrying Clifton Coolidge, a member of his Vancouver
Holdings Company staff.

New rumours greeted Stevens' return late in May
to participate in the remainder of the 1938 session
in Ottawa: he would be a candidate at the Conservative leadership convention in July, called after
Bennett announced plans to retire to England. There
was more to these rumours than mere speculation.
His former Quebec organizer, Jacques Cartier, was
working hard to swing the Duplessis-led Quebec
forces expected to attend the Ottawa convention.
"The agitation around your name," wrote Cartier
in mid-June, "seems to bring out the Knights of
the Eleventh Hour. Some of the Duplessis supporters
are openly talking and laying plans to control
both the Convention and the organization of a campaign."[14] A week later he was predicting that Quebec
would form "a Stevens bloc," but Stevens himself
knew better. On the eve of the convention, he outlined the situation to his old friend Warren Cook:

There is, I think, a growing disposition throughout the country in my favour. However, the machine
end of the Conservative organization is dead set
against my receiving the leadership. They are
quite favourable to having me rejoin the party
but on their terms.

The difficulty is, if I attempt to go to the
convention, I will commit myself irrevocably to
their policy without having first seen it. In
the second place, according to the speech delivered by Earl Lawson, acting as financial critic
for the opposition in the budget debate, the
Conservatives are going to re-emphasize the old
high tariff doctrine, whereas the tariff is no

longer the issue in Canada. Neither the farmer
nor the worker is interested in the matter ...
and unless they show interest in modern problems
such as we have outlined, there is no remote
chance for them.

So, as matters now look, it is unlikely that
I shall be at the convention at all, but I am
assured that, if either Manion or Lawson is the
choice, I will be the first man they will seek
out, and I am under the impression that we will
be in a stronger position to discuss matters
with them after, than now...[15]

At the eleventh hour, Stevens nevertheless did
accept an appointment to the convention as delegate
from Rosemont-Maisonneuve, "which is the largest
labour division in Canada."[16] The convention went
as he had predicted. Manion won a close victory
on the leadership contest, not over Lawson but over
M.A. MacPherson, a last-minute candidate from
Regina, who had entered after Bennett finally
decided against re-offering. However Manion did
not immediately seek out Harry Stevens, even though
his former desk-mate and colleague sent his congratulations and offers of support. It was not until
23 December that Manion replied, asking Stevens
to attend a caucus on 11 January 1939. And he
added: "I hope, my dear Harry, that you will avoid
taking too extreme a view on any subject that you
may discuss... Confidentially quite a few businessmen are naturally a little uneasy and of course
you will realize that we don't want to alienate
too many."[17]

On 25 January 1939, during the throne speech
debate, Harry Stevens marked his return to the
Conservative benches by congratulating Manion.
His "approach to the various social and economic
problems of Canada" had "always given due weight
to the human equation. It is that element in him

211

which appeals to me strongly." For the rest of
the session Stevens talked mostly about economic
issues, preferring to ignore the war clouds that
would soon provide Canada with a solution to the
depression. During the special war session in
September, Stevens assumed the role of chief opposition spokesman in the budget debate. He warned
of the dangers of inflation and the folly of nationalizing industry. "We have a magnificent economic structure in Canada," although "it is not
working with complete equity - not by any means."[18]
But Parliament and the government must always
safeguard the public against exploitation. This
had been Harry Stevens' main theme throughout
nearly three decades as an M.P.; it proved to be
the final note of his parliamentary career. He
had not intended to make this speech his valedic-
tory; he had expected to be serving the House of
Commons throughout another war. It was not to be.
In the snap election of 1940, Harry Stevens again
re-offered, but was defeated.

What does a man of 62 do after devoting most of
his life to federal poltics? If his party is in
power at the end of his career, he can expect a
good appointment, probably to the Senate. In 1940
the Conservatives were a weak and poorly led opposition and they were no stronger two years later
when they gathered once again in Winnipeg to choose
a successor to the inadequate Manion. Arthur
Meighen had convinced many delegates that John
Bracken, the Manitoba Progressive premier, was the
logical choice, but when M.A. MacPherson decided
to try again, others followed suit. First John
Diefenbaker and then Howard Green entered their
names. Finally so did Harry Stevens. According to
R.K. Finlayson, who had helped to organize the
convention, "Stevens made the only good speech".[19]
After it ended, Finlayson's companion turned to
him and lamented: "Oh, what a pity! What a pity!
There was our leader."

It was the last time that Harry Stevens challenged the inner circle of the Conservative party. He did not enter the 1945 general election but ran again in Vancouver Centre in 1949 and again in 1953. It was to no avail; his political career was over. However, he had too many talents to be put on the shelf, as the war years had proved. Supported in his business, Vancouver Holdings, by Patricia's husband, Clifton Coolidge, and Gordon Keatley, a niece's husband, he had found the time to turn to other interests. He became active in the Vancouver Kiwanis and in 1952-53 was president of the Vancouver Board of Trade. He wrote a weekly column for the _Province_, and he made numerous radio broadcasts and public speeches to promote the war effort and Victory Loan drives. For the latter part of the conflict he operated Hotel Vancouver as a rehabilitation centre for veterans and their families. In 1952, as president of the Vancouver Board of Trade, Harry and Gertrude toured the Kitimat area of northern British Columbia, where he had staked mining claims half a century earlier. Later that same year he served as chairman of a provincial government commission that revised British Columbia's liquor laws. Throughout these years he never lost touch with federal politics: he always read Hansard and was frequently visited by Tory MPs. In 1948, while in hospital recuperating from a gall bladder operation, he sent John Diefenbaker a five-page memo to assist him in his speech at the Conservative convention. In 1949, George Marler, a CPR vice president, asked him to draft a new labour code for Canada, a request which implied a certain regard for him among the conventional business community.

To younger Vancouverites, Harry Stevens was best known for his birthday walks around Stanley Park. He had begun them in 1932, and by the time his 76th birthday rolled around in 1954 this annual six-mile jaunt was being followed by television

crews. "Guess the stiff headwind on the First
Narrows side must have slowed me down a bit," he
said by way of apology for his slow time: 95 minutes.

In 1966 Gertrude Stevens died and Harry made a
solitary and last trip east to visit Francis, now
living in Toronto, and to wander through the House
of Commons. He got a rousing desk-thumping welcome
and much satisfaction when Prime Minister Pearson
introduced him as "my old chief" - a reference to
Pearson's role as secretary of Stevens' price
spreads commission.[20] He continued to live in Vancouver until his death on 14 June 1973.

Harry's 90th birthday in December 1968 had found
him once again walking around Stanley Park - in
slightly over two hours. Among the scores of relatives and friends helping him celebrate the occasion was John Diefenbaker. The caption under the
Canadian Press photograph read "Old Warriors."
They are more than that. Stevens and Diefenbaker
epitomize the spirit of Tory democracy that has
kept the party alive - and divided - for most of
the twentieth century.

Notes

CHAPTER ONE

1 Saint John (NB) Daily Telegraph, 21 November 1911.
2 Canada, House of Commons Debates, 1911–12, vol. I, 20 November 1911, p. 25; hereafter Debates.
3 Ibid., 24 November 1911, p. 289.
4 Public Archives of Canada, Stevens Papers, H.H. Stevens to Professor John Munro, recorded interview, 10 May 1966 (hereafter 1966 Interview); much of the information on Stevens' early life is based on this lengthy interview. Additional information and substantive views were obtained from interviews and correspondence between the author and the Rev. Francis Stevens, elder son of H.H. Stevens.
5 Montreal Daily Star, 14 May 1887.
6 1966 Interview. This was L.B. Pearson's father, who later moved to Toronto where Lester was born.
7 Ibid.
8 Ibid.
9 Rev. Francis Stevens to author, 20 January 1969.
10 1966 Interview.
11 Margaret Ormsby, British Columbia: A History (Toronto 1958), p. 315.

12 1966 Interview.
13 Stevens Papers, Stevens to Joseph Atkinson, 16 December 1929.
14 1966 Interview.
15 Ormsby, British Columbia, p. 336.
16 1966 Interview.
17 Rev. Francis Stevens to author, 11 February 1969.
18 1966 Interview.
19 Ibid.
20 Rev. Francis Stevens to author, 11 February 1969.
21 Ormsby, British Columbia, p. 354.
22 1966 Interview.
23 Stevens Papers, speech to Progressive Thought Society, 6 April 1910.
24 H.B. Parkes, The United States of America: A History (New York 1954), p. 474.
25 Richard Hofstadter, The Age of Reform (New York 1955), p. 207.
26 Stevens Papers, Stevens to Joseph Atkinson, 16 December 1929.
27 Rev. Francis Stevens to the author, 11 February 1969.
28 Ibid.
29 Ibid.
30 1966 Interview.
31 Canadian Annual Review of Public Affairs, 1913 (Toronto, 1914), p. 668.
32 1966 Interview.
33 Ormsby, British Columbia, p. 370.
34 Ibid. See also Robie L. Reid, "The Inside Story of the Komagata Maru", British Columbia Historical Quarterly, vol. 5 (January 1941), cited in Ormsby.
35 1966 Interview.
36 Rev. Francis Stevens to the author, 11 February 1969.
37 Monetary Times (Montreal), 8 December 1916; clipping in Stevens Papers.
38 Ormsby, British Columbia, p. 391.

39 Stevens Papers, taped interview between Stevens and Dr. W. Kaye Lamb, 27 July 1955. Hereafter the 1955 Interview.
40 Ibid.
41 Debates, 1917, vol. III, 18 June 1917, pp. 2423-27.
42 Ibid., vol. V, 27 August 1917, p. 4967.
43 Canadian Annual Review of Public Affairs, 1917 (Toronto 1918), p. 617.
44 Donald Creighton, Canada's First Century (Toronto 1970), pp. 168-69.
45 Canadian Annual Review, 1917, p. 618.
46 Debates, 1919 1st session, vol. IV, 24 June 1919, pp. 3951-55.
47 Stevens Papers, Canadian Press despatch, n.d.
48 Debates, 1919 1st session, vol. III, 30 May 1919, p. 2953.
49 Richard Allen, The Social Passion (Toronto 1971), p. 232 and passim.
50 Stevens Papers, clippings, n.d.
51 Ibid., speech, 25 March 1920, Washington, DC.
52 Ibid., clippings, letter reprinted in Vancouver Daily World, n.d.
53 Cited in Roger Graham, Arthur Meighen, vol. II (Toronto 1963), p. 30.
54 Ibid.
55 Cited in Ormsby, British Columbia, p. 419.
56 Stevens Papers, clippings, dated 8 February 1922.
57 Debates, 1922, vol. III, 8 June 1922, p. 2651.
58 Ernest Watkins, R.B. Bennett (Toronto 1963), p. 78.
59 Stevens Papers, Stevens to Meighen, 17 July 1924.
60 University of New Brunswick, Harriet Irving Library, Bennett Papers; also Calgary Weekly Herald, 1905-9, containing references to Bennett and McRae's combined efforts at mining promotion.
61 Ormsby, British Columbia, pp. 420-21.
62 Stevens to Meighen, 28 May 1923, cited in

Graham, <u>Arthur Meighen</u>, vol. II, pp. 225-26.

63 <u>Debates</u>, 1923, vol. III, 7 May 1923, pp. 2527-28.
64 <u>1966 Interview</u>.
65 Stevens Papers, Stevens to A.H. Douglas, 31 May 1924.
66 <u>Ibid</u>., telegram to Stevens, 28 May 1924.
67 <u>Ibid</u>., Stevens to F.W. Rounsefell, 29 May 1924.
68 Ormsby, <u>British Columbia</u>, p. 423.
69 Stevens Papers, Rev. J.W.D. Woodside to Stevens, 28 June 1924.
70 <u>Ibid</u>., Stevens to Meighen, 17 July 1924.
71 <u>Ibid</u>., Meighen to Stevens, 18 July 1924.
72 <u>Ibid</u>., Borden to Stevens, 22 September 1924; Sir Frederick Williams-Taylor to G.C. Cassels, 24 September 1924.
73 <u>Ibid</u>., clipping, London <u>Evening Standard</u>, 25 November 1924.
74 <u>Ibid</u>., Stevens in cable to H.C. Hooper, 26 November 1924.
75 <u>Ibid</u>., Henry Thompson to Stevens, 5 December 1924.
76 Cited in H.B. Neatby, <u>The Lonely Heights: William Lyon Mackenzie King</u>, vol. II (Toronto 1963), p. 42.
77 Stevens Papers, Stevens to Joseph Atkinson, 16 December 1929.
78 Graham, <u>Arthur Meighen</u>, vol. II, p. 379.
79 <u>Ibid</u>., p. 374.

CHAPTER TWO

1 Public Archives of Canada, Stevens Papers, Arthur Meighen to Stevens, 29 December 1926 (pencilled notation: "copy of letter & data sent Stevens & Bennett care of Station Agent, Sudbury, Jan. 4 1926").
2 Canada, House of Commons <u>Debates</u>, 1926, vol. I, 8 January 1926, p. 4; hereafter <u>Debates</u>.
3 <u>Ibid</u>., 14 January 1926, pp. 150-1.
4 <u>Ibid</u>., 1 February 1926, p. 584.

5 H.B. Neatby, <u>The Lonely Heights: William Lyon
Mackenzie King</u>, vol. II (Toronto 1963), p. 114.
6 <u>Ibid.</u>, p. 115.
7 This visit was revealed by G.H. Boivin when he
first answered Stevens' charges of customs
irregularities. See <u>Debates</u>, 2 February 1926,
pp. 703-4.
8 <u>Debates</u>, 2 February 1926, p. 687.
9 Neatby, <u>Mackenzie King</u>, vol. II, p. 116.
10 Stevens Papers, A.J. Jackson to Stevens, 15
April 1926.
11 <u>Debates</u>, 1926, vol. V, 18 June 1926, pp. 4694-97.
12 Roger Graham, <u>Arthur Meighen</u>, vol. II (Toronto
1963), p. 396.
13 <u>Debates</u>, 22 June 1926, p. 4819.
14 <u>Ibid.</u>, 23 June 1926, p. 4890.
15 <u>Ibid.</u>, p. 4891.
16 Cited in Rev. Francis Stevens to author, 11
February 1969.
17 Cited in Neatby, <u>Mackenzie King</u>, vol. II, p. 151.
18 Stevens Papers, Stevens to his children, Marjory,
Sylvia, Patricia and Douglas, 19 July 1926.
19 <u>Ibid.</u>, P.T. O'Farrell to Stevens, 6 August 1926,
20 August 1926.
20 <u>Ibid.</u>, clippings, 13 September 1926.
21 Rev. Francis Stevens to author, 11 February 1969.
22 University of New Brunswick, Harriet Irving
Library, Bennett Papers, George Black to Bennett,
14 August 1928.
23 See Graham, <u>Arthur Meighen</u>, vol. II, p. 380.
24 Rev. Francis Stevens to author, 11 February 1969.
25 <u>Debates</u>, 1926-27, vol. I, 8 February 1927, pp.
104-8.
26 Bennett Papers, Hugh Guthrie to H.H. Stevens,
15 February 1927.
27 <u>Debates</u>, 17 February 1927, p. 395.
28 Stevens Papers, Stevens and John Munro, taped
interview, 31 May 1966.
29 <u>Ibid.</u>

30 Stevens Papers, clippings, 13 December 1927.
31 Ibid., 21 January 1928.
32 Graham, Arthur Meighen, vol. II, p. 336.
33 Stevens Papers, Stevens to R.B. Bennett, 26 April 1928.
34 Ibid., Bennett to Stevens, 3 May 1928.
35 Bennett Papers, Bennett to George Black, 4 May 1928.
36 Ibid., telegram from Stevens to R.B. Bennett, 11 June 1928; Bennett's telegram in reply, 13 June 1928.
37 Stevens Papers, Arthur Meighen to Stevens, 23 July 1928.
38 Bennett Papers, George Black to Bennett, 14 August 1928.
39 Ibid., Bennett to Senators G.H. Barnard, R.F. Green, and Charles Dickie, 9 November 1928; Dr. S.F. Tolmie to Bennett, 8 November 1928; Stevens to C.M. O'Brien, 22 November and 5 December 1928 (copies sent to Bennett by O'Brien).
40 Debates, 1929, vol. I, 12 February 1929, pp. 61, 65, 69; 5 March 1929, p. 691.
41 Bennett Papers, H.H. Stevens to A.D. McRae, 24 April 1929.
42 Ibid., C.J. Lang to Bennett, 15 August 1929; clipping enclosed from Vancouver Sun, 12 August 1929.
43 Ibid., Walter Hamilton to Bennett, 17 August 1929.
44 Stevens Papers, Stevens to R.B. Bennett, 31 October 1929.
45 Ibid., telegram from Bennett to Stevens, 5 November 1929.
46 Ibid., Stevens to Bennett, 7 November 1929; Bennett to Stevens, 9 November 1929.
47 Bennett Papers, Stevens to Bennett, 15 November 1929.
48 Stevens Papers, Stevens to R.J. Manion, 6 December 1929.

49 Ibid, W.F. Nickle to Stevens, 13 December 1929.
50 Ibid., Toronto Star clipping, 6 December 1929.
51 Ibid., Stevens to J.E. Atkinson, 16 December 1929.
52 Ibid., Bennett to Stevens, 27 December 1929.
53 Ibid., A.J. Anderson to Stevens, 30 December 1929 and Stevens' reply, 6 January 1930.
54 Ibid., Vancouver Daily Province, 16 January 1930, clipping.
55 The Stevens Papers contain much correspondence on this bankruptcy case, which subsequently became a political issue in the 1935 election when Ontario Liberals, notably one Arthur Slacht, publicized it.
56 Margaret Ormsby, British Columbia: A History (Toronto 1958), pp. 442-43.
57 Debates, 1930, vol. II, 3 April 1930, pp. 1227-28.
58 Bennett Papers, J.D. Clark to Stevens, 17 April 1930; Stevens to Bennett, 23 April 1930.
59 Debates, 8 May 1930, p. 1880.
60 Bennett Papers, Bennett to Dr. S.F. Tolmie, 23 May 1930 and Tolmie's reply, 29 May 1930.
61 Canadian Annual Review of Public Affairs, 1929-30 (Toronto 1930), p. 85.
62 H.H. Stevens to Rev. Francis Stevens, 16 May 1930, cited in Rev. Francis Stevens to author, 2 March 1969.
63 Vancouver Daily Province, 26 July 1930, cited in Canadian Annual Review, 1929-30, p. 85.
64 Stevens Papers, Stevens and W. Kaye Lamb, taped interview, 27 July 1955.

CHAPTER THREE
1 Escott Reid, "The Effect of the Depression on Canadian Politics, 1929-32," American Political Science Review, vol. XXVII (1933), p. 465.
2 Canada, Imperial Conference, 1930; Part II, Appendices (Ottawa 1931). Also Canadian Annual Review of Public Affairs, 1930-31 (Toronto 1931), pp. 320-21.

3 University of New Brunswick, Harriet Irving
  Library, Bennett Papers, Stevens to Bennett,
  22 December 1930.
4 Rev. Francis Stevens to author, 2 March 1969.
5 Public Archives of Canada, Stevens Papers,
  Bennett to Stevens, 31 January 1931, 18 May 1931.
6 Canada, House of Commons, Debates, 1931, vol. II,
  6 May 1931, p. 1308.
7 Ibid., 14 May 1931, p. 1618.
8 F.H. Soward, "The Canadian Election of 1930,"
  American Political Science Review, vol. XXIV
  (1930), pp. 995-1000; cited in J.M. Beck,
  Pendulum of Power: Canada's Federal Elections
  (Toronto 1968).
9 Debates, 1931, vol. III, 8 June 1931, p. 2373.
10 Ibid., 25 June 1931, p. 3071.
11 Margaret Ormsby, British Columbia: A History
   (Toronto 1958), pp. 444-45.
12 Cited in Michiel Horn, ed., The Dirty Thirties:
   Canadians in the Great Depression (Toronto 1972),
   p. 325.
13 Ibid., p. 327.
14 Ibid., p. 329.
15 James Gray, The Winter Years (Toronto 1966),
   pp. 147, 149.
16 Debates, 1932, vol. I, 10 February 1932, p. 93.
17 Ibid., 16 February 1932, p. 255.
18 Ibid., vol. II, 15 March 1932, p. 1124.
19 A.R.M. Lower, Colony to Nation: A History of
   Canada (Toronto 1964), p. 504.
20 Debates, 1932, vol. II, 15 March 1932, p. 1126.
   Section 98 was repealed by the Liberals in 1936.
21 Debates, 1932, vol. II, 11 April 1932, p. 1904.
22 Montreal Gazette, 27 January 1933.
23 Public Archives of Canada, Manion Papers, R.J.
   Manion to James Manion, 21 January 1933.
24 Rev. Francis Stevens to author, 2 March 1969.
25 Debates, 1932-33, vol. IV, 28 March 1933, p.
   3471.

26 Canada, House of Commons, Journals, vol. LXXXI
   (1932-33), p. 563.
27 Stevens Papers, Stevens to Bennett, 25 May 1933.
28 Montreal Gazette, 6 June 1933. For a description of the unrest and political disarray in
   British Columbia politics, see Canadian Annual
   Review 1933 (Toronto 1934), pp. 293-300.
29 Ottawa Journal, 7 June 1933 and Montreal Standard,
   10 June 1933; from clippings in Stevens papers.
30 Stevens Papers, Stevens to A.S. Dymant, chairman
   of the board, Canadian General Electric Company,
   10 June 1933.
31 Toronto Globe, 1 September 1933.
32 Ibid., 5 September 1933.
33 Stevens Papers, interview between Stevens and
   Dr. W. Kaye Lamb, 27 July 1955.
34 Ibid., Stevens to Bennett, 6 September 1933.
35 Ibid., Mark Senn to Stevens, 7 September 1933.
36 Winnipeg Free Press, 20 October 1933.
37 Stevens Papers, W.B. Connack to Stevens, 7
   November 1933.
38 Ibid., W. Dick to Stevens, 16 November 1933.

CHAPTER FOUR
 1 Public Archives of Canada, Stevens Papers,
   Stevens' speech to Conservative Study Club,
   27 June 1934 (called 'The Pamphlet'), p. 30.
 2 Toronto Globe, 16 January 1934.
 3 Ibid., 18 January 1934.
 4 Stevens Papers, Bennett to Stevens, 27 October
   1934. This letter, written after Stevens'
   second and final resignation from the cabinet,
   contains Bennett's account of their meeting on
   18 January 1934.
 5 Ibid., Stevens to Bennett, 19 January 1934.
 6 Ibid., Warren K. Cook to Stevens, 17 January
   1934.
 7 Cited by the Rev. Francis Stevens in a letter
   to the author, 7 March 1969.

8 Canada, House of Commons, Debates, 1934, vol. I,
  2 February 1934, pp. 188-89, 200, 202; hereafter
  Debates.
9 Stevens Papers, R.H. Coats to Stevens, 30 January
  1934.
10 Ibid., W.H. Grant to Major J.G. Parmelee, 30
   January 1934.
11 Cited in A.M. Schlesinger, Jr., The Age of
   Roosevelt: The Coming of the New Deal (Boston
   1959), p. 110.
12 Canada, Parliament, House of Commons, Special
   Committee on Price Spreads and Mass Buying,
   Proceedings and Evidence (3 vol., Ottawa 1934),
   vol. I (15 February 1934), p. vi; hereafter
   Price Spreads Proceedings.
13 University of New Brunswick, Harriet Irving
   Library, Bennett Papers, Arthur Meighen to
   Bennett, 8 February 1934.
14 Ibid., Geogre Henry to Bennett, 15 February 1934.
15 Debates, 1934, vol. I, 19 February 1934, p. 729.
16 Ibid., p. 734.
17 Ibid., 2 February 1934, p. 199.
18 Canadian Annual Review of Public Affairs, 1934
   (Toronto 1935), p. 29.
19 Price Spreads Proceedings, vol. I (22 February
   1934), pp. 16-18.
20 Ibid. (27 February 1934), pp. 20-53.
21 Ibid., p. 69.
22 Ibid. (28 February 1934), p. 93.
23 Ibid. (7 March 1934), pp. 272-73.
24 Ibid. (8 March 1934), p. 291.
25 Ibid. (8 March 1934), pp. 353, 355.
26 Debates, 1934, III, 19 April 1934, p. 2353; 30
   April, pp. 2642, 2653.
27 Stevens Papers, Sir Robert Borden to Stevens,
   23 April 1934.
28 Ibid., Stevens to Borden, 25 April 1934.
29 Price Spreads Proceedings, vol. II (8 May 1934),
   pp. 1569-73.

30 Ibid. (23 May 1934), p. 2220.
31 Ibid., vol. III (8 June 1934), p. 3036.
32 Cited by the Rev. Francis Stevens in a letter to the author, 7 March 1969.
33 Walter Gordon in an interview with the author, 24 February 1960.
34 Price Spreads Proceedings, vol. III (11 June 1934), p. 3118.
35 Ibid. (13 June 1934), p. 3293.
36 Stevens Papers, Stevens to D.M. Sansom, 14 June 1934.
37 Price Spreads Proceedings, vol. III (20 June 1934), p. 3691.
38 Ibid. (22 June 1934), p. 3815.
29 Canada, Royal Commission on Price Spreads, Report (Ottawa 1935), p. xxvi.
40 Stevens Papers, Dr. Fallis, Trinity United Church, Toronto, to Stevens, 28 March 1934. Other references are found in similar letters in the Stevens Papers.
41 Bennett Papers, Stevens to Bennett, 8 March 1934.
42 Stevens Papers, Stevens' speech to Conservative Study Club, 27 June 1934, pp. 7-8.
43 Bennett Papers, James Muir to Bennett, 26 August 1934.
44 Ibid., John T. Haig to Bennett, 9 August 1934.
45 Ibid., W.W. Kennedy to Bennett, 21 August 1934 (Bennett sent Stevens copies of this correspondence); George Matthews to Bennett, 25 August 1934; W.D. Herridge to Bennett, 20 August 1934.
46 Stevens Papers, clipping from Prince Albert Daily Herald, 15 September 1934.
47 Ibid., Prince Albert Daily Herald, 19 September 1934.
48 Bennett to Stevens, 26 October 1934. This letter was tabled in the House of Commons by Cahan on 12 April 1935; see Debates, 1935, vol. III, 12 April 1935, p. 2671.
49 William Marchington in Toronto Globe, 27 October

1934 (in a column that appeared irregularly,
usually once a week; many columns were based
on the Price Spreads inquiry proceedings).
50 Bennett Papers, Miss Alice Millar, Bennett's
personal secretary, to General J.S. Stewart,
9 November 1934. Also Stevens to author, 10
June 1960; R.K. Finlayson, formerly Bennett's
executive assistant, to author in an interview
9 May 1963; Marchington in Toronto Globe, 27
October 1934.
51 Cited by the Rev. Francis Stevens in a letter
to the author, 7 March 1969.
52 Stevens Papers, Stevens to Bennett, 26 October
1934. Both this letter and Bennett's reply
were published in Montreal and Toronto newspapers on 29 October 1934. Relevant also is
an interview between the author and R.K.
Finlayson, 11 November 1967 (Finlayson was the
prime minister's executive assistant in 1934);
its information is supported by views expressed
by the late Grant Dexter and the late Harold
Daly, in interviews with the author 5, 6 April
1960.
53 Marchington in Toronto Globe, 27 October 1934.
54 Stevens Papers, the Rev. Francis Stevens to
H.H. Stevens, 29 October 1934.

CHAPTER FIVE
1 Evidence from Minutes of Proceedings and Evidence of the Royal Commission on Price Spreads,
no. 3 (1 November 1934), p. 187.
2 William Marchington in Toronto Globe, 29 October
1934.
3 Ibid., 5 November 1934.
4 Public Archives of Canada, Manion Papers, R.J.
Manion to Stevens, 6 November 1934.
5 Public Archives of Canada, Stevens Papers,
clipping from Ottawa Journal, 29 November 1934.
6 Montreal Gazette, 27 November 1934.

7 Ottawa Journal, 29 November 1934, clipping in
  Stevens Papers.
8 Ottawa Journal, 30 November 1934; also Toronto
  Globe, 1 December 1934.
9 Toronto Globe, 4 December 1934.
10 Ibid., 6 December 1934.
11 Ottawa Evening Citizen, 17 December 1934;
  clipping in Stevens Papers. The speech was
  carefully noted and forwarded to Washington
  by the United States ambassador to Canada.
12 Stevens to the Rev. Francis Stevens, 23 December
  1934; cited by Francis Stevens in a letter to
  the author, 7 March 1969.
13 The Rev. Francis Stevens to the author, 7 March
  1969.
14 Bennett Papers, Ward Pitfield to Bennett, 2
  January 1935; Bennett to Pitfield, 8 January
  1935.
15 Ibid., speeches file; also Toronto Globe, 3
  January 1935.
16 William Marchington in Toronto Globe, 3 January
  1934.
17 R.K. Finlayson in an interview with the author,
  6 April 1960; also Bennett Papers, W.D. Herridge
  to Bennett, 16 January, 17 February, 20 August,
  11 September, 15, 20 November 1934; also Manion
  Papers, Herridge to R.J. Manion, 26 January 1935.
18 Stevens Papers, Warren K. Cook to Stevens, 10
  January 1935, and Stevens' reply 12 January 1935.
19 Manion Papers, Manion to R.B. Bennett, 14
  February 1935; Stevens Papers, Stevens to Bennett,
  25 February 1935.
20 R.K. Finlayson to the author, 9 March 1963.
21 Bennett to Lord Beaverbrook, 19 November 1938,
  cited in Beaverbrook, Friends: Sixty Years of
  Intimate Personal Relations with Richard Bedford
  Bennett (London 1959), p. 89.
22 Bennett Papers, Herridge to Bennett, 8 March
  1935.

23 Manion Papers, Herridge to Manion, 22 March 1935; Manion to James Manion, 11 March 1935.

24 Toronto Globe, 21 February 1935, 4, 11 March 1935.

25 Ottawa Journal, 15, 16 March 1935; clipping in Stevens Papers. These recommendations were also widely reported in the other major Canadian dailies.

26 Canada, House of Commons, Debates, 1935, vol. II, 15 March 1935, pp. 1757, 1749-50; hereafter referred to as Debates.

27 Editorial in Toronto Globe, 4 April 1935.

28 Debates, 1935, vol. III, 12 April 1935, pp. 2668-69, 2670-71.

29 William Marchington in Toronto Globe, 13 April 1935. The Globe also printed Stevens' speech verbatim.

30 R.K. Finlayson to the author in various interviews from 1960 to 1969.

31 Debates, 1935, vol. III, 12 April 1935, p. 2676.

32 Manion Papers, Manion to his son James, 15 April 1935.

33 Canada, Royal Commission on Price Spreads, Report (Ottawa 1935), p. 274.

34 Stevens Papers, J.B. Thompson and J.N. McCarter in separate letters to Stevens, in which each enclosed clippings of Burton's speech.

35 Toronto Globe, 19 April 1935.

36 Ibid., 11 May 1935.

37 A copy of this issue was found in volume 31 of the Stevens Papers.

38 Manion Papers, Manion to his son James, 13 May 1935.

39 Toronto Globe, 20 May 1935.

40 Manion Papers, W.D. Herridge to Manion, 23 May 1935.

41 Debates, 1935, vol. III, 23 May 1935, p. 2996.

42 Toronto Globe, 25 May 1935.

43 Debates, 28 May 1935, pp. 3128, 3131.

44 Manion Papers, Manion to his son James, 4 June 1935.
45 Toronto Globe, 5 June 1935.
46 Stevens Papers, Stevens to R.B. Hanson, 10 June 1935.
47 Stevens to the author, 2 August 1960; see also Stevens Papers, interview between Stevens and Dr. W. Kaye Lamb, 27 July 1955.
48 Toronto Globe, 20 June 1935.
49 Debates, 1935, vol. IV, 19 June 1935, pp. 3791-93, 3795-96, 3800-1; reference is also made to a speech by Stevens on 11 June, pp. 3157, 3520.
50 Toronto Globe, 20 June 1935.
51 Debates, 19 June 1935, pp. 3801-10.
52 Manion Papers, Manion to his son James, 21 June 1935.
53 Stevens Papers, Francis Wolfe to Stevens, 26 June 1935; H.B. Winters to Stevens, 22 June 1935; Dr. L.B. Wilmot to Stevens, 26 June 1935.
54 Cited by the Rev. Francis Stevens in a letter to the author, 7 March 1969.
55 This account is based on a Canadian Press despatch carried in the Globe, 2 July 1935.
56 Debates, 2 July 1935, p. 4146; see also Debates, 1923, vol. I, 15 February 1923, p. 324.
57 Stevens Papers, Stevens to D.M. Duggan, 4 July 1935.
58 A photostat of the original petition is in volume 125 of the Stevens Papers.
59 Toronto Globe, 7 July 1935.
60 Stevens to the author, 2 August 1960.
61 H.E. Betts in an interview with the author, 5 April 1960.
62 T.W. Learie, in an interview with the author, 28 July 1960.
63 Gertrude Stevens to the Rev. Francis Stevens, 27 October 1934, cited by the Rev. Francis Stevens in a letter to the author, 7 March 1969.
64 Stevens Papers, Stevens to A.J. Anderson, M.P., 11 July 1935.

CHAPTER SIX

1 Toronto <u>Globe</u>, 12 July 1935. Both the <u>Globe</u> and the Montreal <u>Gazette</u> printed the manifesto on 13 July 1935.
2 T.W. Learie to the author, 2 August 1960.
3 Regina Manifesto, reprinted in K. McNaught, <u>A Prophet in Politics</u> (Toronto 1959), appendix, p. 332.
4 Montreal <u>Gazette</u>, 13 July 1935; Toronto <u>Globe</u>, 13 July 1935; <u>Monetary Times</u>, 13 July 1935; Simcoe <u>Reformer</u>, 11 July 1935: all from clippings in Public Archives of Canada, Stevens Papers.
5 The Rev. Francis Stevens to the author, 11 February 1969.
6 <u>Ibid</u>., 10 May 1969.
7 Toronto <u>Globe</u>, 22 July 1935.
8 Victoria <u>Daily Times</u>, 5 August 1935, clippings in Stevens Papers.
9 Harold Daly in an interview with the author, 5 April 1960; T.W. Learie in an interview with the author, 2 August 1960.
10 Stevens Papers, Stevens to H.S. Cawsey, 16 September 1935. (Both Massey and Cahan were successful in the election.)
11 Vancouver <u>Province</u>, 6 August 1935.
12 Stevens Papers, Stevens in a telegram to H.E. Betts, 13 August 1935.
13 H.E. Betts, in an interview with the author, 5 April 1960.
14 See Stevens Papers for a copy of the speech Stevens delivered in Montreal 4 September 1935; see also Montreal <u>Gazette</u>'s report of rally.
15 Ottawa <u>Journal</u>, 15 September 1935.
16 Toronto <u>Globe</u>, 22 September 1935.
17 The Rev. Francis Stevens to the author, 21 February 1969.
18 Ottawa <u>Citizen</u>, 24 September 1935.
19 Montreal <u>Star</u>, 3 October 1935.

20 Toronto *Globe*, 3 October 1935; Toronto *Telegram*, 4 October 1935.
21 The Rev. Francis Stevens to the author, 21 February 1969.
22 Montreal *Star*, 29 September 1935.
23 Toronto *Star*, 30 September 1935. Also carried as Canadian Press despatches in Toronto *Globe*, 30 September 1935.
24 Toronto *Globe*, 2 October 1935.
25 Both Gordon and Beatty had been knighted in the latest King's birthday honours list.
26 Toronto *Globe*, 12 October 1935. T.W. Learie in an interview with the author, 2 August 1960.
27 Toronto *Globe*, 14 October 1935. Both the *Globe* and the *Telegram* carried denials of this charge by King and Beatty.
28 The Rev. Francis Stevens to the author, 10 May 1969.
29 H.H. Stevens to Francis Stevens, 16 October 1935; cited in letter to the author from the Rev. Francis Stevens, 11 February 1969.

CHAPTER SEVEN
1 Public Archives of Canada, Manion Papers, Sir Robert Borden to R.J. Manion, 18 October 1935.
2 University of New Brunswick, Harriet Irving Library, Bennett Papers, Manion to Herridge, 18 October 1935; Manion to Bennett, 31 October 1935.
3 Escott Reid, "The Canadian Election of 1935 -- And After," *American Political Science Review*, vol. XXX (1936), p. 116.
4 Manion Papers, Manion to Herridge, 18 October 1935. Harold Daly, interview with the author, 5 April 1960; H.H. Stevens to author, 2 August 1960.
5 Gad Horowitz, "Conservatism, Liberalism, and Socialism in Canada: An Interpretation," in H.G. Thorburn, ed., *Party Politics in Canada* (Scarborough, Ont., 1967), pp. 64-65.

6 Ibid., p. 58.
7 Public Archives of Canada, Stevens Papers, Canadian Press release, 27 November 1935.
8 Canada, House of Commons, Debates, 1936, vol. I, 12 February 1936, p. 140; hereafter Debates.
9 Stevens Papers, Stevens to A.S. Nicholson, 30 March 1936.
10 Ibid., Stevens to N. Somerville, 9 April 1936; Sommerville to Stevens, 15 April 1936.
11 R.K. Finlayson, in an interview with the author, 3 March 1967.
12 Stevens Papers, Stevens to Ryerson Ritchie, 28 May 1936; Warren Cook to Stevens, 17 May 1938.
13 Debates, 10 March 1937, pp. 1662, 1667.
14 Stevens Papers, Jacques Cartier to Stevens, 15 June 1938.
15 Ibid., Stevens to Warren Cook, 24 June 1938.
16 Ibid., Stevens to D.S. Glass, 30 June 1938.
17 Manion Papers, Manion to Stevens, 23 December 1938.
18 Debates, 1939, vol. I, 25 January 1939, p. 314; ibid., Special War Session, 12 September 1939, p. 149.
19 R.K. Finlayson, interview with the author, 3 March 1967.
20 The Rev. Francis Stevens in an interview with the author, 30 January 1970.

Index

Aberhart, William 191, 194
Aitken, Sir Max (Lord Beaverbrook) 3, 39, 155
Anderson, J.T.M. 82
Atholstan, Lord (Hugh Graham) 48, 71
Atkinson, Joseph 47, 78, 79
Atkinson, Dr. Sam 197

Baribeau, J.L. 116
Beatty, Sir Edward 62, 199, 200
Bell, C.W. 172
Bell, Leslie 48
Bell, Thomas 116
Bennett, Mildred 103, 148, 154, 201
Bennett, Richard B.: early career, 3, 5, 37, 38,
  40; opposition member, 48-50, 66; role in customs
  inquiry, 56-57; 1927 Conservative convention, 62-
  64, 67-68; opposition leader, 69-73; B.C. party
  squabbles, 73-76, 97; and Stevens' 1929 retirement
  plans, 78-82; 1930 general election, 84-87; 1930
  Imperial conference, 91-92; early cabinet relations with Stevens, 92-96; first efforts to fight
  depression, 98-102, 105, 107; talks with Roosevelt,
  102-103; overseas trips and conferences, 103, 106,
  139; reaction to Stevens' speech to Boot and Shoe
  convention, 111-114; establishes Price Spreads

inquiry, 114-115, 117; reaction to first price
spreads hearings, 118, 130; attempts to suppress
publication of Stevens' Pamphlet, 134-136, 140;
Stevens' resignation from cabinet, 140-142, 160-
163; resumes public speeches, 147-149; reaction
to Sylvia Stevens' death, 150; New Deal broadcasts
and reaction, 151-152, 155; attempts at Bennett-
Stevens reconciliation, 153-156, 159, 166-167;
New Deal legislation, 168; Commons clash with
Stevens, 172-176; and Regina riots, 179-180;
bars Stevens from caucus, 172, 181; rumoured retirement, 169-170, 182; 1935 election campaign,
189, 192, 198-200; bitterness towards Stevens,
169, 201, 204, 208

Betts, Harold E. 157, 181, 194
Bisaillon, J.E. 53-56, passim
Bishop, Charles 140
Black, George 29, 63, 70, 71, 72, 73
Boivin, G.H. 52, 55
Borden, Sir Robert: first administration, 18, 20-
24 passim; 1917 Commons debates and general elec-
tion, 28-29, 31, 89; reaction to Price Spreads
inquiry, 124; conservative principles, 143, 177;
reaction to Reconstruction party, 204
Boulanger, Oscar 116
Bowser, William: opposition to Stevens' nominations,
17, 25, 29, 39; purchase of Kitsilano reserve,
21; provincial leadership, 29-40; 1924 British
Columbia election campaign, 42-44; 1926 B.C.
Conservative leadership, 65
Bracken, John 212
Bureau, Jacques 52
Burnham, J.H. 34, 35
Burton, C.L. 110, 134, 136, 140, 160, 165, 166
Byng (Sir) Julian 51, 59, 60, 61

Cahan, C.H.: St. James Street connections, 48, 70,
82; 1927 Conservative Convention, 67; cabinet
appointment, 90; role in Stevens' resignation,

139-141; reaction to Price Spreads inquiry, 146-147; rumoured resignation, 151; Stevens' bitterness towards, 154; Report of Royal Commission on Price Spreads, 158-159; Commons debates with Stevens, 161-163, 167, 169-170, 173; supporter of Bennett, 173-174; Regina riots, 180; 1935 general election, 189, 191; caucus support, 202
Cannon, Lucien 51, 54
Carter, Percy 188
Cartier, Jacques 188, 194, 210
Carvell, Frank 26
Cassidy, Harry 113, 117
Chaplin, James D. 77
Charters, Samuel 72
Chown, Rev. Dr. S.D. 14, 16
Church, Rev. E.F. 190
Church, Tommy 137, 139, 172 '
Clark, J.A. 74
Coats, Dr. R.H. 91, 92, 118
Cook, Warren K.: Select Committee on Price Spreads, 112-113, 117, 121, 122, 129-130; reaction to Bennett's New Deal, 152-153; coast-to-coast tour, 179; Hamilton meeting to draft Stevens, 181; Reconstruction Party Manifesto, 184-186; Reconstruction party organization, 188, 190, 193, 200; post-1935 election and Reconstruction party, 207, 209; Stevens' return to Tory party, 210
Coolidge, Clifton 210, 213
Cox, Senator Herbert 126
Cramp, W.M. 188, 197
Creighton, Donald 30
Crerar, T.A. 31, 32, 47

Dafoe, John W. 135
Daly, Harold M. 140, 141, 190, 205
Diefenbaker, John G. 206, 212, 213, 214
Donaghy, Duguld 58, 63
Douglas, T.C. 206
Duff, Sir Lyman 148

Duke, Thomas 11
Dunning, Charles 33, 67
Duplessis, Maurice 210
Dupré, Maurice 91

Eaton, R.Y. 110, 112
Eddy, Jenny 37
Edwards, A.M. 116
Engels, Friedrich 11

Factor, Samuel 116
Findley, James 17
Finlayson, R.K. 98, 102, 152, 154, 155, 208, 212
Flavelle, Sir Joseph 6, 27, 28, 128, 132, 140, 160
Fleming, Sandford 4
Forke, Robert 47
Forsey, Eugene 63
Foster, Sir George 46
Foster, Tom 9
Francq, Gustave 120
Fraser, J.A. 162, 163

Gardiner, James 198
Gardiner, Robert 35
Glassco, Grant 128
Glover, Mr. and Mrs. 37, 65, 66
Goodwin, Dr. W.L. 167
Gordon, Sir Charles 167, 199
Gordon, Walter 127, 128
Gott, Eccles 167, 188
Gouin, Sir Lomer 38
Grant, W.H. 89, 115, 134
Grassby, A.E. 81, 122
Gray, James 98, 99
Green, Howard 212
Green, Senator Robert 43, 44, 48, 73, 90
Gregory, T.E.M. 123, 184
Gurney, Edward 71
Guthrie, Hugh 26, 29, 51, 64, 66, 67, 86, 91, 168

Haig, Senator John T. 135
Hall, Gilbert 6
Hannam, H.H. 187
Hanson, R.B. 154, 162, 171, 172, 174
Heaps, A.A. 84, 116
Henry, George 117
Hepburn, Mitchell 85, 164, 198
Herchmer, Sherwood 196
Herridge, W.D.: 1930 Imperial Conference, 91;
  Minister to US, 102; reaction to Roosevelt's
  New Deal, 115, 136; speech to Ottawa Canadian
  Club, 148-149; Bennett's New Deal broadcasts,
  152, 154-155; attempts Bennett-Stevens recon-
  ciliation, 156, 201; Bennett's New Deal legis-
  lation, 168; 1935 election results, 204
Herridge, Rev. Dr. William J. 148
Hofstadter, Richard 16
Holt, Sir Herbert 167, 198, 199
Hooper, H.C. 45
Horowitz, Gad 206
House, Mayor Camillien 164
Hougham, George B. 122, 171, 172
Hughes, Sir Sam 24
Hunter, W.S. 193
Hyde, Col. Reid J. 46

Ilsley, J.L. 116

Johnston, General Hugh 115

Keatley, Gordon 213
Kennedy, D.M. 57
Kennedy, W.W. 116, 135, 136, 144
King, W.L. Mackenzie: first administration, 38,
  40; relations with Britain, 46-47; 1925 general
  election, 48; 1926 general election, 50; 1926
  constitutional crisis, 51; customs scandal, 52-
  62 passim; accusations against Stevens, 62-63;
  five cent speech, 84-85; as Opposition leader,

237

94; price spreads inquiry, 118, 156, 158-159; on
Stevens-Bennett rift, 136-137; Ontario 1934 by-
elections, 136-138; Herridge's Ottawa speech, 148;
1935 general election campaign, 189-190, 194-195,
198-200; 1935 election results, 201, 207
Komagata Maru 22, 23, 24, 68

Ladner, Leon 65
Lapointe, Ernest 47, 51, 55
Larkin, Peter 46
Laurier, Sir Wilfrid 18, 22, 23, 41
Lavers, A.W. 119, 120
Lawson, Earl 210, 211
Learie, Tom 182, 190, 200, 201
Lenin 199
Lipsett, Robert 140, 141
Lisson, Thomas 181
Lloyd-George, David 45
Lougheed, Sir James 10
Lovick, James 80, 102
Lovick, Patricia 189
Lower, A.R.M. 100

Macaulay, T.B. 33
McBride, Richard 12, 17, 24, 25
Macdonald, Angus L. 198
Macdonald, Sir John A. 6, 53, 79, 143, 173, 177
Macdonald, John A. 188
McGeer, Major Gerry 165
McGregor, R.H. 188
MacInnis, Angus 180
McInnes, Billy 29
Mackenzie, Ian 86, 95
McKenzie, Robert 118
McLean, Stanley 32, 120, 121, 160
McNaughton, General A.G.L. 98
MacPherson, M.A. 211, 212
McQuarrie, W.L. 192
McRae, General A.D.: Provincial party, 40, 42;

relations with R.B. Bennett, 48, 70; election as
MP, 63; 1927 Conservative Convention, 64-65; party
organizer, 74-75, 81-82; 1930 election defeat, 87
McRuer, J.C. 62
Manion, Dr. Robert: Unionist MP, 29; Stevens' desk-
mate, 70-71; 1930 election, 85; Marjory Stevens'
wedding, 102; Ontario 1934 by-elections, 136;
reaction to Stevens' resignation, 145-146, 183,
202; Bennett's New Deal legislation, 156; Stevens-
Cahan debate, 163; Canadian National Railways, 166;
Stevens' public speeches, 167-168; Stevens-Bennett
relations, 169-170, 204; Commons argument with
Bennett, 170-171; Regina riots, 175-176; Stevens'
1935 re-election, 204-205; Conservative party
leader, 211-212
Marchington, William 153, 158
Marler, George 213
Marler, Herbert 51
Massey, Denton 191
Massey, Vincent 51
Matthews, George 136, 151
Matthews, R.C. 188
Meighen, Arthur: as Borden's solicitor-general,
24; political views, 30-31; assumes leadership,
34; requests Stevens' aid in by-elections, 35-36,
40; opponents to his policies, 36, 48, 72, 175;
British Columbia party quarrels, 39-42, 44; 1926
constitutional crisis, 50-52, 60-61; customs
scandal, 56; ends Commons career, 63-64, 70;
1927 leadership convention, 67, price spreads
inquiry, 117; 1940 leadership convention, 212
Mill, John Stuart 11
Morand, Dr. Raymond 167, 170, 172
Mosher, A.R. 166
Muir, James 135

Nash, A.E. 58
Neatby, Blair 52
Nesbitt, E.W. 32

239

Newburn, Major-General 199
Nickle, W.F. 77

O'Farrell, P.T. 62
Oliver, Premier John 38, 42
Oliver, Frank 21, 40, 44
Ormsby, Margaret 15, 83, 96

Parmelee, Major T.C. 89, 115, 134
Pearson, Rev. E.A. 6
Pearson, Lester B. 134, 163, 214
Perley, Sir George 62, 139, 141, 151, 172, 174, 180, 189
Pilkey, Rev. P.I. 193
Pitfield, Ward 150

Reconstruction party: origins, 142, 177-183 passim; platform, 184-187, 192; press and public response, 186-187, 191-192; candidates, 188, 193; organization, 188, 190-191, 193-194, 208-209; campaign, 189-200 passim; support of Stevens family, 189, 194, 196; Liberal reaction, 189-190, 194-196, 197; Conservative reaction, 198-199; 1935 election results, 201-203, 204-206 passim
Reid, Escott 204, 206
Retail Merchants' Association 122, 131, 144-147 passim, 156, 163, 171, 179, 192-193
Rhodes, Edgar 103, 188
Rinfret, Fernand 94
Robb, James 52
Robson, Dr. Ebenezer 13
Roddan, Rev. Andrew 191
Rogers, Senator Robert 22
Roosevelt, Franklin 102, 115, 132, 148, 169
Ross, General A.E. 159, 172
Rounsefell, F.W. 42
Royal Commission on Price Spreads: hearings, 144; Stevens' public speeches, 145, 147, 153, 156, 157, 166-167, 171; his recommendations, 157-158, 160-161, 169

Ryckman, E.B. 70, 71, 77, 82, 90

Scott, Prof. Frank R. 113, 117
Scott, H.B. 192
Scott, R.J. 197
Select Committee on Price Spreads: origins, 105–106, 108, 112–113; Toronto speech, 108–112; committee formed, 113–114, 116–117; American influences, 115; staff, 116–117, 134; hearings, 118–122, 125–130; public reaction, 130–131
Senkler, J.H. 18
Senn, Mark 105, 116
Sinclair, Upton 16
Skelton, Dr. O.E. 93
Slaght, Arthur 122, 197, 198
Smith, Sidney 135
Sommerville, Norman 117, 119, 129, 208, 209
Sparks, Percy 53, 57, 104, 112, 113, 128, 129, 130
Speakman, Alfred 93, 99
Spencer, Col. Nelson 35
Stapells, R.A. 110, 119
Steffens, Lincoln 16
Stevens, Annie (Mrs. Francis) 203
Stevens, Bessie 5
Stevens, Douglas 20, 27, 61, 80, 134, 194
Stevens, Rev. Francis: on father's career, 12, 19, 142–143, 177, 200; aids father's campaigns, 35, 189, 194, 196, 197, 202; education, 36, 61, 80, 86; on mother's reaction to politics 63, 93; on Stevens' family life, 92, 140, 149–150
Stevens, Gerturde (Mrs. H.H.): courtship and marriage, 8; letters from Harry, 47, 58, 134; life in Ottawa, 36, 61, 89; reaction to politics, 63, 80, 92; family life, 65, 102, 149; attitude towards Bennett, 150, 177; role in 1935 election campaign, 189–192 passim, 194, 196; Kitimat tour, 213; death, 214
Stevens, Henry Herbert: early years, 3, 5, 7, 19, 38; as freshman MP, 3, 17, 18, 20–21, 24, 26, 28; on Oriental immigration, 4, 14–15, 23–24, 68;

courtship with Gertrude Glover, 7, 11, 13-14;
first jobs, 8, 10, 37; Boxer rebellion, 9;
Vancouver municipal politics, 11-12, 15, 16, 20,
23, 25, 38; his Methodism and political philosophy, 10-14, passim, 16, 33, 89-90, 103, 123-124,
133, 144-145, 180; British Columbia politics, 12,
17, 21, 25, 29, 39, 40, 42-44, 64-65, 72-73, 74,
86, 97, 104, 114, 117; business career, 15, 17,
36, 47, 62, 64, 69-70, 78-79, 209-210; family life,
17, 19, 20, 26, 35, 37, 61, 63, 65-66, 80-81, 86,
89, 92-93, 102, 134, 139-140, 149; Komagata Maru
incident, 22-24, 68; First World War, 24, 27;
Parliament Building fire, 27; and Sir Joseph
Flavelle, 6, 27, 126, 132, 140, 160; 1916 Grain
investigation, 31-32; 1919 Cost of Living inquiry,
32, 174-175; and Big Business, 38-39, 40, 48, 67,
70-71, 82, 109-112 passim, 123; and banking, 41,
74; church union, 42-43; overseas trips, 44-46,
69, 91; as opposition critic (1921-1930), 41, 47,
51, 66, 67, 73-74, 84; financial problems, 47,
75-77; Vancouver Holdings, 47-69, 76, 81, 213;
and R.B. Bennett, 3-4, 10, 24, 28, 29, 37, 49,
50, 71-77 passim, 85, 92-95 passim, 100-103 passim,
111, 139-142, 150, 154, 169, 208; and Arthur
Meighen, 29-31, 36, 38, 40, 42, 43-44, 47-49,
50-60 passim, 64, 73; customs scandal debate,
51-60 passim, 77; 1926 constitutional crisis, 60;
illness, 61; and Mackenzie King, 62, 81, 85, 137-
138, 160; federal election campaigns to 1930, 3,
17-18, 29, 31, 48, 63, 87, 135-137; 1927 Conver-
vative leadership convention, 67-68; 1930 retirement plans, 75-82, 85-86; and R.J. Manion, 29,
77, 145, 154, 156, 167-168, 170, 204, 211;
Manufacturers' Finance Corporation, 81, 122, 197,
209; 1930 election defeat, 87, 95; as Minister of
Trade and Commerce, 89-90, 92-95 passim, 123; 1930
Imperial conference, 91-92; unemployment and relief,
98, 103-105 passim; Study Club speech (pamphlet),
131-133, 134-136, 129-141 passim; final cabinet

resignation, 140–143, 160–162; Commons debate with
Bennett, 172–173; Ontario by-elections of 1934, 136–
139; cabinet and caucus support, 159, 161, 163, 166,
168, 170, 172, 176; as Reconstruction MP, 204, 207–
209; return to Conservative party, 210–212; retire-
ment years, 212–214; see also Select Committee,
Royal Commission
Stevens, Louise 5
Stevens, Marjory 17, 20, 27, 61, 64, 80, 83, 102, 104,
189
Stevens, Patricia 19, 20, 27, 61, 80, 102, 134, 194,
210, 213
Stevens, Richard 5–8
Stevens, Sylvia: early years, 17, 16, 61, 80; illness,
102, 104, 134, 139, 141, 202; death, 149–150, 177
Stevens, William 7, 26, 37
Stewart, J.S. 189
Sutherland, Donald 170

Tarbell, Ida 16
Thompson, Henry 46
Tolmie, Dr. S.F. 40, 73, 82, 86
Tory, Dr. H.M. 91
Tupper, Sir Hibbert 29

Walsh, James 104
Weir, Robert 123, 176
White, Frank 172, 188
White, R.S. 48, 70
White, Sir Thomas 28, 41, 45
Wilgress, Dana 163
Williams-Taylor, Sir Frederick 45
Willivery, R.B. 192
Wilson, Morris 199
Wilson, Dr. R.A. 192
Wilson, Woodrow 145
Winters, James 179
Woodside, Rev. J.W.D. 42
Woodsworth, James S.: 1923 Debate on Bank Act

Revision, 41, 90; House of Commons speeches, 47, 58, 96; relations with Stevens, 57; Regina riots, 180; 1935 general election, 189; political views, 206–207

Young, D.M. 116
Young, Edward M. 116, 129

DATE DUE
